No. 6
St James's Library
★
SIR WALTER RALEIGH

St James's Library

*

1. POTTERISM   Rose Macaulay
2. BERNARD SHAW   Hesketh Pearson
3. THE SWORD IN THE STONE   T. H. White
4. BYRON : THE YEARS OF FAME   Peter Quennell
5. SOUTH RIDING   Winifred Holtby
6. SIR WALTER RALEIGH   Milton Waldman

*

*The price of the volumes numbered
odd is 6s.*

*The price of the volumes numbered
even is 8s. 6d.*

SIR WALTER RALEIGH

MILTON WALDMAN

SIR
WALTER
RALEIGH

ST JAMES'S LIBRARY
COLLINS, LONDON

First Published 1928
First Issued in this Edition 1950

To

J. C. SQUIRE

Printed in Great Britain
Collins Clear-Type Press : London & Glasgow

FOREWORD

IT is the ambition of every biographer to be able to work with material not available to his predecessors, and that privilege to a certain extent I have had. The work of the Historical Manuscripts Commissions, the further volumes of the State Calendars and Acts of the Privy Council and the researches of workers in adjacent fields into foreign archives have considerably supplemented in recent years the quantity of material on the life of Raleigh and the time in which he lived. Even where some of this material has been known to previous biographers it has now been put into such shape that it may be more effectively employed.

Nevertheless one's principal obligations must always remain to one's predecessors, who have laid the foundation of the subject and whose structure we can only hope to supplement without changing its essential nature. Whatever merit this book may possess is in large measure due to the studies of such men as Oldys, Edwards, Stebbing and other biographers of Raleigh.

My one endeavour has been to portray the character of the complicated, versatile and gifted hero of this book, to show him against the background of his age, but to judge him by the criteria of greatness in all ages.

Wherever previously unutilized documents have seemed to assist this endeavour, such as the letters which bitterly protest against Raleigh's political advancement and the British contentions in the Venezuelan Boundary Dispute, I have availed myself of them. But where they have seemed to serve only a minor purpose or to supply only incidental details, such as the records of his petty litigations or of his minor official appointments, I have for the sake of proportion omitted specific reference to them. I have tried, however, to give in the bibliography a complete list of all documents employed.

MILTON WALDMAN

CONTENTS

		PAGE
FOREWORD		V

CHAP.

I.	THE FREE LANCE	1
II.	PUTTING DOWN REBELLION	14
III.	THE NEW WORLD PLANTER	25
IV.	THE QUEEN GIVES MONEY	47
V.	THE OCCASIONAL MUSE	78
VI.	TO THE RAINBOW'S END	93
VII.	THE DRAGON'S HEIR	115
VIII.	THE TRIUMVIRATE	130
IX.	THE TRIAL FOR TREASON	152
X.	THIRTEEN YEARS IN PRISON	179
XI.	THE RAINBOW FADES	198
XII.	THE KING'S MISTAKE	218
BIBLIOGRAPHY		239
INDEX		245

CHAPTER I

THE FREE LANCE

A ROMANTIC reputation is undoubtedly the hardest kind to sustain; it is the romantic actor who most strongly tempts familiar and realistic anecdotes. The glamour that surrounds Raleigh's name, after lingering virtually untarnished for two centuries, began to wear off under the dispassionate scrutiny of the scientific historians of the nineteenth century, until there began to arise the danger that we should see him very much as did his contemporaries. And this would have been manifestly unfair, for that reputation was in large part the careful creation of the very gifted artist to whom it belonged.

The history of that reputation may be briefly summarized. To the Elizabethans, save a comparative few, such as his relatives and his fellow west-countrymen, Raleigh was an upstart, untrustworthy, grasping, overbearing, owing his success as much to the capricious middle-aged lady who sat on the throne as to his own versatile talents. The latter were, in a measure, recognized by his equals; the common people considered more closely the patents and privileges which he wheedled out of the doting Queen, the extravagant estate which he supported at their expense. Then, after a manifestly unjust conviction for treason, came the thirteen years in the Tower, whence spread from time to time news of the wizard who was engaged in incredible chemical experiments and of the sage who was writing a colossal *History of the World* from its very beginning. The courtier was disgraced, the Crœsus in rags ; and when he issued forth on the last despairing mission to retrieve his fortunes and restore his fame, his countrymen began to see him as what in fact he was, the last Paladin of that great age which was already fading from memory. They did not inquire too closely into the facts of his death ; he was a sacrifice to the fears, the pedantry, the roguery, of the leaders of the newer and less happy times, and the manner of his death effaced the obloquy and recalled the brilliance of his life so thoroughly, that in it he achieved a vindication and a triumph as complete as his own insatiable soul could have wished.

So he stood for nearly two hundred years, the martyr who had been soldier, sailor, statesman, artist, the inspiration of the Puritan rulers of the coming age, adored by the poets and dramatists, the idol of the historians. The eighteenth century, critical as was its habit of mind, saw little or nothing, in the beginning, at least, to censure in him. Its principal biography, by Oldys, takes it for granted that it was history's business to recompense his memory for the disparity between his deserts and his rewards ; Gibbon for long planned to devote his genius, which later went into the *Decline and Fall*, to another *Life*, and only desisted because he could find no new material—it seems not unlikely that his sound historical instinct warned him that the existing panegyrics were not the definitive story.

Gibbon's contemporary, Hume, suffered from no such scruples regarding research, and in his *History of England* savagely attacks Raleigh as no better than a charlatan. His opinions have been for the most part disregarded or laid aside, even by historians whose religious views inclined them to prejudice ; but the charge was elaborated by a more thorough scholar, Spedding, the biographer of

Bacon, who, in defending his own hero against the universal excoriation which resulted from the latter's indictment of Raleigh at the behest of King James, re-examines the evidence and comes to a somewhat similar, though not so violent a conclusion as Hume. Gardiner, one of the most respected of English historians, while dissenting in certain particulars from Spedding, is in general accord with him. Neither of them doubts Raleigh's abilities : both, in fact, admit his genius. It is his character which suffers at their hands, and the romantic view is tainted with the charges of unscrupulous dealings and common piracy. It remained for the late nineteenth century to question those abilities, and under Sir Julian Corbett's scrutiny Raleigh's stature as a naval commander diminished considerably. His statesmanship has been repudiated, and much of his poetry, if not dismissed, has either been taken from him and re-attributed or ignored.

Yet the reputation remains. The most diligent examination, the severest studies of the historians, have not succeeded in altering materially the conception of him which took hold of the popular imagination three hundred years ago. In this study I shall attempt not only to discover the reasons therefor, but the justification thereof. The public holds tightly to its idols, and the fact that an age of scientific destruction is usually followed by one of equally scientific reconstruction tends to fortify its attitude. I cannot attempt to dispute with so able a commentator as Sir Julian Corbett upon any man's abilities as a seaman, except by the aid of other and equally qualified authorities. On the question of Raleigh's alleged piratical conduct, however, I have fortunately had access to material not available, not even in existence, when Hume, Spedding and Gardiner wrote, and from that, the gravest charge made against him, he can, I believe, be in substance for ever acquitted.

Yet, although a man's reputation be rehabilitated, and

his many and diverse talents admitted, he need not, for all that, be a great man, in the profoundest sense of the word.   Much more than the proof or disproof of specific charges, more even than the long-held admiration of a world, are required to establish that.

The information that has come down to us of his youth is fragmentary and uncertain, but no more so than is the case with most of his contemporaries.   It is not even known for certain when he was born.   The traditional date is 1552, which is in accord with the age given him at his death by Camden, but the inscriptions on the Zucchero portrait in the National Gallery would make it 1554, as would the Dublin Gallery portrait ; from the Belvoir Castle miniature his birth might be assigned either to this year or to the previous one.   Portrait inscriptions are no longer taken very seriously as statements of fact, and the traditional date seems, on the whole, to be open to fewer objections than any other.

His father, also called Walter, was a Devonian squire, originally from Fardell in that county, who settled in about 1520 at Hayes, or Hayes Barton, near Budleigh Salterton, where the younger Walter was born, in a house still extant and inhabited.   It was sold in Raleigh's lifetime, but years later, in the days of his prosperity, a sentimental mood prompted him to buy it back from its then owner. The Raleighs were an ancient stock, not so blue in blood, perhaps, as the most famous of them would have liked to believe in his days of splendour, but nevertheless of creditable importance and tradition.   His parents are both mentioned in important sixteenth-century annals : the father by Holinshed as a stalwart early Protestant, in connection with the Catholic West Country Rising in 1549, wherein the elder Raleigh nearly lost his life, and the mother by Foxe, whose *Acts and Monuments*, more commonly known as *Foxe's Martyrs*, describes her brave and kindly visits to a condemned woman in prison, during the frenzied Catholic reaction under Philip and Mary.

More celebrated than his ancestors were his living kinsmen by blood and marriage. Devonshire was the cradle of English sea-supremacy under Elizabeth ; certainly more than half the great seamen and explorers who were to distinguish the reign were born within its borders, and to a considerable proportion of these Walter Raleigh was related. The elder Raleigh married three times: first, in 1518, Joan Drake of Exmouth, a putative second cousin of Francis Drake ; next a Miss Darell, of London, of whom little is known; and finally, some time after 1548, Katherine, the daughter of Sir Philip Champernoun and the widow of Otto Gilbert. This lady was already the mother of three sons, John, Adrian and the immortal Sir Humphrey Gilbert ; through them and the two sons, Carew and Walter, whom she bore to her second husband, she earned a sentimental recognition by a New World which as yet must have seemed to her a sort of fabled Atlantis. Besides the Carew, Gilbert and Champernoun connections Raleigh was related to the Grenvilles, Courtenays, St. Legers and Russels—household names in the history of discovery and piracy by sea.

From this meagre information may be deduced the influences which turned his energies to naval adventure and his convictions, such as they were, to the vigorous support of an anti-papal policy. Granted his native talents and ambitions, one understands why the son of a reduced country gentleman, given the opportunity, should have schemed and intrigued along the difficult road to distinction and preferment, and marked each step with a gesture designed to attract instant attention. But whence came the poetry, the subtlety, the incredible range of curiosity and intelligence, cannot be discovered in any evidence of hereditary influence or early training.

That his education must have been of a superior order

his works leave no doubt, but of its exact character we can learn very little. From the Oxford historian, Anthony à Wood, it appears that he went up to that University in 1568, entering at Oriel College as an undergraduate in 1572 with one of his Champernoun kinsmen. Of his career in Oxford nothing is known and little is reported save that he was poor in purse and brilliant in his studies. The authority for the former is the amusing but unreliable Aubrey, who says that—

" In his youth for several years he was under straights for want of money. I remember that Mr. Th. Child of Worcestershire, told me that Sir Walter borrowed a gown from him when he was at Oxford (they were both at the same college) which he never restored, nor money for it,"

—a lapse which can hardly be set down to simple dishonesty.

Of his abilities as a student Wood remarks that—

" His natural parts being strangely advanced by academical learning, he became the ornament of the juniors, and was worthily esteemed a proficient in oratory and philosophy."

Much seventeenth-century comment on the man may be regarded with suspicion, it having been written under the spell of his after-career, but of the fact that all his life he was a remarkable student there can be no doubt whatsoever. The basis of his later unpopularity lay largely in the quick impatient facility of a mind which showed its irritation with the slower processes of more experienced if less inspired colleagues.

It is certain, however, that he did not pass the whole, or even any considerable portion of the interval from 1568 to 1572, in residence; for in his *History of the World* he specifically states that he was present in France from 1569 on, taking part in the battles of Jarnac and Moncontour during the Huguenot wars ; and presumably he remained there until after 1572, for in another section of the *History* he describes the smoking-out of the Catholics in the Caves of Languedoc during the third religious war, which took place in the year of the St. Bartholomew's Massacre. It is usually conceded that he could not have been among the English refugees at the Embassy in Paris during that fearful night. The length of his residence in France is fairly well fixed by Hakluyt's dedication to him of Laudonnière's *Florida* in 1587, wherein the editor says, " You had spent more years in France than I "—and knowing from the dedication of the first edition of his *chef d'œuvre* to Walsingham that Hakluyt's own residence had been five years, it seems fairly certain that Raleigh did not return to England before 1575, his name remaining on the books of his College during his absence.

He returned with a sound knowledge of the French tongue and the principles of military strategy, both of which were to be useful to him later, but without a means of livelihood. While waiting for something to turn up he took up his residence in the Temple ; he may have had the intention of studying law, as young men in his transitory position frequently do, but did not do so, if his own answer to accusations many years later is to be believed. He did, however, pass the time by writing verses. Some of these are preserved, and very good verses they are, too, for a young soldier of twenty-four. They were written in commendation of George Gascoigne's *Steel Glas*, and appeared bound in with the first edition, 1576, as was the custom of the time.

There is something especially tantalizing about these years 1576-1577, because in them Raleigh begins to emerge as a personality from a background of known facts; unfortunately the facts are too few and too unrelated. The register of the Temple makes amply clear that he was in residence there from February 23rd, 1575, and the poem in the *Steel Glas* that he had found certain important connections, for George Gascoigne was a person of consequence. Nor was the acquaintance merely a casual one, for Gascoigne would not have asked an unknown young man to contribute laudatory verses to his book. The contact was probably established through Sir Humphrey Gilbert, the half-brother whose activities were shortly to direct the course of Raleigh's life—Gilbert and Gascoigne had served together in Flanders, where the former had an important command. The latter died in 1577, and it has been noted that Raleigh later adopted his device *Tam Marti Quam Mercurio*, which, contrary to the usual custom of such legends, is so perfectly suited to its second wearer.

Whether or not Raleigh went to Flanders during those years remains undetermined. It is not unlikely; a large number of Englishmen, principally young ones, finding their Protestant zeal unoccupied after the lull in the Huguenot Wars, crossed the North Sea to make things even harder than they were for the Spaniards ; the English contingents under Sir John Norris came perilously near constituting an overt declaration of war against Spain. There seems nothing to determine the matter either way ; it is fairly certain that had he been present at the important Battle of Rimenant he would have said so ; his name is also absent from Thomas Churchyard's *True Discourse Historical of the Succeeding Governors of the Netherlands*, although Mr. John Payne Collier believes that this only proves that he was too young to receive special mention ; nevertheless the *True Discourse* was published in 1602, when Raleigh was a great celebrity, and the author would probably have included him with the least justification. Against all this is the fact that Raleigh had a thorough grounding in the practice as well as the theory of war, and went to Ireland in 1580 so experienced a soldier that a most extensive and varied experience must be postulated for him.

Meantime he was living somehow, and amusing himself after the fashion of young men of the day. That he was able to support servants we know, because in December 1577 he had to bail out a pair of them for an embroilment with the watch ; in this process he is described as *de Curia*, that is, of the Court, to which very likely he was precariously attached through one of his influential relatives. And there are strong references to his riotous living, which in him are rather welcome than otherwise ; for quite soon his energies were, if anything, to be guided almost exclusively by his self-interest, and his youth was to cool into a mould of too-considered action, so contrary to his native temperament. The few anecdotes that have sifted down dwell on his wit (of which the specimens now do not sound too convincing), his high spirits and even his buffoonery. Amongst these one recounts how, being annoyed with the loud garrulousness of a companion, later to be immortalized by Ben Jonson in *Every Man Out of His Humour*, he stopped the fellow's mouth by the liberal application of sealing wax to his moustaches.

There is no further suggestion of light-hearted irresponsibility during the course of his many-sided life. Perhaps there was no time, or perhaps the extant stories of these early years are apocryphal and there was in truth no fun in him. One of the gravest defects of his writings is their lack of humour, but it would seem irreconcilable with the man we know, the egoist, the adventurer, the wit, the highly self-conscious personality, to believe that he lacked even in youth the sense of the joy of living, or the will or capacity to excite the admiration of the young men about him.

It was during this period also that there is reported the first of his many differences with prominent people, this time a quarrel merely characteristic of his years and suggesting none of the worldly intrigue which marred his more adult dissensions. The other party to this quarrel was Sir Thomas Perrot, the son of Sir John Perrot, a distinguished man who was later to become Lord Deputy of Ireland. The cause of the trouble is unknown, but the result was a youthful fracas which brought them before the Privy Council, who sent them both to the Fleet Prison for disturbing the peace. The Minutes of the Council record their release six days later and their giving bonds to behave themselves towards each other in the future. It was not a unique experience for either. Perrot had once before been confined for a similar offence, and later was again sent to the Fleet for having clandestinely married the Earl of Essex's sister. Elizabeth tolerated no such freedom of matrimonial arrangements, as Raleigh himself was to learn a dozen years later when he found himself in the Tower because he had not confided in his sovereign his intention of taking a wife.

The next step in his career is also obscured by lack of complete documentation, which is the more unfortunate in that it was the first on the direct path to his greatest fame. Gilbert had been one of the first of Englishmen to be fascinated by the vision of following John Cabot's lead and making good England's claim to the vast heritage which had lain virtually untouched for nearly three-quarters of a century. While the Spaniards pushed on in the West Indies, Florida, Mexico and South America, and the French in Canada and the Mississippi Valley, only a few English fishing vessels and pirate raiders took practical interest in the New World. As early as 1566 Gilbert had prepared a petition to be allowed to search out the North-West Passage, but had been sent to Ireland instead. Nine years later he renewed his petition, in one of the most significant papers ever written relating to English maritime exploration, the *Discourse of a Discovery for a New Passage to Cataia*, which was subsequently edited and published by Gascoigne along with other

writings which Gilbert had shown him. Several historians have conjectured that Raleigh had a hand in its
composition, on what evidence is not clear. It apparently
made a considerable impression on the new generation,
which was reading with avidity Richard Willes's edition
of Eden's *Decades* and whatever other travel material it
could put its hands on. From then on the English
presses, which had issued but one publication relating to
the New World before Eden's first one in 1553, poured
forth masses of such matter, culminating in the first
edition of Hakluyt's classic work in 1589. But for the
moment Gilbert's pioneer *Discourse* did him little good—
it was Martin Frobisher who was selected to search out
the desired new route by the north-west to China, and
who failed, of course, after three successive voyages in the
years 1576 to 1578. Gilbert continued to write petitions
to which the Queen returned answer or not as she saw fit.

Then suddenly she gave him all that he asked, a patent,
dated June 11th, 1578, " to discover, finde, searche out,
and view such remote, heathen and barbarous lands . . .
not actually possessed of any Christian prince or people,
as to him . . . shall seeme good," and further " to have,
hold, occupie and enjoy . . . all commodities, jurisdic-
tions and royalties. . . ." He had not only the right to
explore but to colonize, the importance of which he was
amongst the earliest to foresee, and in the furtherance of
which his more famous brother was to lose his fortune and
gain immortality. The first expedition under the patent
sailed in the following autumn on the 23rd of September.
Alexander Brown, in his *Genesis of the United States*, says
that Raleigh commanded the " Falcon," one of the smaller
vessels, but fails to cite his authority. Before setting out
a dispute arose with a Spanish merchant relative to seized
cargo of oranges and lemons. The merchant brought
suit against the entrepreneurs, amongst whom was
Raleigh, and the Privy Council laid an embargo against

the vessels.   Mr. Stebbing has conjectured that a fine
of three pounds levied by the Council against Raleigh and
others the following year may relate to the violation of
this mandate, but it is unlikely that no more than that
would have been heard of the affair had it not been ad-
justed before sailing.

There followed the usual weary sequence of events
which Raleigh was to experience again and again when he
rose to the stature of a major naval commander—the fierce
dissensions amongst the various captains, as much and
inevitable a part of Elizabethan naval adventures as
the scurvy, and the raging south-west gales which every
autumn and winter made the route from south-west
England to the Azores a perilous nightmare, and which
in this instance forced the vessels, as often later, back into
Plymouth for refitting and a fresh start.

On November 18th the voyage was begun once again,
but this time the Spaniards intervened, and after an
engagement off Cape Verde defeated and dispersed the
English vessels. They were not, after all, men-of-war, nor
was their commander a sailor ; the time was to come and
soon when nearly every English ship and soldier afloat
was to be respectively somewhat of the one and of the
other. The scattered flotilla returned, each ship on its
own, to Plymouth, and amongst the last was Raleigh, his
provisions almost exhausted. Like Drake he began his
career and ended it with a voyage of disaster.

There has been some dispute as to Raleigh's presence on
this voyage, chiefly because his name is omitted from the
account of Hakluyt, written in Latin by the Hungarian
poet Parmenius, who followed Gilbert to his magnificent
fate five years later. On the other hand, the Hakluyt
account is brief in circumstantial detail, though redundant
in eulogy, and the absence of Raleigh's name from it can
scarcely counterbalance the evidence of another contemporary, John Hooker, who in dedicating to Raleigh his

Irish History in the continuation of Holinshed's *Chron-icles* says :

" Then you together with your brother Sir Humphrey Gilbert, travelled the seas, for the search of such countries, as which if they had been discovered, infinit commodities in sundry respects would have ensued, and whereof there is no doubt, if the fleet then accompanying you, had according to appointment followed you or your selfe had asseyed the dangerous sea fights, when manie of your companie were slaine, and your ships therewith also sore battered and disabled. . . ."

This was written within eight years of the day upon which the recipient rode back into Plymouth harbour, and can leave little room for doubt as to its veracity.   Outside the fact it establishes it is interesting because it begins thus early the tradition, of which we shall observe much later, that where others disagreed with Raleigh, they were at fault or in error, and that his wiser councils would have averted the ensuing ill-success.   Those others and their satellites violently disagreed with these conclusions, and many modern historians have tended to sympathize with them in their grievances.   Certainly there is no doubt that the persuasiveness of his tongue affected those who knew him intimately, as has the eloquence of his pen those who came after, and that his reasoning after the event is usually both powerful and convincing.   His friends too often ministered to his natural conceit.

The failure of the expedition left Gilbert discouraged and nearly bankrupt; it took him nearly five years to muster fresh resources for the glorious failure which ended his life.   Meanwhile he turned to the scene of his earlier activities, Ireland, and thither in due course Raleigh followed him.   Ireland, the grave of so many reputations, was to be his stepping-stone to fortune. Luckily, existing material enables us not only to follow this Irish career in some detail, but to begin to understand what manner of man he was.

CHAPTER II

PUTTING DOWN REBELLION

THE impartial observer in the twentieth century finds it difficult to gain a true picture of England's position in Ireland—the complications due to the Irish character and the peculiar strategic position of the smaller island in relation to the larger make it impossible to be merely judicious, whilst the frequent and well-meant efforts of British governments to solve the hopeless tangle render it unfair to regard merely the long and melancholy chronicle of selfishness, misrule and bloodshed. The issue is somewhat clearer in the late sixteenth century, but even then not altogether simple. With Desmonds and Butlers and other wild chieftains cutting one another's throats, it is difficult completely to reprobate the English who were trying to restore order; with rebellion fermented from abroad, from Catholic Spain, it is not hard to understand the savage determination of the English rulers to repress what they considered their unruly and impressionable subjects. Few outside Ireland objected, and none very strongly, to the brutality of the methods whereby English supremacy was established in that country. And although to us the entire chronicle of assassinations and burnings and brutalities on the part of the stronger people may be sickening, yet in attempting a judgment on the Lord Deputies and Governors, on such men as Sidney, Perrot, Grey, Gilbert, Ormond, St. Leger and Raleigh, it should not be forgotten that gentler minds, such as those of Spenser and Hooker, saw the atrocities as a plain necessity in the execution of a plain duty.

On July 11th, 1580, the Privy Council appropriated to Raleigh and Edward Denny each one hundred pounds, for which they subsequently accounted as from the 13th; on the 15th the City of London was notified that one hundred of its quota of three hundred soldiers for service in suppressing the Munster rebellion were to be put under the command of Raleigh, another hundred under Denny and the remaining third to be held in reserve with the fleet.   The exact day of the arrival of Raleigh and his band in Ireland is unknown, but that he was detained for fifteen days at the Isle of Wight, and that another seventeen elapsed before he arrived at Cork, is stated in his first letter from Ireland to the Lord Treasurer, Burghley, on February 22nd, 1581.   It is interesting to observe from this letter that his own pay was four shillings a day and that of his soldiers eightpence, which, translated into purchasing power of our time, is equivalent respectively to about two pounds and six-and-eightpence.   No wonder that the Elizabethans grumbled at the expense of carrying on war !

His arrival may be fixed, then, in August ; and he was immediately detailed on a commission with his relative, Sir Warham St. Leger, to try Sir James Fitzgerald, one of the leaders of the rebellious Desmond faction, and brother of the Earl himself.   He could hardly have fallen into worse hands, whatever his deserts.   The two West Country officers held strong views on rebels, and both were extremely impatient of any show of toleration or mercy on the part of their superiors.   They sentenced Fitzgerald to be hanged, drawn and quartered, and the sentence was promptly carried out.

Every subsequent act of Raleigh's is so complete an illustration of his attitude to the hapless natives that scarcely any comment is necessary. Once, on a march with the Earl of Ormond, he observed the starving Irish soldiery's custom of disbanding before the approach of a strong British force and fleeing into the woods, later returning to glean what they could from the abandoned camps of the latter. Laying an ambush for them, he captured a number, among whom was one carrying withies. Raleigh asked him what he intended to do with them. "To have hung up the English churls," replied the other boldly. "Well," retorted the Englishman, "they shall now serve for an Irish kern," and ordered the fellow "to be immediately tucked up in his own neckbands." He "dealt with the rest of these robbers and murderers according to their deserts" is the comment of Oldys, which was the opinion of his authority Hooker.

The next episode is perhaps the most famous of all of Raleigh's Irish career. The Spaniards, who were in high hopes from the rebellion, had sent over a force to assist the Desmonds ; by November it was beleaguered in the Fort-del-Ore, in the Bay of Smerwicke, Kerry, by Admiral Fitzwilliam Winter from the sea and the Lord Deputy Grey de Wilton by land. Finally, on November 10th, after several efforts to parley, the garrison surrendered and begged for mercy. Lord Grey put aside certain of the officers for ransom, and then sent Captains Raleigh and Mackworth into the fort, who "entered into the castle, and made a great slaughter, many or most part of them being put to the sword," that is, the foreigners ; the Irish, men and women alike, were hanged—the total number despatched was about six hundred, "as goodly personages," says the responsible commander, "as were ever beheld." It was perhaps the most revolting butchery that took place in a struggle notable for pitiless slaughter, nor does any one seem to have seriously deprecated it. The English Vice-Admiral Richard Bingham

attempted to soften the circumstances by aspersing the
conduct of the garrison : Lord Burghley, as a matter of
policy, disassociated the Queen from public approval of
the event, but there is no doubt that it was greatly to her
liking, as she wrote to Grey in felicitating him ; even the
Spanish minister, Mendoza, made no protest, perhaps
because he knew it would be unavailing. His slaughtered
countrymen were the Pope's Crusaders, and the Pope,
as English Protestants firmly believed, had just had a
fine chalice wrought out of which he would drink
Elizabeth's blood when the Spaniards and Irish between
them should beat Elizabeth into submission.

Of Raleigh's part in this event it is painful to think.
Grey does not mention him in his despatch of November
13th—probably he would have done so had he thought
that his subordinate's conduct was discreditable. He did
not like Raleigh, and for good reason, as will appear
shortly. But the principal chronicler of the affair praises
him highly, and there is no indication that he suffered
the least doubt or compunction. Only the finest souls
amongst his contemporaries, such as Philip Sidney,
perhaps, would have deplored these happenings, and
Raleigh, although an excellent soldier and a shrewd
observer, was in the spirit of his day.

That he was a splendid soldier is admitted even by
the Irish, who execrate him.   All his energy, his astounding personal courage, his mental resources, delighted in
the hazards of this guerilla warfare.   His feats of bravery
are almost legendary.   On one occasion an ambush was
laid for him at a ford between Youghal and Cork by the
Seneschal of Imokillie, through whose country he was to
pass.   Raleigh, riding carelessly ahead of the rest of
his company with his guide, was trapped but succeeded
in escaping over the river.   Looking back he saw one
of his followers, Henry Moile, floundering in mid-stream,
his horse having thrown him.   The man desperately

cried out to be saved. Raleigh dashed back and with pistol and quarter-staff held off twenty men until his own half-dozen stragglers came up, when the ambuscading party fled. A note of verisimilitude is added to the story by the chronicler, who mentions that Raleigh's servant Jerkins, riding behind, had two hundred pounds of his master's money on him—Raleigh's heroism was quite sufficient to account for his risking his life for Moile, but the money alone in any stage of his career would have been nearly as powerful an incentive. His own reference to the affair is extremely modest ; in a letter to Walsingham dated from Cork, February 23rd, 1581, " the manner of myne own behavior I leave to the report of others, but the escape was strange to all men." He was by no means a modest man, yet throughout his career there may be observed this reticent touch in describing his own feats, especially where he was assured that others would elaborate what he suppressed. It was a trait not common in the Elizabethans, who were usually in a great hurry to demand due recognition from court and public ; but Raleigh, wiser than they and the most finished actor of his time, appreciated better how effectively a reputation may be enhanced by the unspoken word. It was a perception which would one day enable him to enact one of the most moving and dramatic scenes which history records.

Another resemblance of our hero's life to the theatre is the number of scenes in which he is definitely in conflict with an antagonist. Most men live out their lives, even in the military or political arenas, with no definite personality arrayed against them. But the story of Raleigh is largely the story of Raleigh versus Grey, or Raleigh versus Essex, or Cecil, or Gondomar. In Ireland the man who seems to have crossed his path as regularly as did the Sheriff of Nottingham Robin Hood's was the Seneschal of Imokillie. During a parley, after the ambush above described had failed, Raleigh contemptuously accused the Seneschal of cowardice, and challenged him to single combat in medieval fashion. The Seneschal and his party hanging back, the Earl of Ormond suggested an extension of the idea, namely that the Seneschal, and Sir John Desmond, accompanied by a small picked number, should meet him and his lieutenant with a like number. The combat in this attractive form never took place however—our source of information against it being English, it is naturally said that the rebels were afraid.

Not long after his rescue of one of his servants he was compensated for his devotion ; during a desperate skirmish, when his horse was killed under him, and he was on the point of being shot, another of his servants, with furious loyalty, flung himself on his assailants and diverted them long enough to allow Raleigh to extricate himself. It was curious how all his life long he could command the worship of his immediate friends and followers, while the rest of the world, aristocrats, politicians, and the poor, longed to humble his pride.

One last military exploit in Ireland completes the picture of the young Raleigh as soldier. His cousin, Colonel John Zouch, commanding in Munster, despatched him with a company of ninety men to capture Lord Roche, one of the influential Anglo-Irish landlords who were suspected of fostering the rebellion. By a forced march at night, through dangerous and hostile country, he reached his destination at dawn. Disposing of his men secretly about the castle, he marched up to the door accompanied only by six of them, where he found five hundred of Roche's tenants prepared with stones and spears to give resistance. They permitted him to parley, and after a time he received permission to enter with two or three attendants. Agreeing to this, the door was opened to him, but instead of the two or three the entire

ninety were craftily smuggled in by some stratagem which
is not described.   Lord Roche received him cordially and
invited him to breakfast, but firmly declined to surrender
himself and return to Cork with his uninvited guest.   He
had no option, however, and the resolute Captain, threatening the hostile tenantry with death to his captive if he
were interfered with, departed again unmenaced at
midnight.   The return journey was fearful.   Amidst
torrents of rain his weary men stumbled on ; the twenty
miles, over rough and pitted country, had to be traversed
again by daybreak, lest the enemy fall upon them.   As
it was, they barely escaped attack and massacre by
Raleigh's old enemy, the Seneschal of Imokillie, who was
waiting for them with eight hundred men, but missed
them in the dark.   One of his men dropped dead with
exhaustion, but the morning found them under the walls
of Cork, where the garrison greeted them with great
enthusiasm.   Contrary to custom, the capture did not
end in an execution ; Lord Roche was later released and
gave three sons in defence of English authority in Ireland.
Raleigh gained notoriety alike for his exploit and his ruse.
The perfidy of the latter seems not to have struck his
biographers any more than it did his contemporaries ; to
stress it in the circumstances would be hypercritical, but
it is interesting to observe the quality of a mind that
knows no scruple in the effective attainment of a desired
end.

Just how far Raleigh had advanced on the path of his
ambition before he went to Ireland it is impossible to
ascertain exactly ; probably no further than the right
introductions and a strong personality could take a young
man of twenty-eight.   But when he quitted this first
Irish service, in December of 1581, he was a figure of
considerable importance, a fact not entirely due to his
distinguished military record.   He returned to London
merely as a bearer of despatches from Colonel Zouch, for

which slight service he was liberally rewarded: but he remained as an unofficial Councillor of State on Irish affairs, the adviser of the Lord Treasurer, Burghley, and the Secretary of State, Walsingham, the two most important men in the kingdom. How this came about is evident from a perusal of his correspondence for the previous year and of the Privy Council Minutes for 1581-1582.

Raleigh's method of bringing himself into prominence was by criticizing his superiors to their superiors. He did not hesitate to inform Lord Grey, the principal English official in Ireland, of the incompetence of Ormond, the governor of Munster. He challenged the attention of the powers in London by asserting the pusillanimity of Grey himself in dealing with the rebels, and offered his own counsel on the subject freely. There are occasions, no doubt, when a subordinate may be justified in so expressing himself ; it is very likely that Raleigh was irritated by the slow and indirect methods employed to attain a very definite end, and it is quite possible that Grey could have reduced the rebels in a shorter time. Like many another impatient and brilliant subordinate, however, Raleigh did not reckon on the factors with which the higher officials had to contend, the avarice of the Queen, her neglect of her army, her capricious disposition ; he did not have to contend with divided counsels, a cabinet that knew nothing about Ireland and took advice from men who either had failed or were to fail in its government.

But the basis of his differences with Grey reveals a defect in his nature graver than impatience, for he charged the Lord Deputy with a lack of severity in dealing with the Irish, a lack which is nowhere evident in that terrible three-year calendar of cruelty. And even if his charges were true, even if still greater barbarism was necessary than was practised to re-assert English

dominion, it scarcely endears him to us to find him its
advocate.

His first criticism of Ormond was written on February
25th, 1581, wherein he complains in general of Ormond's
futility :

"Considering that this man, havinge now been Lord Generall
of Munstre now about too yeares, theire ar at this instant a thowsand
traytors more than ther were the first day.   Would God the service
of Sir Humfry Gilbert might be rightly lokt into ; who with the
third part of the garreson now in Ireland ended a rebellion not
miche inferior to this in to menethes."

The reference to Gilbert may be discounted ; these West
Country kinsmen had a way of grinding one another's
axes for their mutual benefit—the praise of Raleigh by
Zouch and St. Leger is enthusiastic, but no more so than
his of them.   Later, on May the first, he writes to Grey
that Ormond had sent him and his soldiers on a fool's
errand into Canoloch, wherein, from privations and
hardships, they lost two for every " churell of a traytor "
they despatched, and adds with an astute thought for his
correspondent's vanity, " the poore bands have curst the
change they made in levying to follow your Honor, as
they have tould the Lord General many tymes."

It did him no good with the honest Grey, who a year
later informed Burghley that Raleigh's plot for Munster
was impracticable, and Walsingham that " he likes not
Captain Rawley's carriage or company," and it was
Ormond who received official thanks for the suppression
of the rebellion.   But, although Raleigh's methods are
open to censure, his intelligence may have been sound for
all that.   Undoubtedly, despite the handicaps mentioned
above, there must have been some weakness in an ad-
ministration which would spend hundreds of thousands of
pounds and utilize thousands of trained soldiers to put
down a trivial rebellion amongst half-starved, unarmed

peasant factions, who hated one another almost as cordially as they hated the cursed invader.

And although the Cabinet took a diplomatic public attitude regarding its chosen commanders and their policies, it is certain that they regarded with high respect the views and the mind of the young captain who came to tell them what was wrong with Ireland.

But prestige and influence, however useful in their way, was not all Raleigh had gone to Ireland for. That he loathed the service he said several times, and more than once asked to be relieved. Even after he was joined with others in the government of Munster he was not reconciled to a long stay in what, with his remarkable instinct for the poetic phrase, he called " This lost land " and " The Commonwealth of Woe." He was " on the make " as the current saying goes, and the process entailed the acquisition of money. In addition to this, of course, it is in the nature of restless temperaments like his to seek constant change and new adventures.

Before he left Ireland, he laid the foundation of his future there—" The eagles took wing for the Spanish Main, the vultures descended on Ireland," was Goldwin Smith's pregnant remark. Happily for Raleigh's fame he was, like Gilbert, eventually to be numbered more prominently amongst the former than the latter. But he began like any other poor and unscrupulous younger son of his time by petitioning for Barre's Court, a pleasant estate on Cork Harbour, the property of David Barre, who it was alleged had taken part in the rebellion. The details of this transaction are not clear. In the letter to Walsingham of February 25th, already quoted from, he apparently offered to purchase it ; in any event he urged the need of protecting it from burning at the hands of its owner by placing it in safe English custody. Walsingham instructed Grey to allocate the estate to his suppliant, which the latter did, as appears in a list, dated January

27th, 1582, of " gifts " made by the Lord Deputy, of confiscated lands awarded to his followers ; but Burghley prevailed on the Queen not to confirm the gift, either because he distrusted these alienations of Irish property, or because there was another side to the story of the owner's treason, for we find Ormond, in a letter to Grey on March 13th, 1581, forwarding a complaint by Barre that Raleigh and St. Leger had conspired to procure commissions for killing him and warding his father's castles. It seems probable that Ormond, on the spot, would have made short work of such a petition by an overt traitor, had Barre been one.

But Raleigh, disappointed this time, was to get far, far more than Barre's Island. He was to obtain estates in the hapless Western Island which would make him one of the largest English landholders of his generation. And yet even that was to do him no good. For by the very nature of the policy approved by him, the extirpation of the Irish and their supplantation by English, with the murder and arson entailed in effecting this policy, the lack of labour and the destruction of timber, his most valuable asset, consequent upon it, there resulted the very negation of what he sought, and he was to relinquish his eagerly-grasped estates without reluctance. The residuum of what he gained in Ireland was, in the end, to remain intangible—his reputation for gallantry, and much more, his intimate association with Spenser and the composition of *The Faerie Queene*. And by the irony of fate, he who had thought to enrich himself at the expense of Ireland and failed and gained eternal odium for his desire, though he brought little wealth out of the country, is credited with having brought its chief source of wealth into it. But these occurrences belong to later chapters of his career.

CHAPTER III

THE NEW WORLD PLANTER

RALEIGH's leave from Ireland was intended to be merely a temporary one, as may be seen in a letter from Elizabeth to Grey some time in April, 1582, directing the Lord Deputy to give this insubordinate officer the command of a company of infantry in succession to Captain Appleby, recently deceased; the reason given is explicit : that " our pleasure is to have our servant Walter Rawley trained some time longer in that our realm for his better experience in martial affairs," which indicates that the first seed of that long though intermittent favour which the Queen was to show him had been already planted. But he did not return at once to Ireland; Elizabeth had other and more pleasing work for him to do. She first sent him to Holland, where the English were playing a subtle game in the Spaniards' struggle to put down their refractory dependency; his mission included personal contact with the illustrious William, Prince of Orange, and " Monsieur " the Duc d'Alençon, the ten-years-long suitor for the Queen of England's hand. Exactly when he left Holland is unknown, but by his own statement it was after the departure of his chief, the Earl of Leicester, which was in February, the month Alençon quitted England for Holland.

This year, 1582, marked the beginning of his rise at court. It is not clear whether Elizabeth even knew him by sight before his departure for Ireland, but it is obvious that immediately after his return he won his way into her notice. Just how this was achieved and who brought about his presentation is unknown ; the anecdotes repeated by the pretty story tellers Fuller and Prince, of the cloak and the puddle and of his writing with the diamond on the window-pane to catch her eye—

"Fain would I climb, yet fear I to fall"

to which she answered in the same manner :

"If thy heart fail thee, climb not at all"

are sufficiently familiar to every school-child ; of little more value as historical truth is Sir Robert Naunton's statement that the Queen became interested in the young soldier through observing how ably he conducted himself in a dispute with Lord Grey before the Council-board. It is unlikely that any such dispute would have taken place without there being a record of it in the Council Minutes, which I have searched in an effort to find what Edwards, Raleigh's most industrious biographer, overlooked—a task in this case, as in most others, not likely to be crowned with success. The simple truth is probably that the Queen saw him and liked his appearance, as she had that of others before him. All of his contemporaries, even those who disliked him, agreed as to his good looks, strength of personality and readiness of tongue— Naunton, who as James's Secretary of State in 1618 was one of the instruments of the opinion which sent him to the block, wrote that :

"He had a good presence, in a handsome and well-compacted person ; a strong natural wit and a better judgment ; with a bold and plausible tongue, whereby he could set out his parts to best advantage."

His various portraits agree in presenting him as a striking figure, with pleasing features save for his heavy lidded eyes and unhumorous mouth ; the full-length ones show him to have been tall, and confirm the tradition of his passion for fine dress—he was noted for his jewels, his pearls and silver, his raiment of silk and velvet and delicate lace in an age accustomed to every delight in apparel. All his contemporaries make mention of the fortune he wore on his person, even on his shoes.   On board a foul-smelling, disease-laden ship he dressed himself as for a ceremony at court, and no mental picture of him is complete which does not glitter with the grandeur of his costume.

Two facts from which inferences may be safely drawn that the Queen met and was attracted to him as early as 1582 are his growing wealth at that period, which enabled him to finance in part or whole certain maritime expeditions, and her unwillingness to permit him to leave England to take part in them, as he undoubtedly wished to do.   To what degree this favour rose may be gathered from the fact that Burghley, the Queen's principal adviser and right-hand man throughout forty years of her reign, writes to Raleigh on May 12th, 1583, begging him to intercede with Elizabeth for Burghley's scapegrace son-in-law, the Earl of Oxford.   Were not the fact indisputable one would be reluctant to believe it—that the venerable Lord Treasurer's access to the Queen's ear was less certain than that of the Devon newcomer.

Another bit of evidence of the degree of Raleigh's quick ascendancy with the Queen and in the eyes of men is patent in the diary of the quaint astrologer and mystic, John Dee, who in conversation with his familiar spirit records " In respect of the Lord Treasurer, Mr. Secretary and Mr. Rawley, I pray you what worldly comfort is there to be looked for ? "   Raleigh is here mentioned as one of an overshadowing triumvirate at the age of thirty-one—

as a matter of fact he did oblige Dee and established a long acquaintance with him, as he did with nearly every odd, interesting or unusual intelligence of his time.

What precisely were the relations of the Queen and this particular favourite have never been determined. Elizabeth was at this time fifty years old, a striking woman, but certainly no longer beautiful, her red hair dyed, her high nose over her thin mouth and withered cheeks giving her an appearance more formidable than feminine. The gossip of continental diplomats and agents in London put at once the same construction on her intimacy with Raleigh as they had put on that with Leicester : in neither case judging by anything, so far as we now know, save appearances, which were certainly in accord with their view. English contemporaries often held the same opinion, for similar reasons. My business here is not to expound the puzzling and complicated character of the great Queen ; the verdict must simply remain " not proven."

Yet one cannot help gathering impressions, and mine is that, whatever were her relations with Leicester, with her subsequent favourites, Hatton, Raleigh and Essex, they remained platonic, if that word of fine associations may be used to describe personal intercourse which was more ugly than any sensual one could have been. Certain historians have pled guilty on Elizabeth's behalf to her having been the mistress of each of her so-called lovers, on the ground that it was slandering her more to believe her guilty of the kind of hard amorousness the other would have implied. Yet it is just as uncritical to acquit her of the one as of the other without sounder evidence than we have. There was unquestionably something abnormal in the character of Elizabeth, and we must accept it as it was. The woman with the mind and resolution of a man, who could yearn for glory and pinch the fleets that were bringing it to her, lavish thousands on personal display and ruthlessly squeeze pennies required for the public service, who could lie and cheat her way through a French marriage negotiation and exploit the financial needs of a desperate little ally, to rise in the end to a position of virtual supremacy in Europe, such a woman was quite capable, I take it, of flirting with handsome youths as the fancy took her without feeling that her dignity was in the least compromised by yielding to them, or her character by not doing so.

Elizabeth's medical history is a curious one ; it is quite possible that, as with many another woman, her sex satisfied itself by constant flattery from attractive men. Never for a moment did she show feminine weakness towards them when they displeased her ; whatever favour they received did not prevent Leicester from being insulted, nor Raleigh from being imprisoned, nor Essex from having his face slapped in public. She demanded their single adoration, their unquestioning obedience—when they were remiss in one regard or the other, they heard from her in no ambiguous terms. What enraged her most of all was to have one of them contract a marriage of love —which does not so intensely enrage women who have enjoyed their lovers and discarded them, however much it may annoy their vanity. Nor is there any reason to believe that Raleigh would have objected to entering into such an arrangement as is suggested above. It advanced him in the world, it flattered his powers and gave an outlet to his masterful personality. And the fleshly side would have troubled him little, as he was in very small degree sensual ; the affair which resulted in his marriage is, with perhaps one doubtful exception, the only one we know of in the life of a man more gossiped about than almost any other in English history.

If any single fact in Raleigh's life may be considered decisive it is the favour of Elizabeth which made him a courtier. Nothing else could possibly have so altered

the character of his destiny as this.   As courtier the best
of his talents were bound to lie unutilized and only the
worse part of his character and intelligence brought into
constant activity.   His appearance, his facile mind, his
knack of intrigue, served to obtain him easy substitutes
for what he should have earned by his energy and his
genius.   Whilst the less favoured Drake was using the
abilities God had given him to make his country's fortune
and his own, while the ugly little Robert Cecil was by
rigid discipline preparing himself to follow in his illustrious father's footsteps, Raleigh relied to too large an
extent on his figure and his tongue to bring him those
material rewards the seeking of which made other men
great.   The result is that he never became the sailor that
Drake was nor a statesman of the stature of Cecil ; he
remained a courtier, and the cunning Elizabeth, while
free with her gifts, took care that he never became more.
She admired, perhaps loved, him ; but her astute mind
was fully aware that he relied too much on his lesser parts,
that he had not sufficiently trained himself for more serious
service ; hence he was missing from the list of commanders who were to defend England in the perilous
days of the Armada, and she never admitted him to the
Privy Council, the inner circle wherewith she governed
the State.   It was only in time to come, when an act of
passion had brought him her active hostility and he was
compelled to exert himself to win back her countenance,
that he justified the high expectations of his youth.   What
redeems these years at all is the fact that his imagination
refused to be tied down to mere court rivalry and the
business of getting rich ; although he did not follow his
obvious destiny and set out to found that Colonial Empire
which was his dream and became his monument, he did
send out other, unfortunately lesser, men to realize it for
him.   Greedy as he was for money, he never stinted it in
attempting to convert that dream into reality, and hungry

as he was for easy success, he in this instance persisted
through one depressing failure after another.

Of this life at court the poet Spenser has written
vividly, and it is impossible not to believe that he had his
hero, his Shepherd of the Ocean, Raleigh, in mind when
he says of the court :

> " And, sooth to say, it is no sort of life
> For shepherd fit to lead, in that same place,
> Where each one seeks with malice, and with strife
> To thrust down other into foul disgrace,—
> Himself to raise ; and he doth soonest rise
> That best can handle his deceitful wit
> In subtile shifts, and finest sleights devise,
> Either by slandering his well-deemed name
> Through easings lewd, and feigned forgery ;
> Or else by breeding him some blot of blame,
> By creeping close into his secrecy ;
> To which him needs a guileful hollow heart,
> Washed with fair-dissembling courtesy."

It is melancholy to realize that Raleigh knew this full
well. He lived amongst the Hattons and Bacons and
Cecils and Leicesters, but the country of his mind was that
of Shakespeare, Spenser, Marlowe and Hakluyt, the last
three of whom were his close friends. No man ever
wrote more eloquently of the vanity of human desires,
none knew better than he how hollow were the ambitions
of the courtiers. Not only does the thought run like a
grand and swelling theme through his *chef d'œuvre*, the
History of the World, culminating in the most beautiful
passage of prose in the English language, but it is implied
in much of his verse :

> " Tell potentates, they live,
>   Acting, but O their actions !
> Not lov'd, unless they give,
>   Not strong, but by their factions.
>   If potentates reply,
>   Give potentates the lie.

"Tell men of high condition,
   That rule affairs of state,
Their purpose is ambition,
   Their practice only hate.
   And if they do reply,
   Then give them all the lie.

But as I have suggested above, if he thwarted his own destiny for years in these occupations, he enabled other men to fulfil theirs. If he devoted altogether too much of his time intriguing with or against the officials of the realm and incurring their hate, there are records of many kindnesses, such as his forwarding the interests of that curious early spiritualist, John Dee, with the Queen and his intercession for the unfortunate scholar Udall. He used his power as well as his money in aiding the navigators of the age to carry the English flag into the remote portions of the globe, and to plant it firmly in an English dominion in the New World.

The first instance of his intervention of this sort was undertaken on behalf of Sir Humphrey Gilbert, whose patent to colonize in North America and the failure of whose first attempt in 1578 has already been described. Another expedition in 1579 had been prevented from sailing by the Privy Council, who feared that Gilbert was planning acts of piracy—a difficulty Raleigh was to encounter nearly forty years later. Gilbert had tried various occupations since then, but all had proved barren, and in 1582 he was again attempting to fit out a fleet in order to realize his ambition before his patent expired. This time the Queen was extremely reluctant to let him go ; Gilbert had the reputation of " a man noted for no good hap at sea," and no wonder, because he was no sailor, as he himself uneasily realized. But his financial condition was acute ; the patent had but a year to run, and he enlisted the aid of his thriving younger brother both to equip him and to obtain the royal permission.

He was successful in both endeavours ; while not a principal factor in the first, to which Sir George Peckham, that Mæcenas of explorers, contributed largely, he spent £2000 in equipping the two-hundred-ton "Ark Raleigh," a name destined, although not because of its conduct on this occasion, to become resplendent in the long muster of famous English ships. Just to what extent Raleigh was able to influence Elizabeth to change her mind and permit Gilbert to sail is uncertain ; John Payne Collier shrewdly guesses that he had a hand in drafting a very eloquent letter of February 7th, 1583, from Gilbert to Her Majesty, in which the former sets forth the advantages to be obtained by the journey, defends his competence for undertaking it, and pleads movingly his previous services and the necessities of his wife and children.   Certainly any reader of Raleigh's own letters will find the concluding passages very reminiscent of his style and manner :

" . . . But how little account soever is made either of the matter or of me, I trust her Majestie with her favour for my twenty-eight service, will allow me to gett my livinge as well as I may, honestlye (which is every subjectts right) and not to constrayne me, by my idle abode at home, to begg my bred with my wife and children ; especially seeing I have Her Majesties graunt and lycense under the Great Seale of England for my departure, withoute the which I would not have spent a penny in this action, wherein I am bounde to Her Majestie for her great favour, which of all things I most desyre ; and take comfort in protesting, that noe man living shall serve her Majestie more faythfully and dutifully during my life, with all the good fortune that God shall bestowe on mee."

If Raleigh did not write this, it served him regularly as a model when he himself came to write pleading letters to the recipient of this one and to her successor on the throne.

In the end Gilbert obtained his permission ; the Queen sent by Raleigh her good wishes and a token in the form of an anchor guided by a lady, requesting Gilbert's picture in return.   On June 11th the five vessels left Plymouth on a favourable wind, carrying artisans and miners for the projected colony, and " Morris dancers, Hobby horses and Maylike conceits to delight the Savage people."   On the second day a fierce thunderstorm broke, and on the following midnight the " Ark Raleigh " deserted and returned, pleading sickness on board, a plea which was reported with contempt by the rest.

The details of the voyage were fully reported by a survivor ; it was not successful in its primary aims, and in August Gilbert turned towards home, with only two vessels, the " Golden Hind " of forty tons (this was not Drake's vessel, which had returned from its triumphant circumnavigation two years before, and was now being shown to the public at Deptford) and the " Squirrel," of ten, with the terrible autumn gales ahead of them.   The commander himself trans-shipped from the larger to the smaller vessel, saying " I will not forsake my little company going homewards, with whom I have passed so many storms and perils "—no doubt he also did it to refute the suspicion that he was afraid of the sea.   On Sunday the eighth of September, north of the Azores, they encountered a storm with the sea breaking " high as Pyramids."   The water seemed to boil, running in all directions as if a thousand fiendish winds were blowing from all points of the compass.   No one on the " Golden Hind," though many had spent their lives at sea, had ever seen such a storm as this—and as night fell they observed upon their mainyard " an apparition of a little fire by night, which seamen doe call Castor and Pollux.   But we had onely one, which they take an evel signe of more tempests. . . ."

The following day it seemed that both vessels were near the end—control was virtually lost, and they were tossed about in the mad waters, sometimes far apart,

sometimes perilously close together. In the late afternoon they came within hailing distance, and the crew of
the "Hind" were amazed to see the Admiral sitting
calmly in the storm with a book in his hand ; on perceiving them he called out cheerfully above the wind :

"We are as neare to heaven by sea as by land,"

a remark, says the reporter, "well beseeming a soldier,
resolute in Jesus Christ, as I can testifie he was."

The vessels parted for the last time ; after dark the
larger vessel for a space followed the "Squirrel's" light,
as was appropriate and according to the discipline of the
sea, it being the Admiral's ; but at midnight they could
follow it no longer, for the sea had swallowed up the little
frigate and spared the commander the need of coming
home to report that once more he had failed.

Even before it was certain that Gilbert would never
return his relatives prepared to continue his work. A
petition was at once put forward for the renewal of the
patent to another association, of whom the best known
members were Adrian Gilbert, Sir Humphrey's brother,
William Sanderson, John Dee and John Davis. A
second draft of, presumably, January 1584 styles the
new company "Colleagues of the Discovery of the North
West Passage," and agrees to pay the Queen one-
twentieth of all the precious metals found instead of
one-fifth ; considering the region which it was intended
to explore, the difference is not so considerable as it may
sound. Davis, a trained sailor, and like most of the other
sailors of his period, a Devonian, was put in charge of the
expedition. Like Frobisher earlier, Davis made three
voyages under this patent, which turned out, of course,
as far as their primary intent went, to be fruitless. His
contribution to geographical knowledge was considerable,
however, and such names as Davis Strait and Mount
Raleigh still remain to bear witness to their importance.

Long before Davis had set out, however, Raleigh was engaged on the first steps in that undertaking which, so far as America is concerned, at least, was the most momentous of his life. He petitioned for and received letters patent, on the same terms as Gilbert's, authorizing him to plant a colony and hold it for ever. The wording of the document is ordinary enough, but the understanding implicit in it, that the colony was to be situated in territory definitely assigned to and actively claimed by Spain under Pope Alexander II's Bull of Demarcation, indicated a new trend in English transatlantic policy. The wording of the patent, with its provisions against trespassing on the lands of other Christian princes, is interesting, for these words, meaningless as they were under an Elizabeth construction, were the very ones for which the grantee was a generation later to lose his life.

As a preliminary to executing his intention Raleigh sent out a small expedition, under the joint commands of Captains Philip Amadas and Arthur Barlowe, to explore for a site. These set out on April 27th, 1584, and, reaching North America by the usual way of the Canaries and West Indies, coasted northwards until they reached the Island of Roanoke, which they called Wyngandacoia. Here they paused, examined the country, and liked it so much that on their return in September they wrote out a detailed and enthusiastic report to the effect that " The soile is the most plentifull, sweete, fruitfull and wholesome of all the worlde " and that the natives were " very handsome and goodly people, and in their behavior as mannerly and civill as any of Europe." In truth they told Raleigh so exactly what he wanted to hear that, in the light of after events, it is hard not to think that their examination was not altogether thorough.

The report of Amadas and Barlowe, confirming, as it seemed, all of their backer's hopes, aroused general enthusiasm at the court and elsewhere for the projected plantation. The Queen herself, highly pleased at the results of this voyage and the prospects held forth by it, graciously permitted the new land to be called " Virginia " in honour of herself. So runs the tradition at least ; others have asserted that the name was taken from that of the local Indian chief, Wingina ; still others have hazarded the guess that it was derived from " Wyngan-dacoia," which was the response of the natives to the white travellers' demand for the name of their fair country— Raleigh explains in the *History of the World* that the word means " you wear good clothes ! " All in all the first suggestion seems most likely to be the correct one.

It is usually accepted that Raleigh was knighted as a recognition of his services in launching the Amadas and Barlowe voyage, but the evidence is very conflicting. The patent of March 25th, 1584, has in its title the words " Mr. Walter Raleigh, now knight," a curious mixture of titles which, as Mr. Collier pointed out, was not un-precedented. On the other hand Raleigh himself had a seal cut *after* the return of this first expedition, in which he styles himself ". . . *Walter Raleigh militis, Domini et gubernatoris Virginiae* "—*miles* being the distinctive word for Esquire as distinguished from *Eques* for knight. Further evidence that the traditional date of the knight-hood is approximately correct is a letter from the Spanish Ambassador Mendoza, dated February 22nd, 1585, which states " The Queen has knighted Raleigh, her favourite " as if it were recent news, and another letter from Hakluyt, in Paris, to Walsingham, of April 7th, 1585, in which he refers to his patron as *Mr*. Ralegh. Hakluyt might not have known of Raleigh's knighting till after two or three months, but that he would be ignorant of it after a whole year is incredible. It would seem that Collier, whose reasoning at first sight is so convincing, was misled by the descriptive matter on the outside of the patent ; the text itself refers to its holder simply as Walter Ralegh, Esquire. What probably happened was that the endorsement of the outside of the document was put on after the approval of the grant by Parliament in December, and that in putting it on the clerk suddenly remembered that Mr. Raleigh was now a knight and added that information. In any event, to be a knight at that time was an honour ; at the end of Elizabeth's reign it was commonplace, and by James's a joke, even conceivably a disgrace.

The observant reader will have noticed by this time, no doubt, the various spellings of Raleigh's name. It is true that both he and his contemporaries varied it considerably, in fact employing almost every conceivable variation. From 1584 he himself always spelled it Ralegh, but later his contemporaries, in England at least, favoured the one used in this volume. It is certain from the weird attempts at a phonetic reproduction of it in their own language by Frenchmen, Spaniards and Italians—Rallé, Ralli, Reali, etc.—that it was pronounced then much as it is now, although it is quite likely that his first name sounded more like Vawter.

Throughout the winter Raleigh worked diligently to organize his colonists, to prepare for their transportation and equip them with what they should need. On April 9th, 1585, they set out, seven sail from Plymouth, under the command of Sir Richard Grenville, another of Raleigh's Devonshire cousins, destined in a few years to win immortality even more picturesquely than had Gilbert. The leadership of the colony was given to Ralph Lane, also a Devonian, and with him were men whose names have survived even outside their part in this adventure—Thomas Cavendish, the second Englishman to circumnavigate the globe, Thomas Hariot, one of the leading scientists of his day, and Amadas, who had been given the title of " Admiral of the countrey " ; along with these is to be seen in the list a name which was to be detested above all those connected with the career of Raleigh—that of a Mr. Stukely, the father of the " Sir Judas " who betrayed his great cousin and countryman.

The grievances between the Stukelys and Raleigh are supposed to have begun on Grenville's return voyage from Roanoke, where he deposited his charges at the end of June. Returning by way of the Spanish Main, it was natural that he should commit a little incidental piracy. On August 31st he captured a " Spanish ship of 300 tunne richly loaden," and the younger Stukely wailed that his father had been entitled to a vast sum of money as his share of this exploit, out of which Raleigh had cheated him. The story seems improbable, since Stukely senior never pressed his charge in law, as he would surely have done with so much at stake, nor does Raleigh at any time seem to have gained a considerable amount from his Virginian ventures, which in the end attenuated even his bulging purse.

The progress of this colony and of the succeeding one, important as they are to Raleigh's fame, has little to do with him personally, except in so far as their success or failure may have affected his fortunes, and their history may be told briefly. The first reports from the colonists were optimistic ; they thought that they had stumbled into an earthly paradise. But soon finding that the Deity had been in earnest in the book of Genesis when He decreed that a Paradise without the necessity of labour should no longer exist on earth, there began grumblings and recriminations. The Indians turned out not to be angels after all, in fact they quarrelled with the settlers, in turn harassing them or withdrawing and leaving them without means of getting food. It was a bitter winter, and when Sir Francis Drake turned up in the late spring of 1586, with a trail of devastated Spanish towns and sunken Spanish ships strewn behind him, the less resolute of Lane's followers begged to be taken back to England.

The great Admiral offered as an alternative to supply them with what they needed until the expected relief expedition should arrive from England. To this Lane and others would have acceded gladly, but a storm coming, the supply ships foundered and Drake was forced out to sea. He could thereafter not offer such generous provisions as before, and the majority of the colonists grew frightened and voted to go home. Drake consequently fitted them out with a ship, the "Bark Bonner" of 170 tons, and departed for England, whence they soon followed him, arriving at Plymouth on July 27th.

It was by the narrowest margin that Lane missed the relief expedition which Raleigh had sent out, and lost for himself the glory of founding the first English colony in the New World ; for within a day or two came those other ships, with all needful supplies, and the news that Grenville, delayed since Easter, was shortly to arrive, which he did. The latter, attempting to carry out what he knew to be Raleigh's wishes, planted a miniature colony of his own, fifteen in number, and after equipping them for two years sailed away.

The shock to Raleigh when his discouraged and half-starved colonists turned up in the midsummer of 1586 must have been very great, as he had had such bright hopes of their success. Without repining, however, he set to work to build up a new organization and in the following spring had it ready. On the 8th of May he sent out one hundred and fifty householders, organized under John White and twelve chosen lieutenants as " the governor and assistants of the City of Raleigh in Virginia" to renew the attempt. Again ill-luck and the disposition of his company doomed the expedition from the outset. The master of one of the three vessels deserted in the Bay of Biscay ; during a temporary landing in the West Indies some of the settlers indulged themselves in poisoned green apples and after terrible agony barely escaped with their lives. Like their predecessors they were enchanted at the sight of their new land, but the first omen to strike them after landing was that Grenville's fifteen of the previous year had totally and unaccountably disappeared, obviously murdered by the savages—a guess which they were presently to discover was in substance correct. The difficulty of choosing a site at once presented itself, the low marsh lands at first selected being too unhealthy and too exposed. They had hardly unloaded the provisions when they grew frightened at the thought that these were insufficient and decided that emissaries should return immediately to England to obtain more. The governor himself was prevailed upon to go, while his followers decided to move inland. Before he departed in August his daughter Eleanor, wife of Ananias Dare, one of the " Assistants," gave birth to a daughter, the first English child ever born on American soil—she was appropriately christened " Virginia."

During the governor's absence bickering and intrigue defeated whatever chance the colony had of survival. He himself remained abroad longer than he had intended, partially, as historians usually explain, because of the crisis the country was passing through, partially, no doubt, because funds for and patience with a now apparently hopeless venture were giving out at the same time. There is no least justification, however, for the suggestion often made that Raleigh had lost interest in his infant enterprise, to which some general words of White seem unfairly to have given this interpretation. During the next fifteen years he sent out no less than five relief expeditions. The first, and the only one that might have saved the little colony, was frustrated by the stupid determination of its leaders to join in the universal game of piracy which was going on, with the result that they were driven back to England.

The subsequent history of the Virginian Plantation is

no more of Raleigh's making.   In March of 1589 he
assigned his patent, with certain reservations which passed
to the Crown on his attainder in 1603, to a company of
London merchants got together by John White and
others of the Virginia venturers ; that this step was taken
through lack of funds rather than diminution of interest
is proved by the fact that he never lost the latter as long
as he lived.   He talked and wrote about the plantation
continually.   On his return from Guiana he proposed to
pass that way, but was unable to because of the season ;
he sent out another and highly important expedition in
1602 ; from the Tower he begged Queen Anne, James's
consort, to be allowed to join the Jamestown Colony which
other men had founded.   On his return from his last
desperate and fatal voyage, when he was harassed by a
thousand fears and torments, he was only prevented by
his own mutinous crew from stopping to observe its
progress.   He never lost the fervent faith which he
expressed in the words " I shall yet live to see it an
English nation."

Of the colony left by White nothing more was ever
definitely known.   He himself made several efforts to
find its remnants or ascertain its fate, as did John Smith
and his colleagues in 1607.   They had simply disappeared, victims to Indian wrath or their own feckless-
ness.   The tradition has lingered for centuries that they
wandered off into the mountains to the West, and only
about sixty years ago an investigator described a tribe of
Indians who spoke almost pure Anglo-Saxon and whose
oldest members believed themselves to be descended from
Raleigh's lost colony.

No other verdict may be applied to Raleigh's colonizing
ventures in Virginia than that of failure ;   when he
assigned his patent the English were little nearer to a
permanent settlement in the New World than they had
been when he received it.   The causes of the failure were

various, and some of the blame may be laid on him.   His primary fault lay in not having gone out himself ; just what he would have accomplished is uncertain, but there can be no doubt that the influence of his presence, the force of his personality and the keenness of his mind would have removed certain of the major obstacles.   It is quite possible that he would have decided, what the wise Hakluyt three thousand miles away advised, to abandon the Roanoke for the Chesapeake site, where twenty years later, while he brooded in the Tower, strangers were realizing his dream, though the same forces of internal dissension, starvation and native hostility were trying to beat them down.   It is just possible that he would have conciliated the Indians, with whom he dealt so success-fully in Guiana, when he personally led an expedition there.   It is true that Elizabeth would have placed every obstacle in the way of his going, but it seems equally true that had he been strongly enough possessed of the deter-mination to go he would have risked her anger and gone anyway, slipping away as Essex did some years later in defiance of the royal command.

Yet though he must bear some of the blame for the failure, the quality of the personnel and the lack of organ-ization which caused it, he in no way forfeits the respect due to him as the first Englishman to set to work practi-cally to colonize America.   His vision was great, his methods, save in their details and execution, sound ; compared to Sir Philip Sidney's grandiose scheme of the same time for combined piracy and plantation, they suggest thoroughness and practicability rather than wild day-dreaming ; at least with somewhat better luck and more careful supervision, they might have succeeded, whereas Sidney's never could have.   Although he took no direct part in the settlement of 1607, it stemmed from his efforts, and might have been very long deferred without them.   Had he ventured his personal energy as prodigally as he did his money, he would have lived as the greatest man England ever contributed to American history ; even as it is there is no one who can unquestionably dispute that place with him.

Certainly in the minds of his contemporaries no one took rank with him as the patron of exploration.   Of all men none were more fitted to judge his services in this direction than Richard Hakluyt, who as author, editor and propagandist did more than any other man or score of men to waken Englishmen to their obvious destiny : and Hakluyt by his series of dedications to Raleigh, by his continual grateful acknowledgment of the latter's services to himself and by his admiring references to Raleigh's character and service in his many published writings, bears constant witness to the other's pre-eminent position in the field of activity which engrossed the great editor's life.   Raleigh's position in literature, both as creator and patron, will be referred to later, but the gratitude of Richard Hakluyt is pertinent here as testimony to the fact that his part in the great endeavour of the Elizabethan age was not the casual one of the brilliant dilettante.

It has been generally accepted that amongst the results of the Virginia voyages was the introduction of the potato and tobacco into England—two plants which considerably affected the life and habits of this island and the troublesome neighbouring one.   The potato story is probably legend : in a paper by Mr. W. E. Safford, printed in the *Annual Report* of the Smithsonian Institute for 1925, it seems to be proved beyond doubt that the ordinary potato, as distinguished from the sweet potato, was not introduced into North America until 1719, where it was brought from Europe, the Spaniards having originally transplanted it from Chile and Peru.   No plant resembling it is mentioned by Hariot, whose *New Found Land of Virginia* seems to be a complete catalogue of every natural product that that trained observer found as member of the Lane Colony.   How the legend that Raleigh first planted it in Ireland first grew up I am unable to discover, but it is of a very early date and has persisted almost unquestioned from the seventeenth century until now.   It seems too late now to controvert it.

As to tobacco, there is not only not the least doubt that its introduction into England resulted from the 1585 Virginia Expedition, but that Raleigh's example was responsible for the general adoption of the habit.   Hariot describes its preparation for smoking by drying and pulverizing and the great importance the Indians attach to it both as a factor in preserving health and as part of their religious ritual.   It immediately caught the fancy of Europeans, both Catherine de' Medici, the dowager Queen of France, and Elizabeth patronizing it by their interest if not by practice.   It is no wonder that hard-pressed rulers favoured it, for during the next century it became and remained the principal source of national revenue and justified in an unexpected fashion Elizabeth's quip that " she had heard of many who had turned gold into smoke, but that Raleigh was the first who had turned smoke into gold."   In Charles II's time, when the habit had grown into general fashion, it brought the Treasury an annual income of over £400,000, an enormous revenue for those days and greater than the sums for which previous monarchs had exhausted their subjects' patience and risked their thrones.   Even nowadays embarrassed Chancellors of the Exchequer frequently find their way made easier by turning to the subject of Raleigh's importation from Virginia.

The stories about his own first indulgence in the habit, including his alarmed servant and the bucket of water, are too well known to require repetition.   He undoubtedly became a confirmed smoker, and it is impossible to visualize him thereafter in his comparatively infrequent hours of leisure, studying the abstruse writings of the Church fathers in crisp brown pages, or composing his grave *History* to the sound of the river-tide lapping the stones of the Tower, or earlier, uttering his opinions in his small thin Devonshire voice to the circle of wits at the Mermaid Tavern, without seeing his long carved silver pipe resting on his knee and the thick smoke curling up into his beard and the beautiful white lace about his throat.   It appears again, a gleaming spot against the black velvet of his gown, in the last unforgettable picture on the scaffold, aiding him, as he confessed, to meet his ultimate ordeal with a composed and tranquil mind.

CHAPTER IV

THE QUEEN GIVES MONEY

Save for the attempted plantation of Virginia, the years between 1584 and 1592 were those of Raleigh's smallest personal achievement but of his greatest material success. He sent out other fleets or assisted financially or morally in their expedition, but took no part in their activities; he encouraged literature and wrote some himself, although it is difficult to allocate particular pieces to particular years; he managed his properties, became involved in lawsuits, gave his counsel in the great national crisis of 1588, and in other ways kept his exuberant temperament chained in the narrow grooves that his royal mistress approved; in return he received from her gifts of every variety, valuable privileges, vast tracts of confiscated land, offices of prestige and profit. It is in its pomp the most brilliant period of his life, in its achievement and the expansion of his genius so comparatively empty that, if it stood alone, it would scarcely be worth recording, save as a detail of the Elizabethan pageant. One rejoices at the act of passion which tore him from her apron strings and hurled him into the rapid succession of adventures which constitute so vivid a portion of his history.

Whichever of the diverse conceptions of Elizabeth one prefers, none will include an acceptance of her as a generous person; nor indeed was she. Nevertheless the catalogue of her gifts to her favourites is astounding, and can only be explained on the ground that with shrewd instinct she wished to keep them all heavily indebted to her, in which to a large extent she succeeded ; very likely her rage when they went off and did as they pleased occasionally was the very natural manifestation of a woman who thinks herself the victim of ingratitude.   Gifts may be a somewhat euphemistic term for the properties and privileges which she showered, as they were usually taken from those who incurred her enmity rather than from her personal fortune.   Amongst the estates which Raleigh received were at least three such, his 40,000 acres in Munster, part of the land forfeited by the conspirator Babington, and later, Sherborne, the spot in the world he was to love most, which was detached from a bishopric to please him.   His town house, Durham Palace, the historic residence of Elizabeth's parents, was likewise alienated from the bishopric of that name.   In these alienations lay some of the causes of his unpopularity with those whom Elizabeth had robbed to favour him and with the scrambling courtiers all desirous of the same things.   When to these she added the licences for exporting certain cloths, a privilege highly desired by the traders and merchants, and for selling wines throughout the realm, she put him in a position to be hated by almost the whole country, since to most it seemed that his jewels and finery and even his naval expeditions were subsidized by these contributions.   Not one of the gifts mentioned but brought him litigation and curses.   With several he parted gladly— the rest were taken from him by Elizabeth's successor within a few months after her death.

The Wine Licence was the earliest to involve him in difficulties.   In the very year of its bestowal, 1584, there were riots and brawls in the streets of Cambridge, where the University authorities claimed the exclusive rights of licensing under old charter privileges ; the victuallers rose up against Raleigh's new licensee, John Keymer, and nearly murdered his wife. Raleigh proposed to Dr. Howland, the Vice-Chancellor, a peaceful enquiry into the rights of the matter and the punishment of the rioters, which proposals it would appear were ignored. The tone of Raleigh's first letter is conciliatory ; the two subsequent ones became more peremptory, but still the University would have no dealings with the man they obviously considered a grasping upstart ; the letters still remained unanswered. The controversy was at length decided by Burghley, who appears to be constantly cropping up in the path of needy and ambitious young men, in favour of the University.

This dispute was only a detail, however, as compared with a major one which arose on the same subject. Raleigh's method of collecting his taxes from the licensed victuallers was the old and iniquitous one of farming them out. The intermediary in this case was one Richard Browne, who paid £800 a year for the privilege. Either Browne's methods or the amount of his payments did not satisfy Raleigh, who early in 1588 took legal advice and found that if he were to have his own licence cancelled, Browne's would immediately expire with it, whereafter he could have a new one made to himself. Through the instrumentality of Sir Thomas Egerton, the Solicitor-General, this was acomplished, and Egerton's note on the subject to Raleigh still exists ; it provides for a fair adjustment of accounts between the two disputants and the repayment by Raleigh of £1300, whose origin is unexplained, but which I take to be a sort of advance payment against royalties by Browne, before the old licence could be cancelled and the new drawn. Egerton hints that Raleigh would be dissatisfied with this arrangement, of whose fairness there seems to be no doubt. The matter was finally arranged, and the income under the privilege rose to about £1000 a year—a small portion of Raleigh's income, yet £10,000 in the money of our time.

The Universities, it is interesting to note, were excepted from the application of the terms of the new licence.

One of the least attractive sides of Raleigh's character is his desire for wealth, and even more his methods of encompassing it ; yet one can entertain a certain sympathy with him, for his was one of those temperaments of which one feels that it cannot flourish in poverty, or even outside luxury. The extravagances of his character and of his aims demanded a corresponding extravagance of expenditure. He was utterly free of the vices of the miser ; he never hoarded money for its own sake, as his wretched poverty after his downfall proves. He rarely devoted his gains to purely personal ends, save the comparative little which he spent in his childish fondness for self-adornment and on the improvement of his properties, a labour of love which it is hypercritical to deprecate. His money was cast out on the four winds, in raiding expeditions whose equipment cost more than they brought back, in explorations which served his country better than his purse, in disinterested services to learning, into the pockets of dishonest underlings. It is a curious fact that this courtier of the school of Machiavelli never, even after many illuminating experiences, developed a cynicism with regard to other men and his own money. One lawsuit after another never taught him to be watchful over those whom he trusted, any more than poverty made him niggardly. One may deplore the source of his wealth, even his pursuit of it, but there is little to condemn either in his use of it, or, more important, in his attitude towards it.

The list of gifts and honours mounts rapidly and with it the hostility he evoked amongst competitors. When in July 1585 he was appointed successor to the Earl of Bedford as Lord Warden of the Stannaries, a lucrative position which put him at the head of the militia in the mining (or Stannaries) counties of Devon and Cornwall, the appointment called forth the following explosion of wrath from one of Burghley's correspondents :

" Her Majesty and you have placed Sir Walter Raleigh as Lord Warden of the Stannaries, but amongst so rough and mutinous a multitude, 10,000 or 13,000 the most strong men of England, it were meet their governor were one whom the most part well accounted of using same familiarly and biding amongst them ; whereas no man is more hated than him ; none more cursed daily of the poor, of whom in truth numbers are brought to extreme poverty through the gift of the cloths to him ; his pride is intolerable, without regard for any, as the world knows. . . "

It is easy enough to believe that these sentiments of the writer were prevalent generally, but not in Devon and Cornwall ; for Burghley's own son describes a few years later the outburst of joy with which these same strong West of England folk greeted their brilliant countryman on his return amongst them after his first brief sojourn in the Tower.

Previously he had been chosen their representative in Parliament, but in those days election was scarcely a matter of local popularity. Not long after he was made Lieutenant of Cornwall and Vice-Admiral of the two counties of Cornwall and Devon. And in the following year Elizabeth gave him the one appointment which, at the time, at least, must have caused him more satisfaction than any other—the Captaincy of the Guard. It was not a remunerative position, the yearly pay being one uniform of " tawney medley with fur of black budge," but it provided her with what most pleased her, a handsome and distinguished figure to command the fifty handsome and stalwart youths who perpetually guarded her person, and him with an enviable position in the public eye and constant access to her person ; furthermore the Captain of the Guard, by tradition, was accustomed to rise to the highest offices of state.

Meantime he was accumulating those vast estates which were the necessary accompaniment to and support of his brilliant position. First he was given twelve thousand acres in southern Ireland, to which he added by purchase or lease, acquiring in the latter manner Lismore Castle, which is now the property of the Duke of Devonshire. In 1587, after poor Anthony Babington's futile plot to assassinate Elizabeth on behalf of Mary Stuart had been exposed by the omniscient Walsingham, his lands were divided according to custom, and Raleigh found himself the proprietor of estates in five Midland counties. This last acquisition, valuable as it was, seemed to interest him least and least arouses our own interest in him. He never devoted himself to it and its improvement, as he had done with his Irish and was to do with his Dorset properties. There are no pictures to be evoked of his improving, planting, building, occupations to which he devoted loving energy whenever he was weary of activity or out of favour at Court. Furthermore there is an unpleasant suggestion about the whole Babington affair ; the unfortunate conspirator made an attempt to bribe Raleigh to intercede with the Queen for him, and although there is no evidence that the favourite pressed his power, since Babington was actually executed, the pity that his absurd but unselfish plot and tragic fate arouses makes it difficult to view with equanimity the rapacious seizure and partition of his property.

The last of Elizabeth's gifts to Raleigh, just before the sun of her favour set on him, was made on January 19th, 1592, in the form of the Manor of Sherborne in Dorsetshire. This property, with its ancient town and abbey and delightful country seat, she compelled, by some means, the Bishop and Chapter of Salisbury to lease to her that she might assign it to Raleigh ; he had undoubtedly seen and desired it during his many trips from Devon to London, on the route between which it lay.

More than any other single possession he cherished this one, and so lovingly did he undertake its reconstruction and improvement, that to-day his very spirit hovers there amongst the bricks he laid.   He sold his Irish properties without reluctance and suffered the attainder of his Midland ones without undue complaint ; but when Sherborne was torn from him by a shady legal device he moved heaven and earth, so far as a convicted felon might, to revoke the merciless decision of James and his advisers, but to no avail.   It was a legend that the owners of Sherborne before Raleigh had all died unhappily; a curse, so the story goes, had been laid by St. Osmond, Bishop of Sarum (the then name of the See), on all who despoiled his beloved Sherborne.   It was so effective that three of his lay successors in its possession died on the scaffold, and two in prison, while another was murdered.   Robert Carr, Earl of Somerset, vilest of vile Jacobean favourites, to whom James gave the place when he took it from Raleigh, fell from high fortune to imprisonment and disgrace ; death would have been better than the long wretched life he dragged out as a dishonestly acquitted poisoner.

Yet, despite the offices and properties Raleigh now acquired and the odium which their acquisition aroused against him, it cannot be said that he abused the one or neglected the other.   More astounding, perhaps, even than the succession of heroic episodes with which his life is more replete than that of almost any other human being, is the amount of leisure which it seemed to contain for the performance of the more commonplace routine of existence.   We see him sitting in grave judicial pose deciding customs questions in his capacity of Lord Warden of the Stannaries, or consulting with his lieutenants for the regulation of the militia, which in that part of the country, until the Great War at least, retained a large proportion of the rules and government he laid down for it.   We see him in the fine regalia of Captain of the Guard, interviewing hopeful fathers who wished to place their sons in that select body, refusing some and accepting others, brave youths who gladdened the Queen's eye as they carried in platters of silver and gold for her dinner.   We find him called in to advise the Privy Council on a complicated matter arising from the ransom of an Englishman by the Barbary pirates, and drawing up with Thomas Heneage an admirably lucid report on the rights and wrongs of the diversion by the Lord Mayor of the money intended for the ransom.   Later we are to see him as the champion of free speech in Parliament and as the Solon amongst the governors of Jersey.

But these, peaceable as they were in contrast with the occupations to come, are yet in the nature of public services.   There are even quieter pictures of him—as Mayor of Youghal, his maps and charts spread before him in the dark wainscotted study with the carved oak mantelpiece reaching from floor to ceiling, while through the deeply-recessed windows blew in the rich perfume of the yellow wallflowers he himself had planted—the while he vigorously assisted in the ridiculous and savage policy of extirpating the Irish and replacing them by colonists from Devon ; at Sherborne, consulting with architect and gardener, directing the construction of his noble Tudor mansion, laying out his gardens, each hedge and border, the artificial lake and the great row of trees, beeches and limes and sycamores, finally selected and arranged by his own pure taste ; and even in London we may catch many a glimpse of him in his study at Durham House, which stood where Adelphi Terrace now stands—Aubrey saw this study and so described it :

" . . . a little turret that looked into and over the Thames, and had the prospect which is as pleasant as any in the world, and which not only refreshes the eye-sight, but cheers the spirits, and (to speak my mind) I believe enlarges an ingeniose man's thought."

In this little turret he composed a few immortal verses, wrote one bit, at least, of enduring prose, had conversations with Marlowe and Hariot and Dee and others of the choice spirits of his age, and from its windows no doubt his imaginative spirit followed the ebb of the Thames out to sea, to conquests and riches in the Main or El Dorado. Time and again one finds oneself wishing that Raleigh were less Cecil and more Drake or Shakespeare ; that, instead of leaving that little window to increase his own stature or diminish another man's in the sight of the Queen, he had allowed his imagination to lead him out on that tide, or even, staying where he was, sent it out by itself to enrich men's thoughts with poetry . . . the latter, perhaps, was his true destiny ; in the days and nights of loneliness in the Tower, loneliness of which he could have had but moments in Durham House, there sprang from his profoundest spirit words which showed how well he realized the vanity of just such activities as those which were then absorbing him, " the long day of mankind draweth fast towards an evening, and the world's tragedy and time are nearly at an end." He contemplates even now the pettiness of man against that vast vault of Eternity called death—but his spirit is not great enough to accept the truth which it perceives, and he turns again to occupations which do not torture it by these questionings.

One of these occupations was making war against Spain under the cover of freebooting ; at this period he was more detested and feared by that country than any other Englishman save Drake. Hakluyt, writing to Walsingham from Paris in the spring of 1585, says :

" the rumours of Raleigh's fleet, and especially the preparation of Sir Francis Drake, so vexes the Spaniard that I wish, if Drake's voyage be stayed, the rumour of it be continued."

The Queen was obviously in one of her better moods these days ; as she grew older she became more cautious, and elaborate preparations by her admirals and statesmen often ended with ships rotting in harbour and crews eating up in idleness the entire finances of a voyage. Drake sailed and ravaged the Main more thoroughly than he had ever done before or would ever do again ; Grenville varied the monotony of transporting settlers to Virginia by capturing and burning what escaped the terrible Dragon's maw ; Raleigh sent his brother Carew to capture Spanish fishing fleets wherewith to pay the cost of feeding Spanish prisoners.

In the following June two more of his ships, the " Serpent " and the " Mary Sparke," pinnaces of 35 and 50 tons respectively, set out for the Azores, the route by which the Spanish treasure fleet invariably returned from the Indies. Presently they sighted a vessel obviously Spanish ; the Captain, Jacob Whiddon, doubting that the Spaniard shared his own thirst for a fight, put up a white ensign to entice it nearer in the belief that he was a countryman ; which ruse succeeding, he quickly ran up the Cross of St. George, and promptly took possession of her. Amongst her passengers was Don Pedro Sarmiento, Governor of the Straits of Magellan, whom Whiddon brought to London and introduced to his superior. Raleigh entertained his captive graciously, and spent much time discussing, as he relates, the Americas with him ; he might have been less cordial had he been able to foresee how ominously the name of Sarmiento was written across his future.

Other expeditions of his followed in quick succession after the coming and defeat of the Armada, a gesture of Philip's which he and others like him did most to provoke. But in the meantime he was also playing heartily at the game of politics, in which, though he never became a leader, he seriously occupied the attention of such masters as Burghley and Walsingham. It is difficult, if not impossible, to understand Raleigh's exact rôle ; he belonged to no party, was claimed by no faction. In that highly individualistic age he seems the most isolated of all—he was to write of himself " there is none on the face of the earth that I would be fastened unto," and despite his wide cultural contacts, the forced intimacy of months on end aboard ship and the close rub of political and social intrigue, it is true that in his whole life he never attached himself completely and unreservedly to any one. It is one of the reasons, no doubt, along with his self-consciousness and the impatient quickness of his intellect, which gave him his reputation for haughty and overbearing pride.

In this quality of pride he resembled his predecessor in the Queen's favour, Robert Dudley, Earl of Leicester, who probably regarded him with more suspicion than actual dislike. It seems certain that Leicester had been of service to him early in his career, very likely during the French wars. It is also possible that the Earl had secured the young soldier's appointment in Ireland ; at any rate it was to him that Raleigh turned when, sated with Ireland, he asked to be released. His letter of August 25th, 1581, protests extravagantly his devotion to Leicester, saying " . . . . if your Lordshipe shall please to thinke me yours, as I am, I will be found as redy, and dare do as miche in your service, as any man you may commande." The following year Leicester took him to Antwerp, to the pageant in honour of the Duc d'Alençon, the Queen's suitor, to whom the crown of the Netherlands had first been offered. Raleigh returned and Alençon turned out not to be the saviour of the distracted little country after all. In 1586 Leicester in his turn was offered the practical sovereignty of the United Provinces, which aroused the furious anger of Elizabeth, despite his demurrer that he had not sought the honour. Walsingham, Burghley and Hatton restrained her from any gesture which would have offended their Protestant allies, but Leicester, knowing her resentment and the position Raleigh had by then attained, naturally turned towards him as the instigator of the Queen's wrath. The latter, not yet so sure of his position as to defy Leicester, quietly sought out Elizabeth and at her instruction Walsingham wrote a curious letter to the Earl informing him that Raleigh was ever his earnest friend at court. Walsingham makes no comment of his own, merely adding coldly that " this I write by Her Majesty's command." To reinforce his official exoneration Raleigh himself wrote by the same post :

" . . . In ought else your Lordshippe shall find me most asured to my powere to perform all offices of love, honor and service towards you. But I have byne of late very pestilent reported in this place to be rather a drawer bake (drawer-back) than a fartherer of the actions where you govern . . . but all that I have desired at your Lordship's hands is, that you will evermore deal directly with me in all matters of suspect doubleness, and so ever esteme me as you shall find my deserving, good or bad. In the mean tyme, I humbly beseech you, lett no poeticall scribe work your Lordshipe by any device to doubt that I am a hollo or could sarvant to the action, or a mean-willer and follower of your own, and given so, I humblie take my leave, wishing you all honor and prosperity."

To which he appends in a postscript what the Earl most wished to hear :

" The Queen is on very good tearms with you, and, thank be God, well pacified ; and you are agayne her ' sweet Robyn,' "

an item of information which was premature by a considerable time. The letter, while scarcely a testimonial of its author's sincerity or truthfulness, is proof of his superlative histrionic capacity—his protestations are neither too hot nor too cold, he avoids the air of injured innocence and counter-attacks on Leicester just sufficiently to make the latter regret his unkind haste to so candid a friend.

Burghley's attitude towards him has already been indicated. Burghley was the keeper of the public purse and guardian of the public tranquillity, hence he had no fondness for ambitious favourites who emptied the one or endangered the other. His capacities as a statesman have, I think, been greatly overrated, as have that of most of his contemporaries ; what is usually styled their policy was more often a day-to-day system of deliberate misinformation and furtive espionage with the object of capturing trade and suppressing sedition ; a policy in the large moral sense was usually quite beyond them. Burghley was better than the rest in that he conscientiously tried to serve his mistress as well as himself and opposed measures of extortion and violence ; but in his comprehension of the great question of his century, the conflict between the Church and Protestantism, the old agricultural South and the incipient industrial North, he was behind the less honest Walsingham and the less experienced Raleigh. Furthermore he too was compelled to take part in that desperate social struggle wherein Howards resented the intrusion of Cecils and Dudleys, and they in turn that of later comers. It is fairly plain that, although he opposed Raleigh's desires, he did not take him as seriously as did those others of his generation ; and he probably went to his grave believing the other to be one of the many ordinary gifted, handsome young men whose careers he had kept to proper proportions.

With Walsingham Raleigh's relations were rarely other than strained. He never professed the same devotion to the Secretary as he did to the other two, and the latter certainly looked on him with suspicion. Yet they had more in common than either would have admitted ; a boundless capacity for intrigue, an almost complete opportunism, greed and subtlety ; although they disagreed on many questions of public action, they rarely vacillated, as did the Queen and most of her advisers

at one time or another, on the question of the desirability
of a strong and anti-Spanish policy. Elsewhere their
interest came into conflict too frequently to allow of an
understanding. Walsingham was the largest beneficiary of the licence for the export of cloths (by this is
meant unfinished broadcloths upon which ordinary ex-
porters had to pay a duty in the interests of the English
finishing industry), and Raleigh's early and succeeding
grants of the same privilege must have seemed to him
personal deprivation ; further, on the general policy of
the cloth licences his views were opposed to the younger
man's, his interests lying with the Merchant Adventurers,
who stirred up considerable trouble against Raleigh at
various times for what they deemed his infringement of
their lucrative monopoly, and who twice at least received
royal rebuke for their activity ; in 1584 they went so far
that two of their ships were seized and detained on
Raleigh's behalf.

One of Walsingham's most useful attributes was his
nose for plots ; first as Ambassador to Paris and later as
Secretary he seemed able to detect conspiracies almost as
soon as they had been conceived. He was instrumental
in frustrating the Norfolk and Ridolfi plots and knew all
about Babington's from its very beginning. Not that it
required great diplomatic skill to discover or deal with
sixteenth-century intrigues of this sort. They were nearly
always so clumsily conceived, so tardy in execution and so
extensive in the numbers of their members that they would
be comic were it not for the horrible executions which
as a rule terminated them. Walsingham, by his flair, his
spies and his *agents provocateurs*, undoubtedly prevented
them from becoming more troublesome than they were.
But he exaggerated their danger ; if he for a moment
believed that Babington could have unseated Elizabeth
and put Mary Stuart on the throne of England, he was
more of a police detective than a statesman. From

constant contact with conspirators he developed a tend-
ency to see them everywhere, and it was in this rôle that
he frequently regarded Raleigh. He unquestionably
magnified the importance of the latter's criticisms of his
superiors in Ireland, and credited him with endeavouring
to steal Leicester's ascendancy by misinterpreting to the
Queen the absent favourite's ambitions in Holland.
Earlier in 1583, when he himself was involved in deep
courses in Scotland with the object of undermining the
young James VI, he was unable to persuade the Queen
to sanction his policy and at once jumped to the conclusion that his opponents were plotting against him with
Raleigh as their instrument, when the simple explanation
was that an alternative course was cheaper and less likely
to lead to trouble. His letter to Leicester on the subject
is slightly disingenuous :

"I hear there is a by-course on hand . . . wherein Mr. Rawley
is used for an instrument. I hope he is too wise to be used in such
indirect dealings. Your lordship may do well to give him advice
to abstain from such by-courses."

In this instance his suspicions were probably groundless ;
yet though we may smile at Walsingham and his elaborate
conspiracies real and phantom, we cannot unfortunately
feel that he altogether missed his mark with Raleigh, who
seemed attracted to these underground cabals as if by
some mysterious magnetic force. He was too shrewd
to take active part in them ; his interest lay otherwise and
he was keen enough to appreciate their futility. Yet
time and again their skirts touch him and at last so closely
that they enmeshed him and dragged him down the path
to disgrace and ruin.

Similarly, although his pride and good sense kept him
from becoming permanently involved in the legitimate
court factions of the fifteen-'eighties, his temperament did
not seem to permit him to pursue a single honourable

course independent of any of them.   He trafficked now
with one, now with another, and like the bat in the old
fable was in the end distrusted by all.   It is amazing to
observe with what close scrutiny and strong emotion this
soldier of fortune in his early thirties is regarded by his
responsible seniors, but impossible to detect in them
any respect for his integrity and high-mindedness, even
when they granted his perspicacity and promise.

The day was rapidly approaching, however, when
other tests than success in sordid squabbles and back-
stairs' intrigues would show who were the great men of
the time.   Throughout most of 1587 rumours percolated
through of Philip's tremendous preparations to put an
end to his troubles both in Europe and America by
subjugating once and for all their principal author,
England.   The actual state of affairs was finally recognized ;   trade between the two countries ceased, each
appropriated the property and put restraint on the move-
ments of the nationals of the other.   While the Queen,
torn between patriotic ambition and the double caution
of avarice and fear of war, vacillated and gave ear to
every voice, Walsingham mustered his spies in every
country of Europe, principally in that nest of secret
information, Italy, and Drake, taking advantage of
momentary grace in his sovereign, slipped away and
destroyed at Cadiz the ships' provisions which Philip
had been laboriously accumulating for a year.   Neither
the news that Walsingham gathered nor that Drake
brought back was reassuring ;   Philip's preparations were
on a titanic scale and the Armada would without doubt
sail in the following spring.   Only the dishonest and
the obtuse failed to recognize the peril.

Raleigh was certainly not amongst either of these
groups.   As clearly as anybody he recognized not only
the extent of the danger but the best way of preparing for
it.   His biographers have exaggerated his part in the

actual crisis, some even assigning him a major rôle in the historic battle in the Channel, but there is no doubt that he perceived as clearly as Drake himself what line to take to avert catastrophe, namely a powerful navy on the offensive. In his *History of the World* he sets forth so clearly the necessity of defence by naval attack, the hopelessness of it by dispersed land forces, that outside of all else he takes rank as one of the principal strategists of his day. By acute logic, by an overwhelming list of illustrations drawn from his own and other contemporary experiences, he sets forth the doctrine which saved England in 1588.

And yet by an ironic dispensation he was assigned a post, important though it sounded on paper, which proved empty enough in practice. With Lord Grey, Sir John Norris, Sir Francis Knollys, Drake, Lane and others he was in November 1587 appointed on a commission to prepare for the defence of the realm, and it was his hand that drew up the long and able report which advised on the disposition of troops for the defence of the various points on the coast at which the Spaniards might be expected to land. But it was an academic task ; his more important colleagues, save Drake, who was soon detached for high command at sea, were not sailors, but soldiers ; they seriously set about preparing troops to fight an enemy when resistance should be too late, and Raleigh, as Lord Lieutenant of Cornwall, was sent to muster and train that county's contingent of soldiers.

There is very little record of him during that feverish spring of 1588. While the Queen pressed forward and held back, while Burghley urged caution and others whispered treason, while the shipyards laboured day and night to give Howard and Drake what they needed—the workers, according to Stow, who saw them at Tilbury, gleeful that the long deferred death-grapple was at last to come—while foreign diplomats and agents dashed madly about and wrote streams of letters to their eager or panic-stricken principals, while rumours poured in that the Armada was coming, had actually been seen, only to be followed by others that it had been delayed, would not come before summer, perhaps not before the following year, Raleigh, so far as one can discover, examined rosters of able-bodied citizens and taught them the rudiments of the military art. The man who, in 1583, had with Drake and Frobisher and Hawkins outlined the naval policy which was to be England's salvation, knew only by letter and rumour how at last right counsels, his counsels, had prevailed ; how Lord Howard of Effingham, in supreme command at sea, was preparing his navy at Chatham ; how Drake was fretting in Plymouth Harbour, restrained alternately by the winds and his sovereign's caprices from executing his cherished and hard-won permission to meet the Spaniards on their coast and turn back or annihilate them before they ever got started ; how Lord Henry Seymour had been detailed to take his station at the east end of the Channel to prevent the junction of the Duke of Medina Sidonia's forces with the Duke of Parma's mighty infantry in Holland. All these elaborate preparations, with their hurryings and pauses, the absurd errors and the providential interruptions that nullified them, all the epic story of events from the sighting of the first Spanish sail by an errant English pirate on Friday, July 19th, to the fireships of Gravelines and the final havoc in the North Sea, are outside the scope of this biography because, so far as we know, its hero's name is not mentioned in connection with them. His comments upon and explanations of the tactics of the engagement are however amongst the most important historical information which we possess upon them. His perception of the functions and uses of fighting ships at sea mark him as one of the greatest naval students of his time—whether he actually advised on the spot the free tactics, the employment of the superior sailing qualities of the English ships and abstinence from boarding which determined in large measure the result, he certainly recommended and understood them—but commentator after the event is always an ungrateful, as it is often an undervalued rôle. He was to have the opportunity to test his own theories later, with what success we shall see ; but to assign him any more important part in the drama of the Armada than that of administrator in an inactive department, of one counsellor amongst a number, is merely to hazard a guess where all evidence is lacking.

The great Armada had been overcome, but the danger was only temporarily past. Philip would not rest, as all well-informed men knew, nor would Pope Sixtus V let him ; the Crusade against England must carry on, and so it did. Other Armadas were built, which will be referred to in their turn. None came so near to success as Medina Sidonia's first one, yet from 1588 the Spaniard bettered his position in the long struggle, and English triumphs after 1588 were neither so many nor so complete as before that year—in other words England achieved more during the preliminaries to the war that she precipitated than during the war itself, because Spain was learning a great deal from the tactics of her seamen. But the conflict was now overt ; much might be done which had hitherto been surreptitious and without official countenance. The sea-raiders became Admirals, and drew in their wake the best and most adventurous of their countrymen. As the stars of the older men, Drake, Hawkins and Frobisher, began to set, their juniors prepared to take their places. In this new generation no name is more conspicuous than that of Walter Raleigh.

His actual début as a commander was still to be postponed for several years, but there is no mistaking now his impatient eagerness to be off. In September of 1588, when it was feared that the remains of the Armada would re-assemble on the west coast of Ireland, he was actually ordered to prepare to accompany his cousin, Sir Richard Grenville, in joint command of an expedition to drive them off. The fear proved baseless; the Armada had had enough of fighting for that season. So for that matter had Elizabeth ; over the wails and protests of her commanders and more belligerent counsellors she began paying off her sailors, drydocking the vessels and otherwise indicating that she had no mind to spend more money on her fighting force now that the immediate danger had been averted. The burden of financing the war again fell on private shoulders, which assumed it the more readily in that, as has been said above, there were no longer internal complications owing to an awkward state of peace with the enemy.

The one serious effort by the government was Drake and Norris's attack on Lisbon in 1589, and this was undertaken with a political rather than a military end in view. Dom Antonio, the pretender to the Portuguese throne, prevailed upon Elizabeth and her advisers to send out this expedition with the view of dispossessing Philip and replacing himself thereon—Antonio assured his protectors that all Portugal would rise to welcome him and drive out the Spaniards, and made the most extravagant promises, which would have reduced Portugal to a heavily-mortgaged dependency of England for an indefinite period. The Portuguese did not rise, however, and Drake, showing less than his usual acumen, failed of his enterprise. The particular interest of this episode, so far as Raleigh is concerned, is that, amongst the prominent men at court, he and the Lord Admiral alone advised against the attempt—the latter on strategic grounds, in which he proved only too right. Raleigh's objections have been laid to a mere childish desire to oppose Essex, who favoured the enterprise, but such motives, though perhaps not beyond him, need hardly be postulated here. His hard political sense would have informed him that the whole project was a will-o'-the-wisp, a perfectly comprehensible effort on Dom Antonio's part to get something for nothing.

Raleigh's activities in the Spanish war during the next three years were confined entirely to organizing and financing raiding expeditions to be led by such formidable buccaneers as the Earl of Cumberland, Frobisher, Grenville and Borough. I can find no support for the tradition that he accompanied Drake and Norris to Lisbon, and was honoured with a gold chain for his services there. He himself mentions this expedition without saying that he had been there, an omission of which he would scarcely have been guilty. During the years 1589 and 1590 he was for the most part absent from London ; how he occupied himself during this time will appear in the next chapter. But the two following years saw him back again at court, and at last fervently pleading, planning, intriguing to be allowed to lead his own fleets in the most glorious of contemporary occupations.

He came near to being allowed to go in 1591 ; nearer yet in 1592. On each occasion the aversion of the Queen to permit him to risk himself at sea was at least a partial cause of her refusal to let him go. Her feeling for him was not the same, certainly, as it had been half a dozen years before ; the comely young Earl of Essex had come along in the meantime, and found first place in her heart, the last ever to hold it before it withered and shut itself against all human affection. He too, like his elder rival, ultimately coaxed and stormed to be allowed his part in the age of adventure, and he too was compelled to wait until she reluctantly released him. It would have been wiser on her part to have kept them from too constant contact with each other.

The major expedition of 1591, in which Raleigh was until the last minute to serve as second in command to

Lord Thomas Howard, was largely financed by these two and the Earl of Cumberland. Its primary purpose was to intercept the Spanish Plate Fleet at the Azores, the most profitable type of warfare, when successful, ever devised. On the eve of the sailing Grenville was substituted for Raleigh, who went down to Devonshire on official business. There he learned that the Spaniards, at last grown wise, had prepared and were sending out a great convoy to meet Howard, who, utterly unaware, was lingering amongst the islands wondering why the Plate Fleet had been delayed.

Raleigh despatched a pinnace but it arrived too late to give warning. Howard dexterously extricated himself through the superior speed of his ships, but Grenville, who, like a Roland at Roncesvalles, was detailed to cover the rest of the fleet while it hastily collected its men ashore and got away, was compelled to turn and fight. And fight he did, one of the most amazing actions in the history of naval warfare. His company numbered two hundred, of whom eighty were below deck ill. Yet for fifteen hours, from three in the afternoon of September 10th, this incredible crew and its incredible commander stood the battering of fifteen Spanish men-of-war, each larger than their own. Hemmed in, helpless, reduced to a raft rather than a sailing vessel, her masts and sails levelled, she withstood eight hundred rounds of shot before the giant " Saint Philip " grappled her and succeeded in putting on a boarding party. Hand to hand, with cutlass and knife, the mad struggle continued, the combatants slipping and sprawling on the bloody decks. A thousand Spaniards were slain before Sir Richard saw that the end had come. He decided to blow up his ship rather than surrender, but his subordinates had had enough of fighting and glory. The remnants of the " Revenge's " crew were put aboard the Spanish flagship, where they were courteously treated and eventually ransomed into England. But the commander, with a wound in his brain, was beyond such aid. He lingered a few days, the honoured guest of his captors, amusing them by crushing wine glasses between his fingers until the blood ran and then swallowing the fragments. Before they reached port he died. His last words, as reported by John Linschoten, a Dutchman who had them directly, were :

" Here die I, Richard Grennvil, with a joyful and quiet mind, for that I have ended my life as a true soldier ought to do, that hath fought for his countrey, Queene, religion and honor, whereby my soule departeth most joyfully out of this body, and shall alwayes leave behind it an everlasting fame as a valiant and true souldier that hath done his dutie as he was bound to doe."

Nor did the Spaniards ever bring the " Revenge " into port. The ship which had flown Drake's flag during that momentous week when the Great Armada was being harassed out of the Channel into destruction in the North Sea was not destined to enter a Spanish harbour as a captive ; with her prize crew aboard her she quietly sank one night in the Atlantic. The Spaniard could now boast that he had captured one English vessel in all of Elizabeth's reign thus far, but he could not produce her to point the boast.

Meanwhile Drake, who had first made her immortal, occupied Grenville's house in Plymouth and gave that port the benefit of his genius in the office of Mayor ; while Raleigh, who built her, when he heard the news, set himself down and composed an account of her last fight and the cousin who commanded her, which remains the enduring monument in prose of both. Raleigh's inspiration came not only from the event, but from the desire to vindicate the memory of his cherished kinsman, who was already under attack for his unorthodox methods.

The *Report of the Truth of the Fight about the Azores* has, by the beauty of its style, reduced to comparative un-importance the various other accounts of the battle written by less prejudiced reporters ; it has stirred the imagination of the poets, and is responsible for Tenny-son's ballad of *The Revenge*. But its author did even more for his hero than to glorify him ; he also avenged him when, five years later, he sailed his own ship into Cadiz Harbour, and sailed out of it with the " Saint Philip " at its bottom.

The *Report* was Raleigh's first published work ; it appeared in the autumn of 1591. In it he not only attempts to record a memorable event, but to urge the wider acceptance of the war party's plan of continued aggression against Spanish shipping. His policy com-manded by no means universal assent even at court, and was perhaps no more justifiable in morals than its partial adoption proved successful in practice. But it leaves no doubt whatever of Raleigh's attitude towards Spain and heightens the anomaly of his subsequent conviction for treasonable negotiations with her.

Either because the Queen regretted her disappoint-ment of the previous year or because she wished to re-compense herself for the failure of the Howard-Grenville expedition, she encouraged Raleigh to fit a new one with the same purpose in view. She herself ventured a small sum, amiably compelled the London merchants to assist with a larger one, and lent some ships, including the celebrated " Ark Raleigh " which she had just bought from its owner. The Earl of Cumberland also assisted with a fleet and money. Raleigh pledged everything he had in the world, which was a good deal, in fitting out his own largest part of the expedition. He himself was placed in command of the joint fleet, with Sir John Borough as his Vice-Admiral. All winter he journeyed happily and busily back and forth between London and

Plymouth, buying stores, examining ships, scrutinizing the sailors with whom the nets of the impressment gangs replenished his crews. He sailed at last on May 6th, but only to return as soon as he had reached the coast of Spain. Again the Queen repented his absence and again recalled him from his desire, sending Sir Martin Frobisher to take his place. Before returning, however, he used his authority to direct the plan of action and wisely avoided the error of the previous year by sending Frobisher to divert the attention of the Spanish Navy on their own coast, while Borough went to lay in wait for the Plate Fleet.

His dispositions proved highly successful, resulting in the richest captures yet made by the English at sea. Foremost amongst the prizes was the huge " Madre de Dios," Spain's largest carrack, the value of whose cargo staggers imagination—it sounds like a tale out of the Arabian Nights. The actual capture, however, is a strictly contemporary story, the little English vessels, the " Dainty " and " Roebuck " and the rest, like so many hornets, disabling the monster carrack bit by bit until they were in a position to come on board her and with cutlass and pistol finish the job. No one knows where the larger part of the " Madre de Dios' " fabulous cargo disappeared; the plundering by the sailors was enormous, and the simile of hornets changes to one of mice and a large cheese, as the prize was brought into Plymouth Harbour, where Mayor Sir Francis Drake's constituents fell on her with whoops of glee, only slightly in advance of the London traders and brokers who careered across the width of England, all dashing by horse, coach and foot to get a share in the good things the Lord had provided. The confusion was terrific, the uproar of the mice rushing about and attempting to obtain their nibbles deafening. No one's authority was obeyed, no one knew what to do to restore order and yet be sure of getting his own share.   Robert Cecil, Burghley's son, was despatched to Plymouth in the Queen's name and reported that at every step on the road he met some one carrying a bag smelling of musk.

Meantime the original cause of this confusion was far removed alike from uproar and from plundering, being confined for a second time in prison and for the first time in the Tower.   The Queen would have been better advised to let him go to sea, for at some time during the spring, presumably when his more martial activities were ended, he had observed the attractions of one of her maids of honour, Elizabeth Throgmorton, and, as the gossips report, had an affair with her.   Elizabeth might conceivably have condoned this, but the attachment was so strong that he clandestinely married her, which Her Majesty could not possibly forgive.   Very likely she had reckoned that a lover who had been successfully held until he reached the age of forty was her permanent property.   On hearing the news she exploded in a fury and sent the pair to spend their honeymoon in her gloomy castle on the Thames-side.

Nothing is known of the exact circumstances under which Raleigh courted and married Miss Throgmorton, nor is there any date which can be fixed for the latter event. Various biographers have guessed that Elizabeth recalled him from his command on discovering the intrigue, but since she had already notified him of her intention the previous March, when she could have had no inkling of it, this theory must be declared groundless.   The first public intimation that is recorded is a letter from Sir Edward Stafford to Anthony Bacon, dated July 30th, 1592, in which it is stated that the couple are in the Tower. Another letter, an anonymous one, gives more details, and is obviously of a date prior to the imprisonment, but how much it is impossible to decide.   It is so characteristic of its age that it will bear quoting in full :

" S. W. R., as it seemeth, have been too inward with one of her Mati*es* maides ; I feare to say who, but if you should guesse at E. T. you may not be farre wrong. The matter hathe only now been apparent to all eies, and the lady hath been sent away, but nobody believes it can end there. S. W. R. hath escaped from London for a tyme; he will be speedily sent for, and brought back, where what awaiteth him nobody knoweth, save by conjecture. All think the Tower will be his dwelling, like hermit poore in pensive place, where he may spend his endless daies of doubt. It is affirmed that they are marryed ; but the Queen is most fiercely incensed, and, as the bruit goes, threateneth the most bitter punishment to both the offenders. S. W. R. will lose, it is thought, all his places and preferments at court, with the Queen's favour ; such will be the end of his speedy rising, and now he must fall as low as he was high, at the which manie will rejoice. I can write no more at this time, and do not care to send this, only you will hear it from others. All is alarm and confusion at this discovery of the discoverer, and not indeed of a new continent, but of a new incontinent."

But it does not go to prove, as is generally assumed, that he lied when he wrote to Robert Cecil in March " I mean not to come away as they say I will, for fear of a marriage and I know not what. If any such things were, I would have imparted it to yourself before any man living ; and therefore I pray (you) believe it not ; and I beseech you to suppress what you can, any such malicious report." It is not at all unlikely that in March he had no intention of marrying the lady, but did so later, which if true, casts an interesting light on Elizabeth ; as there was such gossip, though of an intrigue merely, she was certain to have been informed of it by one of Raleigh's many enemies. Yet he did not fall out of favour until he had culminated the affair with a marriage.

Raleigh chafed greatly under his imprisonment at the very moment when he was expecting his ships back—news of their magnificent capture came to him in the Tower, and also of the rapacious spoiling which was hourly diminishing the value of his great prize. He describes himself as " become like a fish cast on dry land, gasping for breath with lame leggs and lamer loonges," flatters the Queen, abases himself before her in the approved manner of the day and, after Borough's sensational return, cunningly appeals to her avarice by suggesting that he alone had sufficient knowledge of the conditions and difficulties involved in securing the fortune aboard the " Madre de Dios," that without him she would lose the greater part of her profits—which proved to be no less than the truth.

To his credit it must be said that neither then nor ever after did he utter a word of regret for his marriage. Unlike Essex, who sent his wife, Walsingham's daughter and Sir Philip Sidney's widow, back to her mother's house and disowned her until the Queen's wrath should abate, Raleigh stood loyally by his wife then, when she cost him his freedom, and thereafter, when she continued to cost him the favour and privileges he too dearly valued. They went together through greater misery than falls to the lot of most human beings, yet under the shadow of the scaffold he was able to say in one of the saddest, loveliest letters ever written by husband to wife :

" My love I send you that you may keepe it when I am dead, and my counsel, that you may remember it when I am no more. I would not with my last will present you with sorrows, dear Besse. Let them goe to the grave with me, and be buried in the dust. And, seeing it is not the will of God that ever I shall see you in this lief, beare my destruction gentlie, and with a hart like yourself."

And she deserved the loyalty and affection which she received. She never pretended to understand him ; her mental equipment was totally inadequate to trace in the vaguest way the grandiose patterns of his imagination. But she accepted with fortitude greater than his the terrible catastrophe which blighted their prosperity and all their

prospects, and only once suffered herself to complain of
him, when scoundrels took advantage of the oversight of
fools to rob them of their home by technical trickery.
Otherwise she staunchly stood by him, did his bidding,
bearded his persecutors, fought for his restitution, and
when he was dead cherished his memory through a long
widowhood.

Meantime the spoiling of the carrack was going merrily
forward and it became evident that committees would be
unable to control the reckless mariners whom Raleigh
had gathered together for his voyages.   They were the
same lot who mutinied against the martinet Frobisher on
this very voyage because they preferred the more lucrative
adventure under Borough ; their regard for the orders
of the querulous old Hawkins and the soft-handed young
Cecil who were trying to control them was no greater
than for the Spanish gunnery.   The cargo kept dis-
appearing, and quarrels broke out everywhere, even
amongst the authorities delegated to act on the Queen's
behalf.   The commander himself, Borough, became
involved in a duel arising from the division of the plunder
and was reported killed.   Eventually it was seen that
only one man could unravel the knot; as Hawkins wrote
to Burghley, " Sir Walter Raleigh is the especial man."

So Raleigh, under charge of a keeper, was released and
sent down to Devon.   What happened there is reported
by Cecil on the spot :

" I assure you, Sir, his poor servants, to the number of a hundred
and forty goodly men, and all the mariners came to him with such
shouts and joy, as I never saw a man more troubled to quiet them
in my life.   But his heart is broken ; for he is extremely pensive
longer than he is busied, in which he can toil terribly . . . when-
soever, he is saluted with congratulations for liberty, he doth answer
' No, I am still the Queen of England's poor captive.'   I wished
him to conceal it, because it doth diminish his credit, which I do
vow to you before God, is greater amongst the mariners than I

thought for. I do grace him as much as I may, for I find him marvellously speedy to do anything to recover the conceit of his brutish offence."

I quote this letter at length because it tells so much, not only of Raleigh, but of the man who was to assume such significance in his later life. One can understand Cecil's bewilderment at the popularity amongst his own people, his formidable Devon sailors, of the most unpopular man in London. To the former he was the great man who understood them, to the latter the haughty favourite whom they could not understand save in his least attract-ive aspects. But more than this, there is such an effective contrast between the politician Cecil, who would tempor-arily exalt his necessary agent by suppressing his disgrace, and the actor Raleigh, who knew the advantages in the larger sense of his pose of humility.

No comment is needed on the concluding phrase " brutish offence "—the pious expression of horror at his rival's act of passion on the part of the man who never shuddered at any human foible when he could make it serve his purpose is eloquent beyond words. It defines its writer as clearly as the act itself must elevate in stature the man who was guilty of it—for in contrast with his ordinary calculated conduct and his dubious relationship with the Queen, the affair with Elizabeth Throgmorton, however reprehensible in its beginnings, is a bright spot in Raleigh's history.

It would be too tedious to describe the elaborate accounting which he was finally able to give of the dis-positions of the " Madre de Dios' " cargo. In the end it worked out, as might be expected, in an enormous profit to the Queen, lesser profit to the other shareholders and an actual loss to himself. Of this loss he complains, and justly, since he took the largest risk. But his grievance was not taken too seriously, even by himself, for he obtained his liberty, and as he fondly hoped, his restoration to the Queen's favour.

In the latter, he was disappointed, however.   He was not allowed for five years or more to resume the Captaincy of the Guard nor given his former access to Elizabeth's presence.   When, after his service at sea and in America, he was finally allowed to return, it was not on the same basis.   Outwardly he eventually regained everything, but the warmth was gone.   The light of Elizabeth's countenance never shone on him again after his marriage.

For him it was far better so.   In the years of her disfavour came the storming of Cadiz and the penetration of Guiana, two of the most important elements of his immortality.   But before coming to these we must take account of two others, his friendship with Spenser and the expression of his poetical genius which was closely allied to it.

CHAPTER V

THE OCCASIONAL MUSE

IT was not alone Raleigh's impulse to adventure which was stimulated by the loss of the Queen's favour and his desire to recapture it; a momentary darkening of her brow caused his connection with one of the greatest of English poems and his own composition of certain verses which one would not spare from any anthology. There is not much doubt that his exile from Court in 1589 was not altogether voluntary; although he specifically denies any such construction of his absence in a letter to his cousin, Sir George Carew, of December of that year, yet another letter addressed in August by Sir Francis Allen to Anthony Bacon states that " My Lord of Essex hath chased Mr. Raleigh from the Court and confined him in Ireland." The *Mr.* would cast suspicion on the date of the letter were it not actually dated and the other circumstances in confirmation. What the actual trouble was is not known—that there was bad blood between the two is evident from a note of Walsingham's which speaks of an averted duel between them. However that may be, it is certain that Raleigh had temporarily lost ground, because the Queen flatly snubbed an appeal which he made for an appointment for the Earl of Pembroke; whether she sent him to Ireland or whether he thought it prudent to absent himself there, is likewise not known. He retired to his seat at Youghal, and in a short time the cloud had passed ; by the end of the year he was again in favour and there he remained until the eclipse brought about by his marrriage.

It was during this brief interval that <u>he bcame intimate with Spenser,</u> who now owned and was tenant of the neighbouring estate of Kilcolman Castle. Whether the two had previously been acquainted is not certain ; probably they had, for the poet, as Lord Grey's secretary, had been present at the massacre of Smerwicke and subsequently wrote eulogistically of the conduct and policy of the young captain. They were both of an age, the traditional year of Spenser's birth being the same as Raleigh's. <u>They agreed on many things, particularly their dislike of living amidst the desolation of Ireland, from which the poet, save for two brief intervals, was destined not to escape until a month before his death.</u> There was at the moment a lull in that unfortunate land : a new governor, Sir William Fitzwilliam, was in charge, with whom Raleigh naturally disagreed, and both the young men were able to rusticate and read their poems to each other. These poems happened to be their respective *chef d'œuvres*, Raleigh's *The Ocean's Love to Cynthia* and Spenser's *The Faerie Queene*.

Of Raleigh's part in the inspiration and launching of the latter masterpiece there is no doubt whatever, for its author, in his autobiographical pastoral, *Colin Clouts Come Home Again*, the very title of which contains the wistful note of exile, gives in detail the story of the other's sympathy and aid. Referring to Raleigh as Shepherd of the Ocean and adopting his nomenclature for Elizabeth as Cynthia, the Lady of the Sea, he sings :

> " One day I sat, (as was my trade)
> Under the foot of Mole, that mountain hoar,
> Keeping my sheep amongst the cooling shade,
> Of the green alders by the Mulla's shore ;

There a strange shepherd chanced to find me out,
Whether allured with my pipes delight
Whose pleasing sound shrilled far about,
Or thither led by chance, I know not right:
Whom when I asked from what place he came,
And how he hight, himself he did ycleepe,
The shepherd of the Ocean by name,
And said he came far from the main-sea deep.
He sitting me beside in that same shade,
Provoked me to play some pleasant fit,
And when he heard the music which I made,
He found himself full greatly pleased at it;
Yet emuling my pipe he took in hand
My pipe before that emuled of many,
And played thereon; (for well that skill he cond)
Himself as skilful in that art as any.
He pip'd, I sung; and when he sung, I piped,
By change of turns, each making other merry,
Neither envying other nor envied,
So piped we, until we both were weary."

From just what " main-sea deeps " Raleigh had come he would have been hard put to it to say, but we can charge this to poetic licence. The excellence of his song is vouched for by the listener ; its subject

" . . . was all a lamentable lay,
Of great unkindness and of usage hard,
Of *Cynthia*, the Lady of the Sea,
Which from her presence faultless him debarred,
And ever and anon with singults rife,
He cried out, to make his undersong :
' Ah, my love's queen, and goddess of my life,
Who shall me pity, when thou doest me wrong ? ' "

which would seem to indicate that he was in temporary disgrace.

The Shepherd of the Ocean was not only struck with the rustic's song, but with the propriety of having it heard in quarters where its excellence would be of some benefit to him. He consequently prevails on Colin to

" . . . wend with him his Cynthia to see :
Whose grace was great and bounty most rewardful.
Besides her peerless skill in making well
And all the ornaments of wondrous wit,
Such as all womankind did far excel :
Such as the world admired and praised it :
So what with hope of good, and hate of ill,
He me persuaded forth with him to fare.
Nought took I with me, but mine oaten quill :
Small needments else need shepherd to prepare."

And after a most fearful crossing, which to the poor
travellers was

" A world of waters heaped up on high,
Rolling like mountains in wild wilderness,
Horrible, hideous, roaring with hoarse cry,"

they arrived at the court of Cynthia, who, to cut the story
short, appears to have welcomed her favourite back and
lavished a bounty of fifty pounds a year on his protégé.
The amount of the pension does not to us seem excessive,
but apparently it struck that watchdog of the treasury,
Burghley, so, for he is reported to have exclaimed " all
this for a song ! " and neglected to pay it. Another
version, more detailed but no better authenticated, is that
when the old Lord Treasurer protested, the Queen
impatiently ordered, " Then give him what is in reason,"
which Burghley interpreted to mean nothing at all.
After waiting for some time in vain the disappointed poet
addressed the following epigram to Elizabeth :

" I was promised on a time,
To have reason for my rhyme ;
Since that time, until this season,
I have had nor rhyme nor reason—

with the result that the Queen called Burghley to account
and Spenser had his bounty after all.

The first edition of *The Faerie Queene* appeared in 1590
—that is, three books of the projected twelve for which
the publisher Ponsonby secured a licence—with a pre-

fatory letter to Raleigh, acknowledging the author's indebtedness and outlining to him the somewhat abstruse allegory of the famous poem.   As was the custom of the time the work was, beside the dedication " to the most magnificente empresse Elizabeth," accompanied by a number of other dedications, in sonnet form, to various important personages, Burghley, Hunsdon, Walsingham, the Earl of Cumberland, etc., and by various commendatory verses by the poet's friends.   Amongst these latter the first pair are by Raleigh, and the former of the two is worth repetition in full :

> " Methought I saw the grave where Laura lay
> Within that Temple, where the vestal flame
> Was wont to burn, and passing by that way,
> To see that buried dust of living fame,
> Whose tomb fair love and fairer virtue kept,
> All suddenly I saw the Faerie Queene :
> At whose approach the soul of Petrarch wept,
> And from thenceforth those graces were not seen,
> For they this Queen attended, in whose stead
> Oblivion laid him down in Laura's hearse ;
> Hereat the hardest stones were seen to bleed
> And groans of buried ghosts the heavens did pierce,
> Where Homer's spright did tremble all for grief
> And curst the access of that celestial thief."

The manner is of the time and of the other laudatory poems in the volume, but the quality of this sonnet, as compared with the others, is as startling as Milton's *Lycidas* beheld in juxtaposition with the other elegies on the death of Edward King.   One would have to range far and wide in the vast field of literature to find a lovelier compliment in the form of one poem to another than this.

And it must be remembered that Raleigh was in no sense a professional poet.   None of his verse was published under his name ; his initials alone identify him as the author of the verses prefixed to Gascoigne's *Steel Glas,* the only poem we can definitely fix prior to 1589, when Puttenham's *Arte of English Poesie* had already declared him to be in the forefront of living lyrists. The majority of his shorter poems are variously identified by various critics amongst certain anonymous pieces in the compilation known as *The Phoenix' Nest*, of 1593, but there is still great dispute as to which may be with certainty assigned to him. The question of dates is equally confusing, and no one can say for certain when most of the poems were written. They were probably intended as mere *jeux d'esprit*, to be passed around, not at Court (Heaven forbid!), but amongst the circle of poets and scholars whom their author valued although he disdained their ambitions. These stray compositions were eventually gathered in various anthologies during his lifetime or recovered in manuscript after his death, and may now be examined together in Dr. J. Hannah's *Poems of Sir Walter Raleigh*, which, disputable as may be some of its authentications and rejections, yet offers a corpus of poetical work by which Raleigh's muse may be soundly judged.

And the final judgment must be high, not only of the genius of the man, but of the man himself: if the only data upon his character were his poems, he would remain one of the most glorious figures in all history, generous, erudite, wise, subtle, a philosopher of life in the profoundest sense and a meditator upon death fit to be ranked with the greatest of the world's poets. The sonnet above quoted is generous as well as able ; the elegy on Sir Philip Sidney, with the moving stanzas—

" And I, that in thy time and living state
  Did only praise thy virtue in my thought,
  As one that seeld the rising sun hath sought
With words and tears now wail thy timeless fate.

Drawn was thy race from princely line ;
  Nor less than such, by gifts that nature gave—
  The common mother that all creatures have—
Doth virtue show and princely lineage shrine

What hath he lost that such great grace hath won ?
Young years for endless years, and hope unsure
Of fortune's gifts for wealth that still shall dure.
O happy race, with so great praises run !

England doth hold thy limbs, that bred the same ;
Flanders thy valour, where it last was tried ;
The camp thy sorrow, where thy body died ;
Thy friends thy want ; the world thy virtue's fame,"

is equally so and remains one of the finest examples of a form of poetry in which the English tongue excels.   But it is also a tribute from Raleigh to a man in whom he is able to perceive the reflection of his best self—the far different style of Spenser's pastoral elegy on the same subject, *Astrophel*, with which Raleigh's appeared, shows how, even more than the poet, the warrior and the man in Raleigh was moved by Sidney's bright fame and gracious death.   It has already been suggested that there was something of Drake, of Spenser and of Cecil in Raleigh, something of the pirate, poet and politician ; there was also something of Bacon too, in that he shared the latter's perception of the new era of science which was to be the distinguishing characteristic of the three centuries after his death.   But stripped both of his improbities and his subtleties he is closer to Sidney than to any other man of his time—both romantics, both poets, both overflowing with imaginative explorations and conquests, both courtiers and soldiers, both capable of dying with a perfect last gesture. But Sidney's was unplanned, Christian, Raleigh's conscious, pagan, and herein a whole millennium of human culture intervenes between them.

It is likely that at the time when Raleigh presented Spenser he made his own plea for restitution to favour in the form of the long *Cynthia* poem above referred to.   This, although a fragment, is the longest of his works in verse which has survived ; it was known only by allusions to it until about fifty years ago, when the

manuscript of the extant portion, which still belongs to
the descendants of Burghley, was discovered at Hatfield House.   It is, as Spenser says, a long lament on the
passing of the Queen's favour, at once full of objectionable
flattery and passages of delightful poetry.   The fragment
is in three parts ; there are two short ones of seven and
fourteen lines respectively, the latter in a different metre
from the rest, and the unfinished portion of *The Twenty-
first and Last Book*, which extends to 526 lines.   It is
impossible to tell from what we have the scheme and scope
of the entire poem as projected.   Certain lines such as

> " But I, unblessed and ill-born creature,
>   That did embrace the dust her body bearing,"

deceived commentators at first into the belief that
Cynthia was written after the death of Elizabeth, but Sir
Edmund Gosse has conclusively proved the metaphorical
nature of such lines, and it is obvious that the death so
often referred to is of the lady's affection rather than her
person.   While granting the merit of various stanzas, I
cannot agree that, in its existing form, the poem is of any
very great importance, although, completed, it might
have been amongst the great long poems of the age.
It seems to have served its end however, and restored him
to grace, which is, no doubt, all that he expected of it.

The note of worldly self-seeking, which sounds so
loudly throughout nearly all of Raleigh's career, is
almost absent from the poems, and this may not be
ascribed to the existing poetical conventions, as are so
many other deficiencies in the manner and matter of contemporary verse.   These conventions did little to hamper
the genuine poetic mind ; Sidney's passionate love for
the Lady Penelope Devereux and the torments of Surrey's
haughty soul employ them but as concealment from
the vulgar—the rest are not left in doubt.   It is only
where the emotion is as artificial as the form that the latter

obtrudes itself ; shackling only where it has nothing to shackle. Of this kind are Raleigh's love poems. Not being by nature an ardent lover of women he merely subscribes to the convention which demands from a fashionable poet certain lines in this vein and produces :

> " Silence in love betrays more woe,
> Than words, though ne'er so witty :
> A beggar that is dumb, you know,
> May challenge double pity.

> " Then wrong not, dearest to my heart,
> My true though secret passion :
> He smarteth most that hides his smart
> And sues for no compassion "—

a mere rhetorical exercise. But then he himself admits that he had no great feeling on this subject, for elsewhere he writes :

> " And yet some poets would prove
> Affection to be perfect love ;
> And that desire is of that kind
> No less a passion of the mind ;
> As if wild beasts and men did seek
> To live, to love, to choose alike.

It was not here that the torments lay which could prod his muse at once into tears and song. Somewhere deep inside himself he must at times have felt that he was trading his talents of gold for the baser metal which vulgar men valued, that he had bound his soaring imagination to the sordid earth, that the passing years were punishing him by giving him only what he sought and not what his Maker had intended him to have. Then a cry of scorn and anger bursts from him, as in the lines quoted in Chapter Three from *The Lie*. The very beginning of the poem is painful in its irony :

> " Go, soul, the body's guest,
> Upon a thankless errand :
> *Fear not to touch the best* "

and in the succeeding lines he pours vitriol on all that he had nearly sold that soul to obtain.   In what Sir Edmund Gosse, rightly I think, selects as the best of his poems, *The Pilgrimage*, there is repeated this cry of disillusion, but combined with it is also resignation, a confidence that a Higher Court will reverse the findings of those whose judgments in Eternity can mean nothing.   One cannot quite share his confidence that the Heavenly Judge will accept his own view of himself as one who had suffered from the malice and misjudgment of his fellow-men, nor does he in his poems, at least, urge this aspect of his case too seriously.   But there can be no doubt of the sincerity of his inmost conviction of the vanity of the world's rewards, his perception, akin to that of all the great tragic poets, of the futility of the aspirations and pride of kings and emperors while God possesses and is able to use, at His own caprice it may be, the solvent Death :

> " Of death and judgment, heaven and hell,
> Who oft doth think, must needs die well."

And die well he did, but if he had thought of these things oftener and harder, he might have lived better, too.

His mind was essentially a serious one ; save for an occasional sarcastic prick he never evinces a gleam of humour either in his verse or prose.   He reflects soberly on the world and a hereafter, but though seeing the futility of the strivings of the one in the light of the uncertainty of the other he is never moved to either laughter or pity, as were Rabelais and Shakespeare.   As a poet the acuteness of his intelligence and his sense of melody enabled him to compete with his contemporaries in setting involved images and complex thoughts to music—a truly Elizabethan occupation.   But the more happy mood of *carpe diem*, of young love and springtime and care-free laughter, were utterly beyond him—it is difficult to conceive him in the raptures of youthful love or heedlessly giving way to mirth. The world was a gloomy place, where men strove for place and expressed the worst in them, or for understanding which might breed contentment but never joy. The point need not be laboured, for he himself illustrates it perfectly, in his reply to Marlowe's exquisite lyric, *The Passionate Shepherd to his Love*. Marlowe's first and last stanzas, it will be recalled, run :

> " Come live with me, and be my love :
> And we will all the pleasures prove
> That hills and valleys, dales and fields,
> Woods, or steepy mountain yields.
>
> " The Shepherd-swains shall dance and sing
> For thy delight each May-morning ;
> If these delights thy mind may move,
> Then live with me, and be my love."

Raleigh's corresponding stanzas are :

> " If all the world and love were young,
> And truth in every shepherd's tongue,
> These pretty pleasures might me move
> To live with thee and be thy love.
>
> " But could youth last, and love still breed,
> Had joys no date, nor age no need ;
> Then these delights my mind might move
> To live with thee and be thy love."

Biographers have endeavoured for nearly three centuries to reconcile conflicting aspects of Raleigh's life and character, to explain how one man could be both a patriot and a plotter, a benefactor of the race and a selfish egoist, a man who was profoundly moved by the contemplation of the divine hand in human affairs and at the same time capable of the most time-serving practices and atheistic speculations. But none of these seem impossible to reconcile, granting his versatility and curiosity, for they are mere inconsistencies between the inner thought and

outer act which are commonplace amongst human beings
—what is far more difficult is that he was at heart simultaneously and during most of his life both a Puritan and a
Pagan.   His habits of abstemiousness, which his worst
enemies never question, are merely incidental ; it is his
cast of mind, his complete emotional separation from
Rome when most of his fellows were still Catholic in mind
if not in profession, his distillation of life into a stern
relationship between conduct and punishment, that stamp
him the Puritan.   His philosopher's mind saw beauty
and gaiety not even as embellishments, but as mere
unimportant distractions, at best manifestations to be
pondered upon rather than enjoyed.   There is no doubt
that a generation later, had the unpredictable factor of
self-interest not swayed him one way or the other, he
would have been found amongst the leaders of the
Puritan rebellion—and it is significant that he was read
and regarded with reverence by Hampden, Milton, and
Cromwell.

   But equally strong in him was the Pagan sense, if not
of the minute, then " of the minute made eternity."   He
was completely apart from the Puritan, from all Christians
of whatever creed, in his inability to merge himself with
the Creator, to view Him from any position save the outside.   Man in the abstract he saw, clearly as any thunder-
ous seventeenth-century divine, as a creature who had a
duty to do and his immortal soul to ponder upon in a
sunless world ; but Walter Raleigh appeared to his vision
concretely as a man who made beautiful gestures which
were to be preserved intact to the end of time.   Every act,
every description of himself, is part of an effort to de-
lineate himself in the rôle of a Curtius doing something
which will leave him grandly fixed in a pose for ever.
There is here none of the Puritan sense of the vanity of
all human gestures ; it is the mere Pagan delight in
capturing momentarily a sort of plastic perfection.   One

has but to read his own account of his return to the council
of commanders in Cadiz Harbour, dramatically reversing
their decisions and changing everything in an instant—
his history is not the unfolding of a beautiful life page
by page, but a self-sought apotheosis in sculpture, himself
caught in his greatest moment for all succeeding generations of men to look at.   It is a propensity utterly alien
to Catholic and Puritan alike, but an Athenian would
have understood it perfectly and admired its resultant
expression.

Despite the frequent references to and preoccupation
with religion to be seen in his verse and even more strongly
in his prose, it cannot be urged that Raleigh was in any
profound sense a religious person.   His Puritanism, as
I trust I have made clear, was a habit of thought rather
than an ecstatic union with the Deity under the peculiar
forms of Puritanism—and that habit of thought merely
led him, if not to constant practice, at least to an Old
Testament view of right conduct as a necessity lest one
be punished.   There was so much more of speculation
than of faith in his attitude that it is not surprising that in
his own day he was widely suspected and at one time
seriously accused of atheism.   His eulogists have taken
this charge so seriously that they have been at great pains
to acquit him of such accusations, a task scarcely worth
the effort in our own day, when few would think the less
of him even if it were proved.   The interest for us lies
in the fact that when he had prevailed on the Queen to
alienate the coveted manor of Sherborne from the Church
and give it to him, the enemies caused by this procedure
attempted to retaliate by circulating charges of free-
thinking, an offence punishable by death.   The specific
form of the charge was that he conducted a school for
atheism at Sherborne, wherein all sorts of heresies were
openly discussed and the youth corrupted.   Among the
young men who were supposed to have given him their

attention were Christopher Marlowe and Thomas Kyd
—the opposing faction may be assumed to have included
the young William Shakespeare, for in the latter's very
bad juvenile play, *Love's Labour's Lost*, is to be seen his
ridicule for the Raleigh group, whose leader it is to be
assumed he intended to satirize under the name of Don
Adriano de Armado.

The matter finally came to a head when the hostile
faction succeeded in having a commission appointed to
examine into the statements of Raleigh and his alleged
colleagues in sin, including Thomas Hariot, the famous
mathematician, already spoken of in connection with the
first Virginia Colony.   Marlowe had been killed a year
and a half previously.   The commission began its inquiry
at Cerne Abbas in Dorsetshire on March 21st, 1594.
The case fell rapidly to pieces, as witness after witness
lamely confessed that he knew nothing save by hearsay
from common gossip about Raleigh's and Hariot's
uttered heresies.   What these were may be gathered
from a small portion of the evidence.   A discussion was
going on as to the immortality of the soul and Raleigh
was endeavouring to obtain a workable definition, saying
" that he had never had one from his learned teacher at
Oxford."   The witness reports himself as saying that
the " soul is a spiritual and immortal substance breathed
into man by God, whereby he lives and moves and understands," to which Raleigh objected " yes, but what is
that spiritual and immortal substance breathed into
man," etc.

" 'The soul,' quoth I.

" ' Nay, then,' saith he, 'you answer not like a scholar.' "

Raleigh was simply trying to enforce a Socratic method
of reasoning at these discussions.   The entire episode, in
fact, is almost like a burlesque of the trial of Socrates, the
godless putting up the godly to charge the philosopher
with irreverence and corrupting the beliefs of the young.

It would have been a classic farce had Raleigh been actually convicted ; how well he would have played out the final scene, with words and gestures modelled on the original, and how little would he have succeeded in making a genuine tragedy of it.   He had something of the Greek's brain, but none of his humour or humility, nor, greatest lack of all, sincere love for his fellow-men.

One frequently feels, apart from this connection, that Raleigh's life is a Greek tragedy which slipped a cog somewhere.   The elements are there—the brilliance and versatility of the hero, his rapid rise to fortune, his swift and unjust fall.   But something at least equal to these in importance is lacking; what it is will appear, perhaps, as the story develops.   No Greek tragedian, be it remembered, made a hero of Achilles, the warrior, the orator, the poet. . . .

CHAPTER VI

TO THE RAINBOW'S END

THE years 1593 and 1594 record numerous un-availing efforts on Raleigh's part to get back into the Queen's good graces. For this purpose he employed principally the Lord High Admiral, Charles Howard, and Robert Cecil as intermediaries. To the former he pleads, in a letter of June 21st, 1594, that he intercede with her Majesty so that he (Raleigh) may be allowed to accompany the Admiral as private soldier or sailor against the Spanish fleet—a gesture whose exact value may be estimated by the immediately following words:

" I have no other desire but to serve Her Majestye. And seinge I deserve nor place nor honor, nor servante, I hope it will be easily granted."

It is unlikely that he expected to be given so lowly a place as that of " poore mariner," nor would he have been happy if he had been; he was easily sea-sick, loathed the stench of the forecastle, and would have had to put by his beautiful raiment. His sincerity was not put to the test, however, for even this profound humility did not melt Cynthia's heart.

It was the other avenue of approach, Cecil, whereby he finally sought to achieve his object, not this time by self-abasement but by a magnificent *coup*. Throughout those two years he was constantly using Burghley's son to keep Elizabeth in mind of him, and if Cecil executed a fourth of the commissions given him by the exile at Sherborne, the Queen must have grown excessively weary of her former favourite's name. These commissions consisted for the most part of small pleas on his own behalf or recommendations to Cecil of various protegés, and are not worth detailing separately, for all the time he had in the back of his mind that great exploit whereby, in the opinion of many, his chief claim to the consideration of posterity depends.

Just when and how his interest in Guiana arose is uncertain, but by the beginning of 1594 it was occupying his mind to the exclusion of all other major matters. In February Lady Raleigh is already writing to Cecil, begging him to dissuade her husband from the dangerous adventure, to employ him, if he must go to sea, in " sure water towards the east than help him forward toward the sunset "—even Elizabeth Raleigh, undaunted by the demands of spelling and syntax, could write fine prose in the age ruled by her namesake—but her intercession was altogether futile, for Raleigh had already sent his old and trusted lieutenant, Jacob Whiddon, on a reconnoitring expedition to the Orinoco. Whiddon arrived in Trinidad, was greeted warmly by the governor, Antonio de Berreo, given a coloured and misleading version of Berreo's own previous expedition into that country, induced to part with more information than he gave and came home no wiser than he went, but poorer by several of his crew whom Berreo had detained.

Whiddon's empty return stimulated his employer rather than the contrary; he now had, in addition to other motives, a score to settle with the Spaniard, which he presently settled in full measure. Whiddon had tales to tell of the country's endless resources of gold, tales which merely corroborated what other voyagers to or near Guiana had reported, and of these reports there was not one which Raleigh had not examined until he knew it virtually by heart.   In addition he had interviewed these travellers when available, and collected and conned maps and topographical data, until his proud intellect assured him that he had as thorough a grasp of the actual facts relating to the country as any living mortal.

It is impossible now to reconstruct the sixteenth-century attitude towards that unknown country which lay between the headwaters of the Orinoco and the Amazon. To the contemporaries of Raleigh it was a part of Eden wherein many of the timeless myths and fables of ancient history were actually reality.   Amazon women who fought like men, tribes of human creatures whose heads sprouted from their breasts, trees on which grew all the nourishment necessary to men, cities of gold towering upon rocks of gold.   The legends were spread in part by design, in part by the eager desire of men to believe.   When suspicion of their falsity began to creep in, it was charged, and with some justice, that the Jesuit Friars had been in part responsible in order to induce the adventurous and avaricious to come and open up the country for them. Before Raleigh's time no one had even penetrated far enough to disprove a single important item ; on the contrary the further they progressed the more did they seem to find confirmation of the Indian traditions, and what the natives did not tell them they interpreted for themselves because of their faulty understanding of the Caribbean dialects.   Their geography of the territory, which placed Manoa, or El Dorado, the golden city, on the non-existent lake of Parima, was based on a mis-apprehension of the Indian description of the river Parima's annual inundation of the adjacent Savannahs. This error persisted for centuries, and a map of more than a hundred years ago contains the mythical White Lake of Parima, which appears on Raleigh's chart as the Lake of Manoa.

The persistence of the fables relating to Guiana's wealth is perhaps naturally explained by the invariably gloomy endings of the expeditions which set out to find it—the more insurmountable the barriers the greater the treasures they guarded, seems to have been the explanation of why eight or nine adventurers followed one another to most shocking fates. Raleigh himself describes, with not too great accuracy, the efforts of his predecessors. Amongst these the earliest was Ambrose von Alfinger, a German, who in 1530 went as far as he could into the interior of Venezuela, whence he sent twenty-five men back to the coast for provisions. The latter callously declined to return to their leader's aid, and he and nearly all his men perished by starvation or the poisoned arrows of the Indians. Ten years later Gonzalo Pizarro, a brother of the conqueror of Peru, on the quest for El Dorado, started from Quito with a large force, which he divided on the banks of the Napo, a tributary of the Amazon, sending a detachment under Orellana down the river for the same purpose as Alfinger. Orellana descended the great river to its mouth, the first European ever to do so, and set sail for Spain, having early determined that to return to his companions was too hazardous a business. They, reduced to a remnant, eventually returned to Quito, looking " as if a charnel house had given up its dead." It was the traitor Orellana who first espied women fighting in the ranks with men, in a skirmish he had with the natives, and identified them with the legendary Amazons, whence the river obtained its name. Admiring contemporaries tried to fasten the name of Orellana upon it, but luckily it did not, as in the case of Vespuccius, stick—luckily, because although technically the Spaniard had a better right to be so commemorated than did the Florentine, he was too great a scoundrel to merit the honour. Several minor expeditions followed, which repeated the tales of the city of gold as if they had actually seen it from afar. In 1560 occurred the most notable of all, that under Pedro de Ursua, who numbered in his band Lope de Aguirre, perhaps the most picturesque, and certainly the most horrible, of the procession of rogues who left Spain for the Americas. The whole story is packed with thrills, intrigues, quarrels over women and money, battles and hardships. Aguirre, a kind of outlaw king-maker, first deposed Ursua and murdered him, setting up a tool Fernando de Guzman in his place, and notifying Philip II that a new prince who did not recognize him now ruled in Peru. Later he sent Guzman to join Ursua. Under Aguirre's erratic and incompetent leadership his men wandered thousands of futile miles, murdering and plundering, through Peru, Brazil and Guiana, down the Orinoco to the sea and along the coast to the Spanish settlement of Basquimento, where Philip II's authorized deputies promptly and fittingly dealt with them. The last expedition before Raleigh's was Berreo's, of whose questionable reports a measure of confirmation has been obtained within recent years and published in one of the Foreign Office Blue Books dealing with the Venezuela Boundary Controversy. Nothing speaks higher for Raleigh's courage than his determination to follow in the grisly tracks of his predecessors, and for his abilities than the skill with which he avoided their errors. To what extent he succeeded where they had failed will presently appear, but he brought back knowledge, in many cases exact and illuminating, of the geography, flora and fauna of the country, where they reported only confusion, and evoked affection where they had planted hatred.

Raleigh firmly believed the stories that the ancient treasure-house of the dispossessed Inca was in this locality ; but it would be doing him less than justice to attribute his undertaking of the perilous and distasteful exploration to a mere desire to possess himself of its wealth. That, no doubt, played a part, but a small part ; there were easier ways of getting rich. Also, of course, he desired to retrieve his position by a sensational exploit, and no exploit could be more sensational than one which resulted in a stream of gold flowing from America to England. But it must be recalled that he had assisted Gilbert and planted Virginia with less immediate objects in view—he held most tenaciously to the conception of England's heritage in the New World, and viewed with resentment the growing monopoly of Spain. He could scarcely compose a paper, on any subject whatsoever, without referring to the support which the King of Spain's power in Europe was gaining from its possession of inexhaustible treasure across the Atlantic, and never ceased to urge, as did Drake, that there was the place to strike if that power were to be sapped. Seeing further than Drake, he realized that occasional sinkings of Spanish Plate ships were but an incident in the major campaign— that the prime necessity was to plant the English flag over at least as large and rich a portion of America as was covered by the shadow of Spain's. The Guiana venture was undertaken in the knowledge that for his country's sake as well as his own he must now adopt the principle of large profits and quick returns—that a policy which might only bear fruits in the distant future would neither serve his personal turn nor engage the enthusiastic efforts of his compatriots.

The necessary permission from the Queen was forth-coming in the form of a commission which significantly omitted the customary words " trusty " and " well-beloved " and which contained the usual prohibition against trespassing on the lands of any other Christian prince—a phrase of ill-omen which was to be the pretext whereby his life was taken. His half-brother, Sir John Gilbert, undertook to collect the crew, which was, of course, obtained by impressment ; he had to be extremely careful, in view of the plague which was then raging, and which had just driven Lady Raleigh and her infant son from Sherborne, that no infected person should be taken aboard.   By September of 1594 the expedition was ready to sail.   The usual last-minute difficulties arose, several ships failed to report, Raleigh was involved in a small but troublesome lawsuit, and the winds kept blowing from the wrong direction—not until Thursday, February 6th, 1595, did the five vessels, most of them small even for those days, since coasting and river works were in prospect, set sail.   They paused at the Canaries for fresh meat, again at Teneriffe, where they waited seven or eight days in vain for Lord Howard's ship " The Lion's Whelp," and Captain Amyas Preston, and at length headed east for Trinidad, arriving at Curapan or Punto Gallo, where Columbus had landed in 1498 (now called Point Içacos), on March 22nd.   Almost his first step was to punish the Spaniards for their treacherous attack on Whiddon the year before, when they had seized several of his men in the act of landing, by permission, in quest of food and water. He burned the new city of St. Joseph and took prisoner Governor Berreo, of whom, however, he made a friend and whom he pumped for information instead of hanging. He displays a curious detachment about this gentleman, whom he described at the same time as a brutal murderer of Indians (Raleigh found five chiefs chained together in an indescribably filthy prison and released them), and yet as a courteous and valiant soldier of Castile.   A polite war of wits between the two followed.   Berreo did all in his power to dissuade Raleigh from his project, exaggerating, if that were possible, its difficulties.   In this he was partially actuated by the knowledge that his own lieutenant, Domingo de Vera, was on his way from Spain with newly recruited forces for precisely the same object which he was now assuring the Englishman was unattainable.   Raleigh, in no circumstances open to con-

viction on this subject, was the less likely to be moved by
Berreo's observations, since he privately knew all about
de Vera's mission to Spain and his imminent return, for
he had been put into possession of an abstract of Berreo's
own correspondence on the subject, captured by Captain
George Popham with a Spanish vessel the year before.
He listened to Berreo, learned what he could, and hurried
on the construction of the little galleys necessary for the
navigation of the tortuous tropical rivers into which his
quest would carry him.

Many English writers have grown eloquent over the
difference in the treatment which the Indians received
from their countrymen and from the Spaniards. This
argument will not bear the closest scrutiny, but in the
main it is true that the former appreciated the wisdom of
conciliating the natives, especially in those territories
where their existing hatred of the Spaniards would make
them valuable allies. Elsewhere the Anglo-Saxons were
at times scarcely more punctilious in the observance of
native rights than the Latins, although the wholesale
savageries which prevailed in San Domingo, Mexico and
Peru were never practised on the same scale in the more
northerly expanses ruled by the British—nor, of course,
were the Indians in them as likely to possess gold or know
where it was to be found as the victims of Cortez and
Pizarro. Of Raleigh little can be spoken save praise in
this respect. He severely repressed the least misconduct
on the part of his men towards the natives and their
women, and gained not only their trust but the admiration
of the Spaniards for his success in dealing with them.
One cannot but applaud his act when he called together
the Indian chiefs whom Berreo had dispossessed, showed
them the Queen's picture and gravely explained that,
having been appointed by God to free Europe from
Spanish oppression, she was now turning her countenance
to the Caribbean with the same intent. So much did

they admire Elizabeth's likeness, that he had difficulty in keeping them from making a religious idol of it—all of which Sir Walter was at pains to set forth for Her Majesty's gratified perusal.

Just after the sacking of St. Joseph, Captains Gifford and Keymis, who had been separated from him on the coast of Spain, turned up. But Preston, owing to a mis-understanding, never arrived at all. Finally giving him up, Raleigh crossed the Gulf of Paria, the " Sad Gulf," in which the torrential outpourings of the Orinoco basin are continually raising great billows and cross-currents, to the danger and discomfort of sailors. What these must have been in his small boats is inconceivable, " worse than the English Channel," he says. His ships he left off Los Gallos, at the southerly point of Trinidad.

For the voyage into the interior he employed an old galley, a refashioned barge, two wherries and a ship's boat of " The Lion's Whelp," carrying in all a total of one hundred men with provisions for a month. He had a curious misapprehension of the distances to be traversed, partly due to misleading information, partly to faulty measuring instruments. Berreo had told him that Guiana was six hundred miles further from the sea than he thought, and this knowledge he kept from his men, lest they should mutiny against so much greater a task than they had anticipated. His own reckoning of four hundred miles as the distance from the Bay of Guanipa to the mouth of the River Caroni, the furthest point that he reached, is considerably out—Sir Robert Schomburgk, who surveyed the territory, says that all the windings of the Caño Mañamo, by which Raleigh reached the main stream of the Orinoco and then the Caroni (see Schom-burgk's maps on endpapers), do not make up a distance of more than 250 miles. It is just as well that he deceived his men as to the extent of their journey, for the hardships they suffered were almost beyond belief. One hundred

men packed together, sleeping on bare boards, their
clothes periodically soaked by tropical rain and dried stiff
by a burning sun, their provisions either undressed meat
which decayed rapidly in that fierce temperature or local
fish whose odour rose to heaven—" I will undertake there
was never any prison in England that could be found
more unsavory and loathsome," wrote the commander,
who was aware that he was not bred to this sort of thing.

The delay caused by Preston's tardiness proved costly.
The rivers were undergoing their seasonal rising, the
currents grew daily stronger and the ten days' wait at
Punto Gallo cost many more in the tedious effort to row
against the heavy waters.   The bed of the river shoaled
and shifted, and twice the galley struck and was got off
with only the greatest effort.   The banks were thick
with tropical foliage, cutting off air from the boats and
making the necessary landings difficult.   " If God had
not sent us help we might have wandered a whole year in
that labyrinth of rivers," declares Raleigh piously, but it
was another case of God helping those that helped themselves, for the help referred to, consisting of a better pilot
than the loyal but useless Indian they had engaged at
Trinidad, was a captive taken by Raleigh himself from an
Indian canoe.   From him they received assurance that
they were getting somewhere, but no evidence of it came
to their eyes.   For fifteen days they pulled their flat-
bottomed boats through the currents and on and off the
mud, and with each pull forward the gold seemed visibly
to recede.   Yet it was gold, or the stories of gold, that
kept them to their labours ; like a shining cord ever more
tenuous it runs through Raleigh's narrative of the voyage.
He pauses time and again during the account of those
miserable fifteen days to recapitulate the old evidence and
offer new to the effect that what they sought must be just
ahead of them.   Every story told by the previous writers
and explorers, of the king whose meanest kitchen vessels

were of precious metals, of Martinez, who descended on Manoa in a manner reminiscent of *Erewhon*, but was robbed of his treasure before he could display it to Berreo, is repeated like a Chanty to keep his discouraged followers tugging at their oars.   Stories a-plenty, but no gold.   Just the same hideous yellow waters, the same rank vegetation.   Had this continued one day more the poor pilot would have lost his life, for his employers began to suspect that their plight was due to his treachery.

Then all at once they seemed to have reached their goal.   The country changed and became to their eyes as fair as Paradise.   Instead of underbrush was velvety open country, with tall trees, which seemed to Raleigh's observant eye to have been planted by some divine landscape gardener ; coloured birds flew overhead, and fresh fruit was to be had.   But most cheering of all, a basket of refiners' tools was found in a bush.   That surely meant that the gold was near.   The crew were impatient to begin prospecting immediately, but Raleigh vetoed the suggestion.   They had not brought mining instruments with them, and to dig with their nails, he decided, would not produce sufficient results to compensate them for the warning a small success would be certain to give to other nations.   The reasons do not sound convincing and might be used to substantiate charges later made against him, but they cannot be proved untruthful.

But courage and discipline were now restored, and the men eager to go on.   On the fifteenth day they debouched into the main channel of the Orinoco (which Keymis named Raleana in honour of his chief, the first Englishman ever to navigate the famous river), from where they could see in the distance their objective, the mountains of Guiana.   The country here was inhabited, and the natives welcomed them hospitably, giving them pineapples, " the princess of fruits " as Raleigh called it, on the juice of which numbers of his men became pleasantly drunk, showing them the antidote against the poisoned arrows of the Aroras, who dwelt on the left of their future route (an antidote futile if the wounded man were intoxicated, warns Raleigh), and supplying them with an experienced pilot, the elderly brother of their prince Toparimaca.

Again they resumed their journey, and on the sixth day, after several pauses, reached the province of Arromaia, which was ruled over by King Topiawari.   Raleigh sent a pilot to ask the latter to visit him, and the next day the old man, now 110 years old, made the journey from his home, fourteen miles distant, on foot, returning the same afternoon.   He brought with him " venison, pork, hens, chickens, foule, fish with divers sorts of excellent fruits and rootes " as well as bread and wine, and gave Raleigh for a pet

" a beast called by the Spaniards *Armadilla*, which seemeth to be all barred over with small plates somewhat like to a *Renocero* with a white-horne growing in his hinder parts, as big as a great hunting-horne, which they use to wind instead of a trumpet. Monardes writeth that a little of the powder of that horn put in the ears, cureth deafness."

With this aged monarch Raleigh promptly arranged an alliance, promising the protection of the Queen if Topiawari would acknowledge her sovereignty, which he readily did.   He probably no more understood what it meant than he comprehended the white man's craving for a certain yellow metal which he amiably assured them abounded not far off.   His reason for joining the English is obvious enough, Berreo having, in true conquistador fashion, murdered his predecessor, and caused the centenarian himself to be dragged about with a chain around his neck until he agreed to pay a ransom of a hundred gold plates.

After a brief rest Raleigh wished to push on, but his

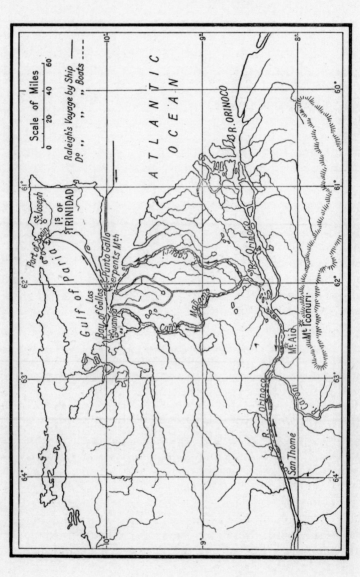

FROM TRINIDAD UP THE ORINOCO

men declared themselves unable any longer to row against that irresistible current.   A land expedition was therefore chosen to ascend the Caroni, and proceeded some little distance accompanied by Topiawari's only son Caworako.   Everywhere they saw evidence of precious metals, bright stones, and glittering ones, which Raleigh gathered and took back to England.   But the year was too far advanced to progress much further.   The annual deluge was imminent, and so he turned back, resolved to return the following year.   Topiawari tried hard to dissuade him from leaving, offering to accompany him to Manoa, which he, like many others, knew all about by report, if Raleigh would leave fifty men to guard his people against Spanish vengeance.   But the offer was declined, and with much goodwill on both sides the Englishmen took their departure, leaving Francis Sparrow and Hugh Godwin of their company, and taking back Caworako, whom he re-christened Gualtero.   Sparrow remained for some years, sketching the country and trading, his principal article of traffic being apparently slaves, for he himself records how he bought eight young Indian women for a red-hafted knife which in England had cost him a halfpenny.   Godwin, a boy, remained by his own wish to learn the language, and succeeded so well that when Raleigh returned, twenty-two years later, he had almost forgotten his native tongue.

Raleigh himself describes his homeward voyage as tedious, and so it must have seemed to his company, for although the passage down stream was easier than up, especially to the " gentlemen " who, as was the custom, accompanied these voyages and whom Raleigh, like Drake, compelled to do their share of the work, hope was now behind instead of ahead.   Actually the downward course was even more fearful than the upward, for the great storms were now raging ; the thunder and lightning were incessant.   The variety they knew in England had

an aspect of only local malignance, but this was as if all
the demons of hell were seeking them out through the
interlaced foliage under which they huddled on the river
banks. They found the route by which they came
impassable owing to the enormous billows, and were
forced to take the lesser tributary, the Capuri, whose
mouth was further from the anchorage of their ships.
Most terrible of all was the crossing of the Serpent's
Mouth, where a storm nearly swamped the galleys.
How it was achieved is stated in Raleigh's own vivid
words :

" The longer we tarried the worse it was, and therefor I took
Captain Gifford, Captain Calfield and my cousin Grenville into
my barge and after it cleared uppe about midnight we put our
selves to God's keeping and thrust out into the sea, leaving the
galley at ancor who durst not adventure but by day light. And so
being all very sober, and melancholy, and faintly cheering another
to shew courage, it pleased God that the next day about nyne of
the clock, we descried the Iland of Trindado, and steering for the
nearest part of it, we kept the shore til we came to Curiapan, where
we found our ships at ancor, than which, there was never to us
a more joyfull sight."

Six weeks later, in August, he arrived again in
England, having sacked three Spanish settlements in the
Main when they refused the necessary supplies.   Raleigh
had planned to stop at Virginia to relieve his erstwhile
colony on the way, but the exigences of the weather
prevented him.

His return did not breed the excitement he had anticipated ; word had already gone forth that the principal
object of the voyage had not been attained—no gold had
been brought back, none had even been found.   This
latter accusation Raleigh set himself resolutely to combat,
in the address " To the Reader " which precedes his
account of the Guiana Voyage.   It seems that while he

was at Trinidad an Indian, knowing the strange cupidity
of the white man for certain kinds of rock, had advised
him of its presence near by, and he had sent forty men
to gather it.   When they returned he examined the
mineral and promptly pronounced it to be worthless
marcasite.   The distribution of these specimens through
London had given the impression that they were the whole
extent of his gleanings.   He, however, placed his faith
on the "white spar" which he gathered on the Caroni, and
submitted it to various public and private assayers, all of
whom, he asserts, declared it to be rich in gold.   As
contributory evidence he offers the fact that the neigh-
bourhood where he had obtained it abounded in El Madre
del Oro, "the mother of gold, or as it is saide by others
the scum of gold," which is the certain sign of the richer
mineral in the vicinity.   There can be no doubt that he
fully believed that he was on the verge of discovering the
hidden source of the treasures of the Incas—whatever
other charges against his good faith can be substantiated,
this one cannot.   The subsequent history of Venezuela
(for his "Guiana" was actually in what is now Venezuela)
shows that although his expectations of its gold resources
were considerably exaggerated, they were not altogether
baseless.   The metal, in limited quantities, has been
mined there consistently during the last century.

Much else of the criticism, both contemporary and
modern, of his conduct of this voyage must disappear or
be modified if we regard it in his own perspective.   He
used gold as a bait, it is true, to lure shareholders and
tenaciously holds to the assertion of its presence when
of his own knowledge and from his own experience he
cannot substantiate that belief.   But, almost despite himself, his mind declined to be concentrated on this one
thought.   If it had been he would have pillaged as well
as burned these three cities of the Main, or run after ships
in the manner of his illustrious contemporaries.   But no,

he wrote, "it would have sorted ill with the offices of
honour which by her Majesties' I holde this day in
England to runne from cape to cape for the pillage of
ordinarie prizes." From the example of the Spaniards
he knew that the richest finds were achieved invariably in
the caves of buried princes, but although he examined
with curiosity the burial customs of the natives and reports
on these with most delightful detail and explicitness, he
declined to be party to desecrating their holy places.
His hope was that by setting forth the wonders of what
he had heard, substantiated in a certain measure by what
he had seen, he would be allowed to lead a larger expedition to reap what he fondly believed he had sown. All
the lengthy conclusion of his *The Discovery of the Large,
Rich and Beautiful Empire of Guiana* is devoted to a plea
that his countrymen arouse themselves to appropriate the
territory and make of it an English treasure-house in
America which should be the envy of Spain and the cause
of her ultimate ruin. Beyond all question of immediate
profit he believed, almost with the fervour of religion,
that England must hasten to dispossess her enemy of this
wonderful land of Guiana—and curiously, in the unveil-
ing of time, long after he was dead, she did. However
disingenuous may seem his excuses for not consummating
the immediate object of the expedition, there is no mistaking his passionate sincerity where the larger issue is
involved.

Most of the censure he met was bred, of course, of
disappointment that he had not persisted if he had
come so near El Dorado as he said he had. Some of this
is justified, no doubt, as is the criticism he brings on
himself by the implicit admission that his preparations
were inadequate. But granting this latter, it would have
been highly dangerous to proceed in the flooded condition
of the country and his ignorance of the topography. He
had before him the tragic histories of Alfinger, Pizarro,

Ursua and the others, and was of no mind to repeat them. His best justification lies in the fact that in those absurd little boats, under the unhealthiest and most hazardous conditions, he brought his men through these hundreds of miles and back again without losing one, save a young negro who fell overboard into the very jaws of a crocodile. His only notable loss on the whole voyage was faithful old Captain Whiddon, whom he buried in Trinidad.

His return gave rise to more than disappointment— it bred slanders of the most serious description. His enemies circulated the report that he had never gone abroad at all, that he had lain hidden in Cornwall while his ships went off without him, buying whatever of true ore they had in Barbary and bringing it back into England from Guiana. It was such assertions as these, he declared, which impelled him to write out his own account of the voyage, whose full title is given above (I shall refer to it merely as *The Discovery of Guiana* hereafter) and upon which I have relied for the bulk of the information contained in this chapter. No one now gives any credence to those silly slanders. If the confirmation of his own description of the country by succeeding explorers like Humboldt and Schomburgk were not enough, the independent testimony of his men would be ample to refute them. More interesting, although no less groundless, are the strictures of David Hume, the historian, on the veracity of the author. The basis of his charges are that Raleigh invented wonders which never existed, cities and figures of gold, the tribes whose heads grew out of their breasts, the women who lived in a segregated community and fought like men. But Hume apparently did not read *The Discovery of Guiana* with sufficient care before damning it. It is true that it is full of tall stories, and to this is due half its fascination. But the strictest line is drawn between what the writer saw and what was reported to him. No doubt he was, in common with the rest of his age, credulous, and accepted literally the kind of folk tales which all primitive peoples have invented since the world began.   But credulity is not mendacity ; it may even be evidence of an active and curious mind handicapped by lack of exact data.   It was at least as creditable for the sixteenth-century explorer to believe as for the eighteenth-century pedant to deride.   One lived in the age of wonders, the other in the age of doubt. Raleigh himself, by anticipation, offers the best defence for his proneness to accept the marvellous, when he answers the sceptics of his own day by retorting that there were in the world " stranger things than are to be seen between London and Staines."

That Raleigh did not intend to mislead is clear—in speaking of the headless men he states distinctly " though it may be thought a mere fable, yet for mine owne parte I am resolved it is true, because every child in the provinces of Arromaia and Canuri affirme the same," and he goes on to say " they are *reported* to have their eyes in their shoulders, and their mouths in the middle of their breasts, and that a long train of hair groweth backward between their shoulders."   When Humboldt and Schomburgk explored the country they found these tales still current and still credited by the natives.   And it would be strange if it were not so.   From the beginning of time travellers have brought back equivalent stories, and men of curious minds have pondered upon them seriously, even where they have not accepted them.   Bacon discusses wilder propositions, and this very idea seized on Shakespeare's imagination, for amongst the wonders which Othello, a truthful man, reports in the recitals which captured Desdemona, is a tale of

> " The Anthropophagi, and men whose heads
>   Do grow beneath their shoulders."

The report of the Amazons has a more familiar ring.

It came down from antiquity, and Columbus was early informed that his New World possessed an island inhabited by these warlike females. Nearly every sixteenth-century history or book of travels gives credence to them, and Raleigh after all was compelled to rely on such information. When he arrived on the scene himself he found an unqualified belief in these Amazons, with most circumstantial descriptions of their habitat, appearance and customs, transmitted by men who were alleged to have seen them. Because he himself was not privileged, owing to the brevity of his stay, to do so, was not in itself a refutation, unless he had been another man and of another age. Even after his time as well as long before it learned men accepted the story as truth. No reader of *The Discovery of Guiana* can possibly regret that its author did so, for if he had not he would not have recorded so conscientiously their tribal *mores* and we should have been deprived of incomparable reading. Just an extract must suffice :

"They . . . do accompanie with men but once in a yeere, and for the time of one moneth, which I gather by their relation to be in Aprill." (What month more natural ?) "At that time all the kings of the tribes assemble, and the Queenes of the Amazons, and after the Queenes have chosen, the rest cast lots for their Valentines. This one moneth they feast, daunce and drinke of their wines in abundance, and the Moone being done, they all depart to their own Provinces. If they conceive, and be delivered of a sonne, they return him to the father, if of a daughter they nourish it and retaine it, and as many as have daughters send unto the begetters a Present, all being desirous to increase their house, sex and kind."

Why should he disbelieve in these things, he who not only saw and pondered daily upon phenomena which had either never been heard of before or confirmed those which had existed in thousand-year-old traditions? Had he not himself seen a tree on which oysters grew, a hill of diamonds, a red mountain ? His successors found different, and to us more convincing, explanations of these curiosities, of the cowls which made the Ewai-panomas seem headless, of the tides which left the oysters on the trees ; but lacking their background and facilities for investigation, he still could believe that nature might be capable of marvels beyond complete elucidation by the human mind.

Those portions of his narrative which tell of his own personal observations have been praised by experts as in the highest degree reliable. Humboldt often confirms his remarks on the flora and fauna of the country and upon the traits and customs of its people. Schomburgk declares that his geographical knowledge was wonderful. Beyond these two we cannot go—it must be accepted that what Raleigh vouches for is as accurate and comprehensive as it is vivid.

Of its quality as literature praise can scarcely go too far. Its author's feeling for the sound of waterfalls, his eye for the colour of the tropical birds as they wheeled about overhead in a clearing, his childlike delight in the difference between the flowers of Guiana and those of England, his endless curiosity for and presentation of detail in the outlook and customs of the Indians, his ability to communicate alternate hope and terror in the rush of his simple prose prove him to have been a consummate literary artist. All one need do is to read through that epic of English travel, Hakluyt's *Voyages*, to realize that *The Discovery of Guiana* is, from the point of view of style at least, the gem of that incomparable collection.

The practical results of the Guiana voyage were very small. Although Raleigh, in his published account and in eloquent letters to Cecil, begged the public and its leaders to follow where he led, every one but himself and his friends remained sceptical or apathetic. He set forth in every possible light, of wealth, of empire, of religion, the advantages to be derived, were England to make herself mistress of Guiana. He sent out Keymis in January 1596 and in December of the same year Leonard Berrie—why he himself was unable to go will be evident in the following chapter. Both returned with reports of the renewed activities of the Spaniards on the Orinoco (de Vera's tragic failure occurred that year) where a trading post, San Thomé, of evil augury, had been established. He undoubtedly encouraged Sir John Gilbert's large but abortive preparations for despatching Captain Samuel Mace in 1602. In fact his mind never left for long the subject of El Dorado during the rest of his life—thither he made his last voyage, and from there returned to climb the steps of the scaffold. But the colony of British Guiana as it exists to-day is only in-directly a fruit of his efforts—he never set foot within its boundaries as now defined.

Although the politicians and business men did not respond to his lead, his fellow-poets found a mine as rich in inspiration as he supposed Guiana to be in gold in the published account of his explorations. This, as stated above, appeared in 1596, a small quarto of 112 pages, and immediately became a best-seller—several re-printings were issued in the same year and translations in several languages appeared on the Continent. Its mark is dis-tinct on the literature of the period. Its language as well as its influence may be traced in *The Tempest* as well as in *Othello*. Chapman took up the author's case and in a poem full of his praise beseeches Elizabeth to

" Go forth upon the waters, and create
A golden world in this our iron age."

So did Drayton and many minor scribes. The Guiana voyage is so important to his fame largely because it made him a hero in the eyes of men whose business it is to preserve memories. Nor is their praise undeserved, for however badly he may have failed, however sterile may have been his achievement, the deed itself was a great one, and the record he left of it a piece of great literature.

CHAPTER VII

THE DRAGON'S HEIR

Although the Guiana voyage did not arouse the public enthusiasm that Raleigh had anticipated, it did him one good turn in that it made it impossible for him to be omitted thereafter from consideration as a naval officer. In a theoretical sense he had already been numbered amongst the available seamen of England for many years, but actually, as we have seen, had not yet exercised an important command. No one who reads his writings can for a moment doubt the extent of his strategic perception of naval affairs, and not merely as a commentator after events have taken place—his letter of November 3rd, 1595, to Lord Charles Howard, shows how graphically he foresaw the situation of Drake and Hawkins, who were engaged in an old-style raid on the Main in ignorance of a fleet which was being sent after them. As in the case of Lisbon in 1589, he guessed aright; the end of the ill-advised, ill-supported raid was the failure and death of the two grand veterans. Whatever younger and more emulous men might say of Raleigh, the judicious, slow-thinking, aristocratic old Lord High Admiral had a deep respect for his powers, to which many a word and gesture bear irrefutable evidence.

It is not known in whose mind originated the idea of striking the Spaniard at his principal port in 1596, both as a retaliation for the Drake and Hawkins failure and to

prevent the sailing of a new Armada, but the project had
no more ardent supporter than Raleigh.   Like every true
military or naval executive he recognized that in an un-
remitting offensive lay the best defence, and particularly
so in the case of England, who was safe so long as
enemy squadrons could be kept from her shores.   In
addition he had an old grudge to settle on behalf of
Grenville, as he himself states.   In one of those great
waves of chauvinistic emotion which periodically swept
over the public the decision was made to concentrate every
effort on punishing Spain as she had never been punished
before.   Even the over-cautious and penurious Elizabeth
could not hold out against the universal feeling, articu-
lated as it was by those whom she most loved or trusted,
Essex, Raleigh and Cecil.   The most formidable force
which had ever been sent to sea from an English port was
gathered together, and placed under the joint command
of the Lord Admiral and Essex, with Lord Thomas
Howard as Vice-Admiral, Raleigh as Rear-Admiral and
Sir Francis Vere, the first of living English soldiers, as
general of the troops.

In many ways it was a singular expedition.   Universal
as was the enthusiasm for it, the jealousies surrounding
were even fiercer than usual.   These expressed themselves at times in amusing fashion.   No one welcomed
Elizabeth's distrustful and often fatal policy of joint
commands, yet when she characteristically vacillated
during the preparations and spoke of sending a smaller
force under a single leader, Thomas Howard, he, like all
those detailed to go with him, arose in protest and refused
to go unless every one else went too—each was afraid of
compromising his dignity by being sent on an expedition
of less importance than the one originally planned.   A
sort of Round Robin was drawn up and the Queen not
unwillingly capitulated.

No one of the commanders aroused more jealousy than

did Raleigh, before, during and after the action. Most of it may be set down to pure malice. Thus, although his eagerness to be off was notorious, the court and naval circles rang with gossip purporting to explain his delay in joining the fleet at Plymouth. There is no doubt that he gave Essex and Howard some anxious moments during that spring of 1596 by not reporting for duty when the fleet was nearly ready to sail, but the explanation was simple enough. There was only one way of making up crews and that was by impressing them ; professional sailors were few and landsmen reluctant to go on foreign service. So Raleigh, the pampered and elegant, had to run, as he himself writes to Cecil, from alehouse to alehouse along the banks of the Thames, dragging his finery and his prisoners through the mire that his ships might have their full complement. Essex must have realised the truth of this explanation, for he himself was only able to stop the wholesale desertions which threatened to defeat the voyage at its very start by a few salutary executions on "a fair green called the Hoe" at Plymouth. Thereafter it seems that discipline improved enormously.

One morsel of gossip relating to Raleigh's delay has been preserved to give rise to the wildest and most comical explanations. It consists of a sentence in a letter from Anthony to Francis Bacon which runs :

"Sir Walter Raleigh's slackness and stay by the way is not thought to be on sloth, but upon pregnant design, which will be brought forth very shortly, and found to be, according to the French proverb, *fils ou fille.*"

Edwards interprets this to mean that Bacon suspected an intention on Raleigh's part to supplant either Essex or Howard as joint commander of the fleet ! Perhaps ; but it would not have been beyond the bounds of probability that a man married nearly four years might be expecting his wife to present him with a son or daughter, who failed to materialize. His first child, Walter, was now nearly two years old, and his second, Carew, was not born until eight years later. Hence my guess is as unsupported as is the other, but seems somewhat less fantastic. Besides his two sons Raleigh is reported, wrongly, I think, as will appear later, to have had an illegitimate daughter, whom he commends to his wife's care when he was about to be executed, but she is never referred to elsewhere and is, in any event, palpably not the *fille* which was shortly to be brought forth.

The long delay at Plymouth did not tend to soothe bad tempers and again Raleigh became the centre of a stormy dispute which nearly resulted in bloodshed. Amongst the commanders none was more consistently hostile to him than Vere ; after a dinner at which Essex and the Flemish admirals were present, the Marshal found inspiration in his cups to state explicitly what he thought of his colleague. Raleigh exhibited his customary self-restraint—no man could rouse him to intemperate language—but his hot-blooded young brother-in-law, Arthur Throgmorton, took up the cudgels and became so violent that the Earl ordered him from the table and later had him cashiered. What the cause of the trouble was we do not know, but can surmise from the words of a witness, Sir Anthony Standen, who refers to a " scandal " as being the subject and from the fact that Lady Raleigh's brother took such umbrage. With jealousy and hatred the momentous undertaking began and with them ascendant it concluded.

Finally, on June the first, the expedition was ready to sail, and a brave showing it must have made in Plymouth Harbour. Nearly one hundred and fifty sail, large and small (the accounts vary), as beautiful a sight as the sea ever held, reported the Spaniards, who beheld it with amazed and terror-stricken eyes as it approached

Cadiz three weeks later. The business in hand was serious, but the officers and the five hundred amateur gentlemen soldiers did not therefore stint their personal displays, and so dazzling an array of gold and silver lace, said Standen, had never yet been seen on shipboard.

The English vessels were divided into four approximately equal squadrons, led by Howard on the " Ark Royal," his flagship of 1588, Essex on the " Repulse," Lord Thomas Howard on the " Merhonour," and Raleigh in the " Warspite." The ships of their allies the Dutch, numbering eighteen men of war and six " victuallers," were commanded by Admiral Jan Duyvenoord ; they had little to do with the principal action. The total number of men is reckoned at nearly 16,000 : 6400 English sailors, 1200 of whom were trained as mariners, 6500 English soldiers and about 2600 Dutch. It was a vast fighting force for those days, but proved to be by no means too large.

A false start was made on the 1st, but the wind dropped and not until two days later did they get away. The arrangements were admirable. Behind a screen of pinnaces and fast small boats, which intercepted every vessel, enemy or neutral, which might convey news of its coming to Cadiz, the Main Fleet advanced in wide formation each day and closed up each night, sealed orders providing for rendezvous at Cape St. Vincent and Cadiz respectively in case of dispersal. By June 9th they were off the coast of Spain and the Spaniards still drowsed tranquilly in the early summer sunshine. The chief of their naval forces, the Duke of Medina Sidonia, lay in his orange groves recovering from an illness and cursing the small boys who teased him by shouting over his garden walls " Viene el Draque," " Drake 's coming," and running away. The terrible Dragon was dead, as he knew, and nothing would now disturb his days or his slumbers, else Philip's crafty spies would have told him

so.   And then a peasant on a mule, exhausted from a
thirty mile ride, burst in to inform him that he had seen
from a headland, four days since, the horizon blotted
out by English sails.

The duke then bestirred himself to save Cadiz.   The
time had gone by to arrest the progress of Howard's fleet.
On the ninth the latter had called a council which, on the
basis of information obtained from captured vessels, had
decided on the various dispositions.   These, so far as
they affected Raleigh, separated him from the rest ; he
was to stand inshore and then cruise slowly down the
coast so as to prevent any enemy ships from slipping away
and out of the clutches of the main fleet.   With a heavy
heart he took up his post ; like the rest he had bubbled
with joy at the news that the principal ships of the
Spanish Navy, notably the "Saint Philip," were in Cadiz
Harbour, and had anticipated taking part in, if not actually leading, a glorious victory.   But he accepted his
assignment without demur.   Creeping slowly along, he
sighted five Spanish ships, members of the *flota*, on their
way to join the convoy waiting at Cadiz.   Giving chase,
he ran into a fog and lost sight of them until the next
morning, when the shoals prevented him from engaging.
One was driven aground, however, and the rest escaped
to San Lucar, all being put effectively out of action.
Raleigh then proceeded south.

Meantime the main fleet had arrived and taken up its
position off the rocky tongue of land called San Sebastian
(see map).   Again a council was called, there being a
wide diversity of opinion as to what to do next.   The
decision arrived at was the worst possible under the circumstances—that troops should be landed and an
attempt made to storm the defences with soldiers.   The
landing place selected was in the angle between San
Sebastian and Santa Catalina, under the very walls of the
town.   Not only was the plan unsound, but its execution

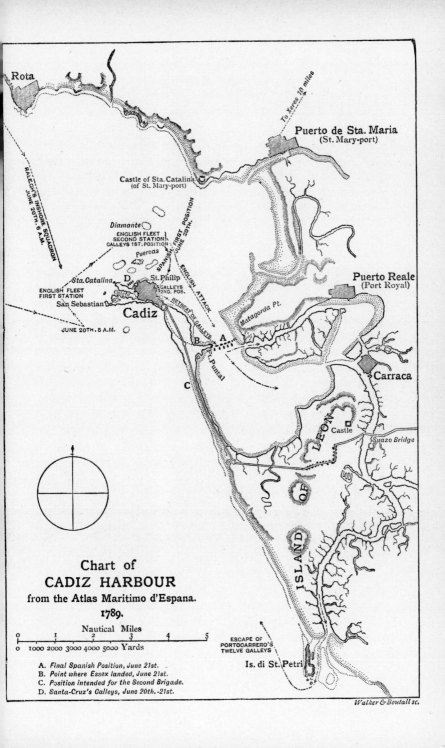

Rota

To Xeres 10 miles

Puerto de Sta. Maria
(St. Mary-port)

Castle of Sta. Catalina
(of St. Mary-port)

Diamante

ENGLISH FLEET
SECOND STATION.
GALLEYS 1ST. POSITION.

Puercas

Sta. Catalina

ENGLISH FLEET
FIRST STATION

San Sebastian

Cadiz

JUNE 20TH. 5 A.M.

St. Philip

GALLEYS
2ND. POS.

RALEIGH'S INSHORE SQUADRON
JUNE 20TH. 6 A.M.

SPANISH FIRST POSITION
JUNE 20TH.

ENGLISH ATTACK

RETREAT OF GALLEYS

B

A

Puntal

Matagorda Pt.

Puerto Reale
(Port Royal)

Carraca

C

LEON

Castle

Suazo Bridge

ISLAND OF

ESCAPE OF
PORTOCARRERO'S
TWELVE GALLEYS

Is. di St. Petri.

Chart of
CADIZ HARBOUR
from the Atlas Maritimo d'Espana.
1789.

Nautical Miles

| 0 | 1 | 2 | 3 | 4 | 5 |

0 1000 2000 3000 4000 5000 Yards

A. *Final Spanish Position, June 21st.*
B. *Point where Essex landed, June 21st.*
C. *Position intended for the Second Brigade.*
D. *Santa-Cruz's Galleys, June 20th.-21st.*

Walker & Boutall sc.

badly prepared, for the English sailing masters, on the evening of the 19th, had misjudged their distance from shore. When they sailed in, early on the following morning, the Spaniards were thoroughly prepared to resist the landing with four strong galleys. A rising north-west wind had sprung up, setting the sea a-roaring and making the debarkation of men into small boats highly dangerous. Several were swamped. To experienced eyes the attempt was seen already to be hopeless. But in a kind of frenzy Essex persisted. The crucial moment of the great venture had arrived and it looked now, if nothing should intervene, that it was doomed to end in a ghastly failure.

Then Raleigh, having finished his assignment, came up. His quick brain took in immediately the impending disaster, and forcing his way through the crowds of small boats into which the frightened soldiers of the " Repulse " were descending, he sought out the distracted Essex. Nothing could move the latter. His own counsel to assault the harbour first and think of the town afterwards having been rejected, he was determined, like a stubborn small boy, to proceed with the substituted design whether it was insane or no.

Raleigh flew back to Howard, demanded that a council be summoned and before it plead that the landing project be immediately given over. It was rarely that his equals or superiors could control their prejudice sufficiently to agree with him—his utter self-assurance, his haughty certainty, alienated them even when he was right. Nothing is more offensive to the mediocre than genius divorced from tact. But now there was no withstanding his arguments—the sea was roughening further, Essex's boats were capsizing faster, and the day was passing while nothing was done. Every wasted moment made the Spanish position stronger, their own weaker. The council wavered, gave in. Raleigh dashed back to the

" Repulse " and, unable to wait, shouted in Spanish across the foaming waters his glad tidings—" Entramos." Essex's response was to toss his white plumed hat exultantly into the air, where the wind took hold of it and carried it out to sea.

The wrong course had been stayed, but the right one was not immediately taken. Essex reassembled his soaked and shivering troops and rejoined his colleagues, who immediately went in for further discussion. Essex himself was for immediate action ; it suited his temperament and he, after all, had more to gain from a theatrical victory than any one else, for his only equal in rank, the Lord Admiral, was presumably past such vanities. Friendly historians have attempted to blame Raleigh for holding back, but such a charge is mere carping. He was not the principal commander ; in principle it took two to decide anything, and in practice four, at least. By the time that the troops were brought back on board, the ships reassembled and the new council had finished its deliberations, the late afternoon tide had gone out and the chance of entering under favourable conditions and utilizing the daylight to fight to a decision was past. It would have been folly to have attempted a decisive action under the changed circumstances.

The subject of dispute for a large part of that momentous night was the question of who was to lead the van in the ensuing day's engagement. Every one wanted the honour, and Essex defiantly claimed it as his right. The Lord Admiral was firm in opposition to this claim, for his order from the Queen had been explicit to keep the young favourite out of harm's way—it was with the greatest reluctance that she had permitted him to go at all. The squabble finally ended by the designation of Raleigh for the coveted post, probably in the absence of the Vice-Admiral, Lord Thomas Howard, who would have had next claim to it after the joint commanders. When he returned he was furious, and resolved, council or no council, that the first blow would be his.

So the council actually decided nothing, but its nominee decided for them by getting up earlier than any one else. Just after sunrise of the first morning of summer, he weighed anchor, and by six o'clock was heading for mid-channel. On his right Vere, with the prospective landing forces, had just engaged in a futile duel with the batteries of the town and seventeen galleys who were sheltering under its walls. These at once turned their fire on Raleigh, but he was aiming at bigger game, the four great Apostles, the SS. "Philip," "Matthew," "Thomas" and "Andrew"; he answered each volley with a scornful flourish of his trumpets, rejoicing mightily in this warlike antiphony. The galleys he left to the mercy of his supporting squadron, and it soon had them in full retreat to the narrow channel in which the great galleons were taking up their line of defence. As the galleys scurried by, hugging the shore and exposing their sides, Raleigh once took notice of them with a single round of shot. "I bestowed a benediction on them," he genially remarks.

The Spaniards had, the night before, designed to fight in a line running N.N.E. from Cadiz itself, the very line the English had planned to take up, but as this position was too extended and exposed, they decided to abandon the town and withdraw to the narrowest part of the harbour off Fort Puntal. But the wind had dropped overnight, and in almost a calm they worked their way up the three miles to their new positions. The calm rendered Raleigh's advance also very slow, and by the time he was within firing range the Apostles had anchored bow to stern athwart the channel, the full force of their broadside armament presented to their assailants and all their attendant vessels clustered about them.

Raleigh paused. For this he has been severely criticized, more by jealous contemporary commentators than

by more judicious modern writers.   The accusation is
that he, a soldier by training, was afraid of the deafening
but comparatively innocuous gunfire of the enemy.   The
charge of physical cowardice in relation to Raleigh is too
ludicrous even to be worth discussion.   He did not know
his ground ; of whatever perilous shoals the Spaniards
had avoided in taking up their position in these, their own
waters, he was naturally ignorant.   Vere, who came
creeping up presently on his right, displayed a similar
caution for a similar reason.   Furthermore close engagement by ships of the size of the " Warspite " was unorthodox—he was waiting for the flyboats to come up
and clear the way.   Meantime he was firing round upon
round into the chastened enemy.

Presently he grew impatient.   For three hours he had
beaten upon the best ships of Spain and they on him, like
cymbals, cannon balls and culverin flying thick as musket
bullets ; he seemed likely to sink on the spot, so he
thought, unless the action advanced a stage.   He leapt
into his skiff and, threading his way through the harbour,
now choked with English ships, great and small, all
scrambling to get in a blow at the enemy, sought out
Essex and demanded the flyboats.   If they were longer
delayed he would venture a boarding with his own, or
rather the Queen's ship, and chance official unpleasant-
ness by risking Her Majesty's property.   To which
Essex gallantly replied " Lead on " and followed his
Rear-Admiral to where the fray was now not only thick
but congested.

This congestion was due to the frenzied but comic
scramble of the English leaders to attain the van.   When
Raleigh returned he found the " Merhonour " ahead of
the " Warspite."   With all due respect to Lord Thomas
this could not be borne.   He slipped anchor and moved
forward, thus answering the charge of fear if that
were necessary.   The next menace from his own side

was Vere, who thought to assure himself of his place by fastening a cable to the " Warspite " and drawing himself alongside. Raleigh, detecting this, promptly cut the cable and the discomfited Marshal of the Forces dropped astern. Meantime Essex was also pressing forward, and in his haste fouled Clifford's ship, the " Dreadnought." But Raleigh was now taking no chances. He manœuvred his vessel across the bows of his zealous neighbours and finally drifted into a position parallel to the Spaniards. Having effectively blocked the channel, he had no further apprehension that any one would get ahead of him, for *that* day at least.

He did more than merely triumph in this private contest of vanity. By his manœuvre he tended to equalize the volume of firing which the English were able to bring to bear on the enemy, for it must be remembered that the latter, in line-ahead position, had the advantage of the use of their broadside guns, whereas the former were restricted by their line-abreast position and could only use their bow or " chasing " pieces. For three hours deadlock had prevailed, the superior quality of the English gunnery neutralized by the greater quantity of the Spanish. For three hours the gunfire had roared and still the great Apostles and their cohorts held firm and Cadiz was as far from falling as she had been the day before—nay further, for the Duke of Medina Sidonia was already mobilizing all effective forces and batteries for the aid of the threatened port.

Then suddenly the deadlock and the backbone of Spain were broken simultaneously. Shortly after noon the flow of the tide enabled Raleigh to do what the wind had hitherto prevented, and as the " Warspite " drifted closer to the line of galleons he was able suddenly to get out a warp and draw himself close to the " St. Philip "—an act which not only renders all reference to fearful hesitation on his part incongruous, but leaves him beyond doubt the

hero of the memorable battle.   For, at the moment that
his joyful boarding party prepared to climb on to the
decks of Grenville's conqueror, all resistance collapsed.
Essex and Lord Thomas immediately closed in ; and the
Spaniards, seeing that the end had come, only thought of
making sail and saving themselves by flight into the inner
harbour.   But it was too late.   All four of the galleons
ran aground, and their crews in a panic began to jump
overboard, setting fire to their ships before they should
fall into the hands of the English.   The " St. Philip "
and " St. Thomas " disappeared in flames ; the other
two were saved ; Raleigh's gifted pen can best describe
the situation :

"The spectacle was very lamentable on their side ; for many
drowned themselves ; many half-burnt, leaped into the water ;
very many hanging by the ropes' ends by the ships' sides, under the
water even to the lips ; many swimming with grievous wounds,
stricken under water and put out of their pain ; and withal so
huge a fire and such tearing of the ordnance of the great ' Philip,'
and the rest, when the fire came to them, as, if any man had desire
to see hell itself, it was there most lively figured.   Ourselves spared
the lives of all after the victory ; but the Flemmings, who did
little or nothing in the fight, used merciless slaughter, till they were
by myself and afterward by my Lord admiral beaten off."

Grave critics have complained that Raleigh has bewitched posterity by the wizardry of his pen, making just
examination of him impossible.   One can understand
the grounds of their complaint when one reads *A Relation
of Cadiz Action*, from which the above extract is taken.
But his conduct at Cadiz required no self-glorification,
nor did it receive any.   The beauty of his style is utilized
to exalt the action itself, not his special part in it.   His
superiors and colleagues receive generous praise, and the
only complaint he has to make on his own behalf is the
characteristic one that he did not get his fair share of the

loot, in which contention, as in his relation of his own part in the battle, the other chroniclers, who were neither dispassionate nor impersonal, on the whole agree with him.

His part in the subsequent proceedings is negligible. The storming of the town, which Essex promptly undertook after the naval engagement was terminated and carried to a successful conclusion, he reports briefly and in the capacity of inactive witness, for during the encounter with the " St. Philip " he received a painful wound in the leg, accompanied by a mass of splinters, the frequent concomitant of gunshot wounds at sea in the days of wooden ships. Even so, he had himself carried on his men's shoulders into the town so that he might see what was going on, and after the horses were disembarked Essex sent him one. But he was exhausted with fatigue and pain, and returned early to the fleet, where he found himself the only high officer, indeed almost the only human being of any kind, for everybody had gone off to help in the pillage. The private soldiers stole, their leaders bargained for ransoms in huge quantities, while the man whose brain and daring had made this triumphant result possible lay in torture on his narrow berth, dreaming of the house of which he would have possessed himself if God had spared him that cursed wound.

All night long the looting and burning continued, and by next day the best part of the hapless town was in ashes. Treasure and ransoms so thoroughly occupied the minds of the English leaders that they forgot the primary purpose of their coming and one by one these slipped through their fingers. Unheeding of Raleigh's plea to be allowed to follow and capture the *flota*, which lay in the roadstead of Puerto Royale, the generals allowed the rich vessels, reputed to be worth twelve millions, to escape up the river and finally were compelled to negotiate for their ransom. But that too eluded them, for the Spanish generals, with true Castilian disdain of merchants' interests on a point of honour, burnt the lot. After a dispute in council Cadiz was abandoned, against the objections of Essex, who wished to hold it. One hundred and twenty thousand ducats were in the end accepted for the hostages within the city, a sum which the noble Duke of Medina Sidonia attempted to pay in mercantile bills, which he might later repudiate, instead of in specie. But the Englishmen, though sailors and soldiers by profession, possessed a modicum of the national talent for banking, and the substitution was refused. Essex and Raleigh alone seem to have been exempt from the prevalent hunt for quick gain, and the latter's forbearance was not, it is to be feared, entirely due to his own choice.

On the fourth of July Cadiz was evacuated and the conquerors sailed away, to the bitter disappointment of Essex, who desired, like Drake, to hold a permanent base on the Spanish coast. As has been said, he was outvoted and probably rightly ; the cost and difficulty of retaining a stronghold at so great a distance would have been insuperable obstacles to the scheme. He had his great moment, however, when, after a banquet of celebration in the Priory of St. Francis, he and Howard began handing out knighthoods. Sixty-six were given in all, and the honour never recovered from the degradation it suffered on that occasion and others when Essex did the same thing in order simultaneously to play Jove and build up a following. He alone created more knights, a contemporary wrote, than had existed in all of England before. The sixty-six after Cadiz may be compared with the five Howard made after the Armada in 1588, amongst whom were such men as Hawkins and Frobisher. Most of the Cadiz lot were such nonentities that a contemporary lampoon calls them:

> " A gentleman of Wales and a knight of Cales
> And a laird of the north Countree "

whom
> " A yeoman of Kent with his yearly rent
> Could buy them out all three."

The return voyage was marked with renewed friction and dispute between the various commanders, who for the most part wished to dash home to enjoy their spoils and report their heroism ; the principal ones had already sent their satellites to see that the Queen and public opinion were properly notified, but they were aware that nothing could equal in value a personal appearance. Essex was for going on to the Azores and waylaying the Plate Fleet, in which he was overruled on the ground that provisions were running low and disease infecting the crews.   Raleigh has been blamed for opposing the Earl's apparently sensible plan, but how just were the reasons for his opposition we cannot now decide.   Essex himself does not blame Raleigh, of whose achievements in the expedition he speaks with the highest admiration.

One tangible result of this after-cruise was the raid on Faro, whence the library of the Bishop Osorius was stolen and conveyed to England, where it was given to Oxford and became the nucleus of the famous Bodleian Library. Then bit by bit the components of the fleet, weary of absence at sea, hungry for ease and their country's praise, separated themselves and flew home.   The leisure that the humbler sort enjoyed was brief, for most of them were immediately pushed off to Holland ; whatever of it their superiors had they devoted to writing or dictating self-laudatory versions of the battle by sea and land.   So in bitterness and animosity between its heroes ended this last great effort, this Trafalgar of Elizabethan naval warfare, which finally determined that England should rise and her ancient enemy descend in the scale of nations.

CHAPTER VIII

THE TRIUMVIRATE*

IT was a not unreasonable expectation on Raleigh's part that his services at Cadiz would reinstate him at Court. His wound and the result of the expedition led him to expect a cordial, if not effusive, welcome. But neither moved the Queen as he had expected, and his return to Court was deferred for nearly a year. Elizabeth was not at all pleased with the results of the Cadiz venture. The blow to Spain and the triumph of English arms mattered little to her in comparison with the small dividends paid on her large investment—£78,000, she claimed. How much she valued the services of her commanders may be seen in the suit instituted by her against the heirs of Drake after that loyal servant's death, on account of expenses incurred on his last fatal voyage, which he had in large measure financed himself. Her complaint against the leaders at Cadiz had more justification—there was undoubtedly a great deal of plunder taken and hidden away, to all or most of which she would have laid claim could she have put her hands on it. But the accounts were so confused that she could find no trace of it, nor of those who were responsible for its disappearance. Raleigh was not likely to emerge from the disfavour with which she regarded the issue of the whole affair; nor must it be forgotten that in the various highly partial versions issued by the various actors in it only a minority gave him the credit due to him. It was only after a

* For map illustrating this chapter see p. 151.

sifting of accounts, friendly and hostile alike, that the figure of the real hero of Cadiz emerged. The final verdict on Raleigh's conduct need not be found in his report or in those of his partisans—a careful comparison of the charges, admissions and inconsistencies of the other extant documents must prove that not only was his own story in substance true, but that in the fierce engagement of June 21st he wrung unwilling admiration from men disposed to hate or mistrust him.

His reinstatement, when it came, was due, unfortunately, not to his deserts, but to the conventional method of intrigue: and his sponsors were his two natural rivals, Essex and Robert Cecil. These three had by now emerged as the most important men in the kingdom, if the aged Burghley, who was to die shortly, be excepted. There was very little common ground between them temperamentally, and their conflict of tastes and interests made an alliance seem unlikely before the two Admirals sailed for Cadiz. It was not very long since Essex had publicly reviled Raleigh and challenged him to a duel; he was furious to find that in his absence the Queen had appointed Cecil her principal Secretary of State over his bitter opposition. The winter of 1596-1597 saw them drawing together, however, probably through Raleigh's instrumentality. The events of Cadiz seem to have healed the breach between Essex and his Rear-Admiral—their comments on each other's actions are generous in the extreme, and whatever distrust the young favourite had of his predecessor seems to have been temporarily allayed.

With Cecil Raleigh seems to have had a friendly intercourse all of his life, even after the Secretary became one of the instruments of his downfall. There is no more inscrutable character in the whole period than Cecil's and occasionally, when one wishes to decipher his feelings towards a given person, one is tempted to believe that he had no feelings at all. But it is certain that Raleigh trusted him as far as he trusted any public man, and believed that the other was disposed to serve him. Most of his existing letters are addressed to Cecil, so many of them in fact that the overburdened Secretary seems at times simply to have given up answering or, I suspect from the endorsements, even reading them. Nevertheless, one, a letter of condolence to Cecil on his wife's death, indicates that a certain warmth must have existed between the two during the period with which we are dealing. It is endorsed " 24th January 1597," and although too long to quote here, may be recommended for reading—it is very close to the source of the spring which a dozen years or so later was to pour forth that masterpiece of prose, the Authorised Version. If Cecil failed to love and admire the writer for at least a moment after reading it, he was of a certainty without ordinary human emotions.

The immediate result of their working agreement to grind one another's axes was that each of the three obtained what he most particularly desired at the moment. Cecil, for the time being the most important of the three at court, bolstered up Essex's failing credit there and secured for him the appointment of Master of the Ordnance, which made him practically Commander-in-Chief of the military forces of the country ; for himself he secured the Chancellorship of the Duchy of Lancaster, and for Raleigh the contract to provision the fleet for the impending expedition against Spain, an arrangement which eminently suited its beneficiary's always ravenous purse. On the following June the first, nearly a year after Cadiz, he was allowed once more to resume his duties as Captain of the Guard.

For a few months the triumvirate flourished, amicably dining together and concluding arrangements satisfactory to all concerned. But the two able-bodied members of it were not long to indulge their leisure thus pleasantly.

Philip had sent out an Armada the previous autumn which had only been prevented by the gales with which Heaven consistently favoured England from forcing a landing and causing considerable trouble in Ireland, if not at home. The wind did the work which the navy should have undertaken, while all the strategists were busy spilling ink in the effort to devise a perfect plan of defence. Raleigh's scheme, for the defence of the Thames-mouth, was soundest, but as far off the mark as any, for an attack there was much too good an idea for Philip or his aristocratic naval staff to have thought of. Nobody knew exactly what the Spanish king planned to do, nor was he quite certain himself. While everybody tried to guess, the reluctant *Adelantado* was ordered out to sea, and all England waited in desperate tension and then relaxed as Boreas tore down on this Armada as he had done on its predecessor, and sent it reeling back shattered to its base at Ferrol.

But no one thought that Philip intended to give up after this failure. The subjugation of England had become a mania with him. While he lay dying of a dreadful disease, unable to imbibe nourishment, all the sights and sounds of the last rites for the dead perpetually ready about him, he still concentrated on plans for one overwhelming effort. He drained his own country of its boys and his dependency Italy of its money, and both flowed in streams to the port in Northern Spain where Don Martin de Padilla, Conde de Gadea, was refurnishing the new Armada.

All this was known in England, and it behoved her to bestir herself, but the question was, as usual, whither and how ? The orthodox method would have been to sit down and wait for the Spaniards to come, trusting to God and the navy to deal with them when they did. But Drake, if he had done nought else, had taught his countrymen one lesson, that attack was the best defence, and what they had failed to comprehend from his practice they were compelled to learn from the eloquent pen of Raleigh, Drake's true heir and disciple.   The Queen herself was in favour of assailing the *Adelantado* in his own stronghold, a decided step in advance for her.   Raleigh as well as Essex preferred taking a leaf out of Drake's notebook and striking at the Indian Plate Fleet in the West Indies, which would divert Philip's preparations if, indeed, his navy were able to issue from Ferrol during that year at all. But as on the similar occasion of 1596, Raleigh's keen intellect was unable to predict what Philip's muddled and half-crazed one would decide.

The Queen held to her decision, however, and her two Admirals were constrained to accept it, or to pretend to do so, and they proceeded with the organization of their expedition along those lines.   It resembled the one of the previous year in many respects.   There were to be only three English squadrons, instead of four, the Lord Admiral being missing, and one Dutch, but the fighting strength was to be approximately as great.   Essex and Lord Thomas Howard exchanged ships, though the former later took back the " Repulse," but Raleigh retained his " Warspite."   At length on the afternoon of Sunday the 10th of July the expedition got away, but almost immediately ran into a storm so fierce that the ships were dispersed in all directions.   The gale was so terrific that leaks were sprung, masts cracked and a number of the soldiers, unaccustomed to the sea, died of a mixture of fright and seasickness.   For a week or more the various squadrons battled on hopelessly in the teeth of a headwind, but gradually bit by bit allowed themselves to be blown back torn and battered into English ports ; all but that of the impassive old sea-dog, Lord Thomas Howard, who brought the bulk of his squadron through the gale and to the coast of Spain, where he dared the *Adelantado* to come out and fight.   But the latter had no

desire to match his strength even against this exhausted
fraction of an English flotilla, and so Howard was forced
to turn and come back for lack of anything else to do.

More terrifying to her commanders than the storm was
the prospect of what Elizabeth would say to this futile
expenditure of time and money, but to their great joy she
said nothing unkind.   Time no longer mattered much
to Elizabeth, and she devised a roundabout means of
making Essex pay for the necessary repairs to his ships
out of his own pocket, so that that item did not trouble
her.   Yet though she was quite willing to have her open-
handed favourite impoverish himself on her account,
she nevertheless in her own curious fashion must have
loved him deeply.   For when Raleigh wrote a letter full
of the most enthusiastic praise of his superior's conduct
and seamanship, a portion of the letter which the cautious
Cecil suppressed, she broke down and wept at the mere
tidings that he was safe.

So in an atmosphere of complete amicability the commanders got together to repair the ravages of the storm.
At the same time they reorganized the expedition to suit
their own ends—on one plea or another, of sickness and
unfitness for sea-service, they reduced or discarded the
military units and by the time they were again ready for
sailing it was obvious that a naval cruise rather than a
repetition at Ferrol of the Cadiz campaign was in their
minds. Most important objects in the Elizabethan annals
seem to have been accomplished by circuitous methods,
and it is amusing to speculate on how often the Queen
was complacently aware that she was being circumvented
for her own good—her temper and her ambition were
able to run in double harness better than most people's
who had a far smaller share of either than had she.

On August 17th they were off again.   In Raleigh's
squadron were the two prizes of the previous year, the
" St. Matthew " and the " St. Andrew," which, according

to the new plan of campaign, were destined for burnt offerings to dislodge the Spaniards and make them come out of their secure nest.   In other words it was intended that Raleigh should repeat Drake's sensational strategy of 1588 at Calais and attempt to force his way close enough to the *Adelantado* to be able to let loose amongst his fleet the two surviving Apostles as fire-ships.   But Fate intervened with a series of events which permitted the English Admirals to discard a project in which they had so small an interest.   Raleigh's mainyard broke in two, he could not tack about in the face of an easterly wind, so, overrunning the first rendezvous at Finisterre, he was compelled to continue on to the second off Lisbon. Essex, having sprung a leak, had to lie by before reaching Finisterre, and the majority of the fleet, not finding him there, continued on after Raleigh.   The result was that when the commanding officer came up, he found very little of a fleet to lead.   This meant the end of the Ferrol enterprise and there were not lacking a crowd of Essex's sycophants to point out that their leader's now awkward position was due to Raleigh's disobedience in running beyond the appointed meeting place.   But in his heart Essex knew that the accusation was untrue ; he knew that Raleigh, and even Cecil, were aware that the course for Ferrol had been taken only as a colourable pretext for evading the Queen's unwelcome instructions, nor is it possible to see how, even if Raleigh cannot be acquitted on the ground that he had a secret understanding with his superior, a court-martial could have reproved him in the state of affairs prevailing.   Essex apparently took this view, for his despatch to the Queen, sent after his council had decided to give up the attempt on Ferrol, in no way blames the absent Rear-Admiral for the failure.

Meantime Raleigh had arrived off Lisbon and there received the tidings from an English bark that the *Adelantado* had put out to sea and was hastening to act as convoy to the returning Plate Fleet.   Raleigh passed this bit of improbable information on to Essex, who swallowed it whole, thanking the gods that his plain duty now consisted in doing what he had long wanted to do. He immediately pressed on all sail and hastened to the Azores, directing Raleigh to do likewise ; which order the latter, in no wise reluctant, diligently obeyed.   At this point, despite the friction caused by the missed rendezvous, they understood each other perfectly.

The whole campaign now grows somewhat ridiculous. It suggests that Essex was thinking more about what was going to happen to him at home than about the immediate business in hand.   He dashed hither and thither, ordering his subordinates to meet him at one place and then running off to another before they could get there.   He listened to every rumour, no matter how absurd, and allowed himself to be drawn into half-a-dozen wild goose chases.   If his motive power had been coal or oil or some other costly fuel instead of the wind, the Queen would have read him a lecture on his return which would have made all previous quarrels seem like lovers' raptures.   He completely forgot his first rendezvous with Raleigh, and only met him off Flores (the places mentioned in this account may be seen on the map on p. 151 after a futile look in at Terceira for the phantom Spanish fleet.

The re-union between the two Admirals at Flores was friendly in the extreme, but it was the very last of its kind, and the rupture was due entirely to the instability of Essex's tactics ; for Raleigh, having asked permission to take on fresh water there, was interrupted in the midst of his occupation by peremptory orders to make for Fayal, whither Essex was flying on the wings of a new rumour. Raleigh did so promptly and arrived the next day, only to find that Essex was not there.   The mercurial Lord General had been blown out of his course by still another rumour, which was now hastening him to the north.

Raleigh waited three days before undertaking the next step, the reduction of the town of Horta. Then his impatient soul would not let him rest longer and he decided to attack. But Essex's toadies, led by Sir Gelly Meyricke and Sir Christopher Blount, burst out into a storm of protest, fearful lest their chief should be deprived of his due honour by that rival of his whom they most detested. Another day passed, and then Raleigh, unable longer to abide the thought that the Spaniards would interpret his delay as fear, decided to land. The Essex faction declined to follow him, but with the rest of his squadron he sailed around the island and came opposite his selected landing place, four miles to the south of the town.

He first sent off a party in boats to carry out his original project of watering, but the enemy, espying him from an adjacent headland, sent down a force to entrench themselves and prevent the English from landing. Thereupon Raleigh, seeing that fighting was obviously called for, took personal command of his two hundred and fifty West Country marines and rowed off to the assault. A brisk hail of shot greeted them, and for a moment the invaders, more sailors than soldiers, wavered. Perceiving this their leader stood up, fully exposed, and with harsh words taunted them as cowards, inviting the fearful ones to drop back and the courageous to follow him. The answer was a forward movement of the boats so brisk that several split on the rocks, and from thence poured the English with wild shouts. Leaping from rock to rock of the protecting reef like goats, they rushed the defenders, who attempted for an instant to hold them at close quarters with pikes, but the impetus of the attack was too great and they turned and fled, leaving their arms behind them.

The way was now prepared for the assault on the town itself and Raleigh sent back his boats for his company of

Dutch War veterans.   These tumbled ashore eager for
the fray, but were drawn up by their leaders into a parade
formation and, in greater dignity but less security than
they were accustomed to, followed a vanguard of forty
gentlemen volunteers, led by Raleigh himself, who
sauntered coolly on with a staff to assist his wounded leg.
Their objective was a group of rocks which would
shelter them from the musketry of the High Fort, under
whose searching fire their entire way led.   " The enemy
troubled us more," he later wrote, " in our march towards
Flores than in our taking the shore."   The situation
proved too much even for the veterans and they broke for
cover.   In untroubled order, but volubly irritated with
the men's conduct, the gentlemen completed their
knightly march until they too had obtained refuge.

The next step was a reconnaissance of the way up to
the town.   Raleigh first called for volunteers, but no one
responded—the area to be reconnoitred was far too
exposed.   He thereupon decided to undertake the
extremely dangerous business himself.   His more intimate lieutenants protested, but without heeding them
he put on his helmet and breastplate, and they were
constrained to follow him, seven or eight in number,
including Sir Arthur Gorges, his cousin and the historian
of this Islands Voyage, and the always loyal Keymis, who
was usually to be found wherever Raleigh was, notably in
dangerous adventure.

Up they toiled, the gallant company, on their rocky
way, their bright armour and coloured garments rendering
them excellent targets for the enemy.   Observing this
Raleigh turned to Gorges and asked him to take off his
red sash.   To which Gorges imperturbably replied
through the din that the other's white one was an equally
good mark ; after a moment's reflection both decided
that Spanish marksmanship was scarcely good enough to
deserve the tribute of compelling them to lay aside these

embellishments. Their conclusion turned out to be erroneous and very nearly fatal. Gorges was wounded in the leg and Raleigh's handsome doublet and breeches were punctured with holes. The reconnaissance completed, the troops were brought up and the assault began. But the Spaniards had had enough of their reckless and apparently bullet-proof opponents ; they turned and ran, relinquishing Horta without further struggle. Raleigh rested for the night, reserving for the morrow the capture of the High Fort on the headland.

Morning proved further action unnecessary, since the Spaniards had decided overnight to relinquish the High Fort too. But before this was discovered affairs took a new turn. Essex turned up, smarting with the disappointment of another fruitless chase, only to be informed by Meyricke and his other sycophants that Raleigh had stolen the honour of carrying out single-handed the most difficult feat, and the only successful one, of the entire cruise.

The enraged Lord General sent a peremptory order to his Rear-Admiral to come aboard the " Repulse " at once. The latter gladly obeyed what he deemed to be a summons to receive congratulations on his achievement. He was soon undeceived—Essex greeted him coldly and accused him directly of disobedience to the general fleet order that no subordinate commander should land without explicit orders from above.

Things looked black indeed for him. Essex's partisans, who loathed the very name of Raleigh, had seized the interval before the latter's arrival to point out to the Earl the gravity of the act of insubordination, and how ridiculous he would look unless he promptly punished this refractory thief of his glory. If Essex had elected he might have constituted a court-martial of these very officers and had his Rear-Admiral sentenced to death and executed without referring the matter back to England.

The consequences to himself might have been serious, but he probably knew that he could, in the last resort, depend upon the secret but all-powerful support of the Queen.

All this Raleigh was able to read in the other's face as they confronted each other. But his mental resources were endless and he promptly seized his one impregnable line of defence. With a lawyer's skill he expounded to the enraged but uncertain Essex the elements of the situation. There was a prohibition, he granted, against subordinates landing without their superior's permission. But this permission he had obtained before leaving Flores—in fact he had been ordered to water at Fayal. Furthermore, he was not a subordinate commander ; he was in the line of succession to the high command itself, Essex and Howard failing, and as successive commander was exempt from the general order and the operations of courts-martial.

Essex's wrath dwindled before this subtle but accurate exposition of the situation and he temporized, going so far as to accompany Raleigh ashore and argue the matter further. There he fell so completely under the other's spell that he was on the point of remaining for dinner at his quarters, which would, of course, have indicated a complete forgiveness, but his alarmed officers persuaded him to come away where they could reinflate his resolution. So well did they pump their poison into him that his vanity again asserted itself and he ordered, as a preliminary step, that all of the officers who had taken part in the attack on Horta should be dismissed the service. Raleigh, fearing that morning would bring forth the worst, spent the night in getting his men and ships into fighting trim—he had resolved that, rather than submit to further humiliation, he would dare the hazards of mutiny and engage the entire balance of the fleet.

Beyond a doubt he would have done so, but luckily this

further blot on an already disfigured expedition was averted. Lord Thomas Howard, that irreproachable man of good sense, went privately to Raleigh and induced him to pocket his pride and tender a formal apology, if the Earl would accept one. This he had already arranged in advance, and the meeting of reconciliation went off smoothly. Essex restored Raleigh's officers to their posts and in his official report makes no mention of the Fayal incident to Raleigh's discredit—nor to his credit either, which somewhat neutralizes the generosity of his forbearance.

Much has been made of Essex's qualities as an Admiral and Raleigh's are often compared unfavourably with them. But if the former's reputation is to rest on his conduct of this Islands Voyage, as it is called, it is a very poor thing indeed. The whole story is one of ineptness and uncertainty of purpose. After ravaging Fayal he finally received word of the Flota and prepared to meet it, disposing his squadrons so as to cut it off from the strongly fortified harbour of Angra for which it would of a certainty head. An inescapable net was drawn—and at the last moment, just before midnight of September 25th, Essex listened to another vague rumour and ordered the whole fleet to change its course for St. Michael's Island. Three hours later the long-sought Flota, one of the richest ever to leave the West Indies, cut across the wash of the English squadrons.

It was an exasperating and inexcusable piece of mismanagement. Four English vessels, which had mistaken their orders in the confusion, alone were left to meet the newcomers. These, with characteristic pluck and persistence, hung on to the eight great galleons of the convoy, imploring them to stop and fight, but were laughed at for their pains. The Englishmen tried every ruse to delay the enemy until their signal guns could bring Essex back, but the latter was far away, beyond hearing, and the

crestfallen quartette were compelled to fall back as the
Plate Fleet and its guardians rode grandly into Angra
Harbour and disposed of its treasure in the vaults of the
impregnable castle of San Sebastian. Essex, when he
returned almost insane with rage, wished to assault the
harbour, but the attempt was obviously hopeless and he
was prevailed upon to give it up. If, as has often been
alleged, Raleigh's pen has bewitched posterity into giving
him more than his due deserts as a seaman, what shall we
say of the praise lavished on the winning, impetuous,
fearless but altogether unstable Essex ?

The expedition's original programme, of which the
destruction of the Armada was the principal number,
had been cancelled and another, calling for the destruction
of the Plate Fleet, had been substituted. This, too, had
now been altered owing to the tardiness of the principal
performer. There was nothing to do but to go home,
which presently they did, in typical Elizabethan fashion,
every unit for itself. Only when they arrived at Plymouth did they discover that they had narrowly missed
taking part in the first programme, with reversed rôles,
after all—for on the very day that they made sail for home
the *Adelantado* put out to sea, and having the shorter
course was hastening to meet the scattered squadrons of
England on their homeward course. It was a peril more
serious than that of 1588 ; the southern ports lay open,
the navy was away, and, what was worse, rushing home
all unconscious of the one hundred and thirty-six ships
spread out to meet them. England was in a panic—the
militia was desperately mustered, frantic messages were
sent to Essex, the entire country was put into a state of
siege—but presently the returning fleet straggled into
Plymouth Harbour, without having caught sight of the
waiting enemy. Once more the winds had protected the
fortunate island country and, in retarding the return of
the fleet, had thoroughly and completely devastated that

of the enemy. It was the end of Philip's ambition. Within a few months he died, his dreams made nightmares by the land whose throne he had once shared.

The simultaneous failure of the Islands Voyage and of the last Armada demonstrated to both combatants that the long war was ending in a stalemate, and in Spain and England alike the politicians began to take over from the soldiers the conduct of affairs. Superficially neither side had won ; but actually the result of the war had been to reveal to the world the decay of Spain and the power of England. The throne which Elizabeth left to her successor was the most important in Europe.

The Islands Voyage also marked the end of both Essex's and Raleigh's careers as admirals, and led to the eventual resumption of that feud which their comradeship-in-arms had temporarily put by. Raleigh was by no means sorry to quit the sea ; he liked life on shipboard so little that a chronicler of the times seriously states that he would go all the way round by London Bridge rather than be rowed from his house across to the southern bank of the Thames ; nor is he alone amongst English Admirals in his distaste for the element whereon he gained so much glory. Furthermore, he was quick to see that the opportunity for regaining his ascendancy over Essex had come. The latter had returned to Plymouth sore and disheartened ; his royal mistress was not deceived as to his failure, and ridiculed in detail his errors. His reception at London in the autumn of 1597 was the preliminary to the last tragic scene of his brilliant, futile career on Tower Hill four years later.

It would too far exceed the limits of this volume to set forth in detail Raleigh's occupations from the time his flag fluttered down from the masthead of the "Warspite" until the death of Elizabeth. His private life was tranquil and unmarked by any conspicuous event ; his public career is a record of services in Parliament, as defender of free speech and expert on economic problems, and in the innermost councils of the nation as high authority on national defence. His speeches in the former capacity are masterpieces of logic and common sense, in the latter of far-sighted penetration ; in both he displays a fund of information amazing in a man who had so much else to do. During this period also he added to his offices the governorship of Jersey, which island still remembers him as the most active as well as the most illustrious of its governors ; but the seat at the Privy Council, to which his services had long since entitled him, was still withheld. It is possible that the Queen would have sanctioned his appointment, but at the mere rumour of it his enemies raised such a storm of opposition and abuse that the weary old lady dropped her half-hearted project.

They were busy years for him and, if the details of his activities are omitted here, it is only because his subterranean occupations overshadow them in importance and interest. All men's minds were now occupied with the problem of the succession, and most of the courtiers were preparing their way to the favour of the new sovereign when he should ascend. There was no longer much question that he would be James VI of Scotland, Mary Stuart's son. Elizabeth had throughout her reign refused to consider the subject and had sternly repressed any open discussion of it, but it was now known that she accepted James as heir presumptive. Essex, Cecil, and Raleigh's bitterest enemy, Lord Henry Howard, were in secret communication with him, each determined that when the time came James should look to him for advice and guidance. Raleigh probably had dealings with the Scotch emissaries, but there is surprisingly little evidence of effort on his part to approach the king himself. Yet he must have known as well as any one else how the wind blew and how necessary it was to ingratiate himself with the future monarch. The suspicion that he was supporting a rival candidate, Arabella Stuart, was prevalent at least as early as 1600, for an anonymous letter of that year says of a plot on her behalf :

" There is likelihood of Raleigh's concurrence—seeing Essex leans to the Scot—having seated himself in that part of the realm, who is the very Achitophel of all plots of this age."

But it would be utterly inconsistent with Raleigh's political acumen to believe that he really thought that Arabella had a chance to succeed. Nor would it be anything but a charitable guess to hold that his self-respect prevented him from flattering James as did the others.   The only reasonable supposition is that he hoped to arrive at so high a place in Elizabeth's esteem that she would hand him on to whoever in the end did succeed as her one indispensable servant.   If so, it was an unlucky reading of the situation on his part, for it put him completely into Cecil's cunning hands.

The latter has covered his trail too well to enable us to do more than reason by inference what his tactics were, but it seems fairly clear that he appreciated, as Raleigh and Essex did not, that in their rivalry lay the means of his triumph. For although he could not hope to eliminate so formidable a pair by his own single-handed machinations, if their struggle should result in the downfall of the one he felt able to cope with the other.   And in the issue he proved himself right.   At first the old triumvirate arrangements were resumed and outsiders were alarmed at the ring of power and patronage which it constituted.   There is no reason to doubt Raleigh's whole-hearted participation.   When Essex grew discontented and restive after the Lord Admiral had attained precedence of him by being created Earl of Nottingham, Raleigh restored the balance by securing the appointment of the other as Earl Marshal of England. But Cecil's perception was shrewder ; he realized that

Essex's vanity had too long been fed on the poison of his satellites' flattery and the public's adoration to allow him to rest tranquil with increasing honours. None of them seemed to compensate him for the sense of the frustration of his powers which he constantly felt. He was a man whose temperament seemed to demand nothing less than complete dominion wherever he happened to be. It was this, as well as his discontent with his associations at court, that impelled him, probably, to the rash mistake of accepting the government of Ireland— " the grave of reputations." Perhaps also the rumour that Raleigh was to be offered the post influenced his decision. It was no more than a rumour, but as we know, Essex was peculiarly sensitive to rumours. He went, and like his father before him, made a failure of the job. His truce with the rebel Tyrone was a mistake, to put the better of two possible constructions on it; the other is that he was attempting to build up a following amongst his country's enemies. He heard of and bitterly referred to Raleigh's opposition in London—the latter had never outgrown his preference for drastic treatment of the rebels, as a letter of a slightly later date proves—and finally, on an impulse, returned to England for what we should now term a show-down. The inevitable was postponed only a very short while. He gained access to the Queen, it is true, and even a sort of pardon for quitting his post without permission, but when she put a qualification on his full return to favour, he forced a stormy interview and informed her that " her conditions were as crooked as her carcass "—a speech which, as Raleigh says in one of his later writings, cost him his handsome head. It was scarcely a tactful remark to make to one whose vanity was as great as his own.

And it was always Raleigh whom his diseased imagination saw as the gaoler who kept him locked in the prison of his ambition. He knew by now that it was his former subordinate who had been placed in command of the defensive forces when his conduct in Ireland had aroused the fears of the court the year before. In every direction he fancied himself blocked by the man who, could he only have known it, possessed a tenure of privilege, and even of life, scarcely more secure than his own.

When finally on the morning of Sunday, February 8th, 1601, his rebellion came to a head, it was the death of Raleigh which was amongst its major objects, and which was nearly attained despite the defeat of the conspiracy. For Raleigh undertook the task of emissary to hear Essex's grievances and demands, and arranged an appointment with the latter's supporter, Sir Ferdinando Gorges, to talk the matter over. Essex declined to allow Gorges to go to Durham House, but agreed to a meeting in open boats on the Thames. The parley was fruitless, but during it Sir Christopher Blount, the man who had refused to follow Raleigh at Horta, fired four shots at him, all of which missed. To this Blount confessed on the scaffold and begged his enemy's forgiveness.

The insane conspiracy was of course suppressed and its ringleaders sent to the Tower. Although the populace had not supported Essex as he had anticipated, it nevertheless idolized him still, and it was on Raleigh's shoulders that most of the blame fell for his execution. It would be hypocritical to pretend that he regretted his rival's downfall or even his death ; and the attempt to twist the meaning of a much-disputed letter to Cecil, wherein he says " if you take it for good counsel to relent towards this tyrant, you will repent when it shall be too late," into a plea for the commutation of Essex's sentence, is quite unconvincing. But he was far from deserving all the opprobrium which he gained from the event. It was Cecil who might have averted it, and refrained, and who gained the most by it. Yet until his own downfall it was almost universally agreed that it was Raleigh's cunning which had lured Essex to his doom, and that as Captain of the Guard he stood before Essex and gloated as the axe fell on Tower Hill. Only when he came to the same situation himself was he able to clear himself of this sinister slander.

The triumvirate had disappeared. But a little while longer and Cecil was to be the sole remaining heir of its power. There is no more poignant irony in that age of rich contrasts than the fact that the two men who succeeded Drake as the hated scourge of Spain should have gone to the block under the suspicion of having treasonably intrigued on her behalf, while the third, after having lived twenty years as her secret pensioner, should have died honoured in his bed, first of the long and illustrious line of the Salisburys.

Slowly the mine was laid which was to blow up the structure of the Elizabethan era and shatter its last surviving ornament. The Privy Council records of this time are full of references which show Raleigh to have been occupied with his private estates, yet constantly employed in minor public matters, as arbitrator on commissions, in Jersey and Devon, as protector of his Devon miners, as expert in Irish affairs, as military governor charged with enlisting and training troops for the service of his cousin Sir George Carew, who was engaged in putting down the new Munster rebellion. It is not in these records however, that we find the key to his destiny, but in another secret batch, the cipher correspondence which was regularly passing between Cecil, Lord Henry Howard, and the gloomy Scotch king. In them Cecil can not only be detected in the business of assuring his own continuation in power when James should become master, but by insinuation and sneers preparing the way for the downfall of Raleigh. On the whole he has covered his traces well, much better than Howard, whose long-winded, tedious epistles are monuments of hatred

and mendacity.   Lord Henry was by no means a genius,
but his prophecies of events to come, as they affect
Raleigh, partake of that quality unless it is assumed that
he had some hand in bringing them to pass.

Between this pair James was completely won to a sense
of dependence on them to guide him through the tortuous
plots with which the country was seething, and a com-
plementary dislike and distrust of the man he was told
was leader of the most active hostile faction.   The
suspicion of Raleigh's part in Essex's downfall, moreover,
contributed to these feelings on James's part, for he had
counted on the Earl's assistance in preparing the way to
the throne.   It would be of the greatest interest to discover how much Raleigh perceived of the web which had
been drawn about him, how far he realized with what
cunning his name had been made a curse in the Stuart's
ear.

He was to learn very shortly.   Elizabeth died on March
24th, 1603, and on April 5th James, having received
the tidings with not too great a show of grief, set out for
his new capital.   He issued a proclamation forbidding
unauthorized persons to seek his presence, but Raleigh,
all innocent that his name in the formal petition of welcome to the new monarch had been viewed with sardonic
eyes, and requiring the king's sanction to the conduct
of certain legal business in Cornwall, came to meet him
and was greeted by the pun " Raleigh ! Raleigh !   True
enough, for I think of thee rawly, mon "—at least so the
tradition goes.   He was forbidden further access, and
shortly thereafter deprived of his prized post of Captain
of the Guard.   Apparently James hesitated for a moment
before deciding on his final course, for he made a slight
recompense in the form of an abatement of rent arising
out of the Jersey Governorship and now due.   Raleigh
must also have been restored temporarily to the freedom
of the court, for it was while he was waiting on the Terrace

at Windsor to accompany the king to the hunt that Cecil
came out to inform him that he was to attend an enquiry
before the Lords of the Council.   A few days later, after
a series of interrogations, he was in the Tower, awaiting
trial on the capital charge of treason.

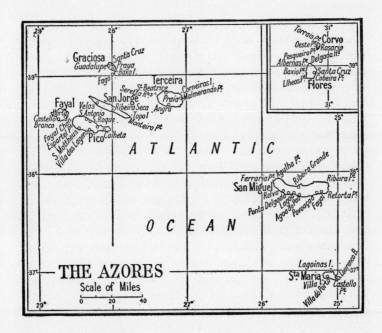

CHAPTER IX

THE TRIAL FOR TREASON

RALEIGH's arrest and trial were the result of one of those absurd and futile plots, or series of plots, which are so characteristic of that age, not only in England but in most of Europe. The original mover was William Watson, a Romish priest who combined the functions of spy and emissary of the Papacy in England. His original intention was, apparently, to seize the person of the King at Greenwich Palace and by pressure upon him compel a favourable attitude on the King's part to Catholics and Catholicism in the country; a list of Catholics had been drawn up who were to supplant certain Protestants in the high offices of state. Watson originally enlisted the co-operation of two discontented Catholics of good family, Sir Griffin Markham and Anthony Copley, but as the plot spread it followed the precedents of its kind and began to take in the strangest bed-fellows, most curious of whom was Lord Grey de Wilton, son of Raleigh's former chief in Ireland and head of one of the most prominent Puritan families in the kingdom. Other confederates included George Brooke, the dissolute brother of Lord Cobham, Warden of the Cinque Ports, who for several years past had been one of Raleigh's political intimates. It was Brooke who provided the link between this original scheme and Raleigh.

Watson's, or the " Priest's Plot," having nowhere in particular to go with its incongruous crew, shortly split up. Watson himself betrayed a portion of his own associates and planned to further his own and the Papal interest by warning the king and obtaining his favour by gratitude instead of coercion. The more straightforward Grey carried on with the original plan under cover of presenting a petition to James for organizing a regiment for services in the Low Countries. It is almost needless to add that none of these intrigues came to fruition. Like Walsingham, before him, Cecil held all the threads of the various unwieldy cabals and dissipated them before they could threaten in the smallest degree.

Meantime Cobham, who, like many another rising star of the end of Elizabeth's regime, saw himself about to be eclipsed by the collusion between James's Scotch courtiers and the astuter amongst Elizabeth's, was engaged in some sort of negotiations with the Count of Aremberg, the ambassador of the Court of England from the Archduke Albert of Austria, the Spanish nominee to the throne of the Netherlands. Exactly how far these negotiations were carried will perhaps never be known, but in substance it was alleged that between them they planned a *coup d'état* whereby Spanish money should foster rebellion in the country and seat the next claimant, Arabella, on the throne. It was intended that thereafter she should be compelled to make peace with Spain, tolerate Catholicism and permit her supporters to dictate her marriage. It is certain that these plans never even approached the stage of maturity. Arabella did not even hear of them and if she had would probably not have been interested ; her heart was engaged elsewhere and the penalty she finally paid was to romance and not to treason.

It was principally through George Brooke that Raleigh was finally accused of complicity in the Aremberg plot. When the principals in the earlier conspiracy were approached they hastened, after the manner of their kind, to confess all they knew, and more, each hoping to get himself off at the expense of the others.   In the course of his examination on July 17th, Brooke let drop the remark that he and his colleagues thought Raleigh " a fit man to be of the action."   In view of the latter's known association with Cobham no more was needed to drag him into the net.   As a matter of fact the conspirators distrusted him as much as they did Cecil, and took elaborate precautions, as one of them admitted, to keep their affairs from his ears, for they were certain that whatever Cobham knew " Raleigh the witch " would get out of him.

On his first examination Raleigh denied any knowledge whatever of the plot, an unfortunate lie which later prejudiced him heavily ; for he subsequently admitted that Cobham had made him some sort of proposition with regard to an uprising and a pension from Spain, to which he had listened indifferently, thinking it was just another of the other's idle vapourings.   And this version bears the stamp of truth.   Raleigh had even a profounder contempt for Cobham's intellect than he had for most men's.   He could not possibly, of course, have restrained his curiosity to learn what was going on, and the occupations of Cobham's mind were as simple and occasionally as amusing to him as a child's primer.   But for this very reason he could not conceivably have involved himself very seriously in any large business which the other had conceived or was prepared to execute.

He got himself in even deeper before he realized how serious the affair was, and how eager James's satellites were to build a case around him.   When he had surrendered the tentative position of total ignorance of the affair he informed Cecil that the key to it lay in the hands of a certain Laurency who had acted as *liaison* between Aremberg and Cobham.   The wily Secretary showed this letter to Cobham, and that wretched weakling, conceiving that his friend had betrayed him in the effort to save himself, burst out " Oh traitor ! oh villain !   I will now tell you all the truth," and proceeded to a circumstantial account of the entire transaction with Raleigh figuring as the instigator.   He later retracted, withdrew his retraction, and again retracted, so that his outburst in hot blood is of not the slightest value as evidence.   But it was enough to warrant joining Raleigh in the indictment.

For a moment his proud spirit broke, as it was to break once more when his series of catastrophes came to a head.   Early during his confinement he attempted suicide.   The wound, in the right breast, was not serious ; in a few days he was reported on the road to recovery, a strange fact in view of the continual references of his contemporaries to his expertness in the use of arms. Stranger still is the conspiracy of silence in the affair. It was barely whispered around, even by his enemies, who might have adduced from it a confession of guilt. The only plausible inference is that it was on his part a gesture whereby he hoped to evoke sympathy, and on theirs taken so seriously that they did not wish the world to think that so great a man had been driven to frenzy by injustice.   Perhaps further light will yet be found on the incident.

This obscure effort at self-destruction and a very dubious letter to his wife from the Tower in July are the only evidences that for a moment he lost his courage. The letter to his wife I call dubious, but it is more than that—it is a palpable concoction which some one has inflicted on posterity in the name of a very great stylist in prose.   Granted even that Raleigh could have in-dulged in the hysterical despair of the epistle, he would never have used such words as :

" I am now made an enemy and a traitor by the word of an unworthy man . . . Woe, woe, woe, be unto him by whose false hand we are lost.   He hath separated us asunder.   He hath slain my honor ; my fortune.   He hath robbed thee of thy husband, thy child of his father, and me of both.   O God ! thou dost know my wrongs.   Know then, thou my wife and child—know then, thou my Lord and King, that I ever thought them too honest to betray and too good to conspire against."

One has only to compare this meaningless transport with that superb letter of the following December, which has already been quoted and will be again, to recognize that both could not have issued from the same mind or been written by the same pen.   Curiously it is this letter which is responsible for the unsatisfactory tradition that its writer left an illegitimate daughter.   In the other, the indubitable letter, there is only a tender care for his cherished son and namesake.

From this time forth until the grand dénouement at Winchester his courage and his resources never wavered. Whilst his conviction was being anticipated, his estates and honours confiscated and parcelled out, he bent every effort to preserve to his family whatever property he could save out of the wreck, entreating councillors, pursuing recalcitrant debtors, searching his memory exhaustively for whatever he could properly lay claim to.   And Lady Raleigh, now as later, acted ably under his guidance. At the same time he was pursuing Cobham with every device to bring him back to his senses.   That smaller Jonathan, Keymis, dared the rack and expostulated with the poor feeble coward on his master's behalf, employing an argument which bears quite certainly the coinage of the latter's subtle brain, to fear nothing because the law required two witnesses before it could condemn him. Cobham did in fact repent and wrote asking to be allowed to make a new statement to the Council, but the Lieutenant of the Tower, Sir George Harvey, suppressed the request until it was too late to be of use.   A few days before the trial Raleigh contrived to throw an apple into

Cobham's window, containing a letter in which he sternly exhorted the latter to pull himself together and not let the preachers seduce him into the same fatal mood of confession which had led Essex to his conviction. Cobham replied by admitting his wrong, but such a confession was useless in so supine a witness, and at length he was moved to write a complete retraction, which its recipient hid away until he could use it with the maximum effect.

The trial was set for November 17th at Winchester, because the plague was raging severely in London, two thousand victims succumbing to it every week. Four days earlier Raleigh was taken out of the Tower and sent in custody to the ancient British capital. If he had had any doubts as to the feelings of the populace towards him, his progress should have completely answered them. His keepers had the greatest difficulty in getting him alive through the mobs, which gathered at every stage of the journey, shouting execrations and threatening violence. Of all menaces this moved him least. His contempt for *demos* was unutterable. Of all men who in the end received its profound respect and even worship, he put himself out least to gain it. Arrived in Winchester he was confined in the old Royal Castle, one of the palaces of the Bishop of Winchester, along with his alleged fellow-conspirators.

On October 18th the Privy Council had sent out notices to the various Earls and Barons to report at Winchester on November 12th, "at which time the Terme was to beginne and the triall (of Cobham and Grey) to be within some few days after." The function of these noblemen was peculiar and has no counterpart in the legal processes of to-day. Although the court was *nisi prius* and tried its cases before a jury, its proceedings were conducted by a mixed bench of commissioners, some of them professional, the majority lay. The commissioners in Raleigh's case included his old colleague-

in-arms, Lord Thomas Howard, now Earl of Suffolk ;
Lord Henry Howard, afterwards Earl of Northampton ;
Robert Cecil, Lord Cranborne and Earl of Salisbury-
to-be ; Sir William Waad ; Sir John Popham, the
Lord Chief Justice of England, and three other judges,
Anderson, Gawdy and Warburton.

How fit were the majority of these men to decide on
the guilt or innocence of the accused may be ascertained
by a glance at their records with relation to him.   Lord
Henry Howard, later to gain perpetual infamy in the
Overbury poisoning, was, on the posthumous confession
of his own secret letters, the concocter of the plot for
participation in which the accused was now on trial ;
Cecil, even if he did not wish Raleigh's death, directly
contributed to put him in his present position ; Waad
had not scrupled to use any means, as the Privy Council's
spy, to get information wherewith to convict the prisoner.
As to the judges, their chief, Popham, had begun life as
a highwayman and ended it with the largest fortune ever
amassed by a member of the English bar ; he gained
respectability in the process, but did not altogether
escape the suspicion of fraud in his decisions.   His professional fitness and that of his colleagues to adjudicate
in a serious legal process involving the life of a man will
appear in the course of this chapter.

The proceedings were opened by the reading of the
indictment by the clerk ; it contained four counts, conspiracy to deprive the king of his government, to raise up
sedition within the realm, to bring in the Roman super-
stition as the State religion and to procure foreign enemies
to invade the kingdom.   The particulars set forth that
on the previous July 9th Raleigh and Cobham met at
Durham House and there decided that Arabella Stuart
should be advanced to the throne of England ; that
Cobham should apply to Aremberg for 600,000 crowns
(£150,000) to further this treason, and when it occurred

to him that Aremberg's employer had not even the money to pay his Army in the Netherlands, that Philip, the Archduke's father-in-law, should be solicited for the same purpose. The three letters which Arabella was to sign on her assumption of the throne, to which I have referred above, are then mentioned. Raleigh is brought in as participator by the assertion that he was to wait in the Isle of Jersey and receive Cobham on his return from Spain, when the latter would turn over to him part of the proceeds resulting from Philip's favourable reply to Cobham's request. The indictment goes on to state that a few days after the conference of June 9th the two brothers Brooke met and uttered the words " That there never would be a good world in England, until the king and his cubs were taken away," and that Raleigh had published a book against the legality of the king's title.

To this indictment and its several particulars the prisoner pleaded not guilty. The jury's names were then read and he was asked if he objected to any of them, to which he replied—" I know of none of them, they are all Christians and honest gentlemen, I except against none." His speech and attitude were quiet and confident, but within he must have felt far different than he appeared without. For before him was a jury overawed by the weight behind this prosecution, a bench as prejudiced and corrupt as official selection could make them, an array of prosecutors led by Sir Edward Coke, as celebrated for his savagery as for his talents, and outside a public opinion waiting to gloat as he was hurried to torture and death. On his side he had nothing save his own wit and resourcefulness. No legal adviser was allowed him, in accordance with the custom of the day ; he was not permitted to call or question witnesses, not even to interrupt the presentation of the prosecution's case though it slandered and belied him outrageously. The only privilege granted him was that he might have

pen and ink wherewith to refresh his memory of the
particulars of the charges, and to answer in general after
they had been brought and elaborated. Whatever
atmosphere his accusers chose to cast could not be broken
through in the process of its construction and dissipated
—only after it had fogged the mind of the jury was
he allowed to say that in this or the other respect his
opponents had misrepresented him.

The Crown's case was opened by Serjeant Heale, who
merely repeated the items of the indictment, praised the
king whose title the conspirators had questioned, made
a few vague assertions and sat down again.

Then the Attorney-General, the great Sir Edward
Coke, arose, and from now on the trial was a duel between
him and the accused, an unfair and one-sided duel, in
which all the weight of official machinery and legal
experience was on one side only.   There is no doubt that
Coke believed as fully in Raleigh's guilt as he had in
Essex's and Southampton's three years before.   His
head was full of Romish plots and Jesuit treasons, and his
ferocity was at least sincere, not the mere acting of a
barrister before a jury.   This was the greatest cause he
had ever had to plead, and he mustered every resource of
his mind and his long experience to the destruction of
this enemy to the king's peace of mind.   And, largely
as a result of his efforts, he consigned himself and his
master to eternal odium and raised his victim to immortal
admiration.

Coke's opening speech was a repetition of the aims of
the Bye plot.   His style of exposition may be observed
in his introductory remarks :

" Here is mischief, *in summo grado*, exorbitant Mischief.   My
speech shall chiefly touch these three points ; imitation, supporta-
tion and defence.   The imitation of evil ever exceeds the precedent ; as on the contrary imitation of good ever comes short.
Mischief cannot be supported but by mischief ; yea it will so

multiply that it will bring all to confusion. Mischief is ever underpropped by Falsehood or foul practices. . . ."

After listening for some time to this tirade on the villainous practices of the plotters of the Bye, Raleigh finally interpolated a remark to the effect that he was not on trial for complicity in that intrigue. To which Coke paid no attention, but following the immemorial custom of prosecuting attorneys, continued the attempt to smirch the prisoner with the taint of crimes which only remotely touched the one for which he stood accused. After which he set forth the Law of Evidence and the Law of Treason, in the following scholarly definition :

". . . there is Treason in the heart, in the hand, in the mouth, in consummation ; comparing that *in corde*, to the root of a tree ; *in ore* to the bud ; *in manu* to the blossom, and which is *in consummatione* to the fruit."

And turning to the impressed commissioners uttered the following praeterea :

" I shall not need, my lords, to speak anything concerning the king, nor of the bounty and sweetness of his nature, whose thoughts are innocent, whose words are full of wisdom and learning, and whose works are full of honour "—

all this of the most repulsive boor who ever occupied the English throne ; so certain was he that the prisoner could not possibly admit dislike of this paragon that he demanded of him, " but to whom do you bear malice ? To the children ? " " To whom do you speak this ? " asked Raleigh drily, " you tell me news I have never heard of."

A sharp interchange followed, one of many. Coke, irritated by Raleigh's not unreasonable remonstrance that he confine himself to the matter in hand and bring some proofs in support, lost his temper and called the other a monster with an English face but a Spanish heart. Refusing to allow the prisoner to answer him in his wildest accusations, he proceeded to give an outline of the Cobham-Aremberg plot, only again to express his horrified disbelief that any man could have conspired to dethrone so good a king.

Again Raleigh declared that it was all news to him. Coke declined to be drawn into details, and when Raleigh pressed him to declare when, if ever, he had spoken with Arabella, on whose behalf he was alleged to be acting, the Attorney accused him of losing his temper. Raleigh coolly pointed out that whatever temper had been dislodged did not belong to him. The ruffled Coke then went on to prove by inference that the plot could not have issued from Cobham's feeble brain, but from Raleigh's Machiavellian one. But the latter instantly pounced on the inherent weakness of the prosecution and pointed out that whatever practices were alleged had all been laid to Cobham, and his own name did not appear save in the disputed and retracted confession:

"I do not hear yet that you have spoken one word against me ; here is no treason of mine done. If my Lord Cobham be a traitor, what is that to me."

"All that he did," retorted Coke angrily, "was by thy instigation, thou viper ; for I thou thee, thou traitor "— the "thou" being a form of deep insult.

"It becometh not a man of quality and virtue, to call me so," returned Raleigh quietly, "but I take comfort in it, it is all you can do."

"Have I angered you ? " inquired the Attorney eagerly.

"I am in no case to be angry," was the prisoner's composed remark, and evidently Coke was again about to burst into rage, for the Lord Chief Justice intervened to save a scene between the two.

I take the risk of boring the reader by these lengthy extracts from the minutes of the trial, for in no other way can the incredible pedantry and savagery of the Attorney-General be conveyed. His whole exposition of the Crown's case was so dull and laboured as the extracts from it which I have quoted. One actually welcomes his fierce personal apostrophes to the accused, grotesquely unfair and irrelevant as these are, before he has even completed his accusation, let alone his proof.

The clerk then read Cobham's first deposition to the commission. It was about 200 words in length and charged at the beginning that he would not have entered the plot but for Raleigh's instigation, and admitted at the end that he thought Raleigh would probably deliver him and his Spanish money up to the king ; in other words, that he doubted Raleigh's loyalty to himself rather than to James. And it is significant that he declared himself unable to recall any of the particulars of the plots and invasions on which he declared that Raleigh and he had frequently conferred.

This vague and incoherent document is the total of the Crown's direct evidence ; in effect it may be said that upon it the prosecution rested. It was Raleigh's first turn to speak.

He began simply by repeating the first circumstances of his examination, his original denial of any knowledge of the Arabella plot and his subsequent admission of knowledge of the Aremberg transactions. He recalled that it was from himself that Cecil received the advice to apprehend Laurency. Why, he demanded, should he have intrigued with Cobham, a man of no importance and no repute, in favour of Spain, a country of waning power and exhausted wealth ? What could he gain, in fame or fortune, in throwing in his lot with either ? Did he not, like any observant man, know that it was just at the moment of the alleged conspiracy that England was stronger than ever, with Scotland united to it, and Ireland at last tranquil, with an active king on the throne instead

"of a lady whom time had surprised."

There must have been a complete hush in that solemn medieval hall as the poet uttered this lovely reference to the old queen, and it must have grown utterly tense as the conqueror of Spanish fleets went on in phrases so brilliantly in contrast with Coke's bombast :

"The State of Spain was not unknown to me ; I had written a discourse, which I had intended to present unto the king, against peace with Spain. I knew the Spaniard had had six repulses ; three in Ireland and three at sea, and once in 1588, at Calais, by my Lord Admiral. I knew he was discouraged and dishonoured. I knew the king of Spain to be the proudest prince in Christendom ; but now he cometh creeping to the king my master for peace. I knew, whereas he had in his port before six or seven score sail of ships, he hath now but six or seven. I knew of 25,000,000 (pounds) he had from his Indies, he hath scarce one left. I knew him to be so poor that the Jesuits in Spain, who were wont to have so large allowance, were fain to beg at the Church door. Was it ever read or heard that any prince should disburse so much money, without a sufficient pawn ? I knew her own subjects, the citizens of London, would not lend her Majesty money without Flushing, Brill and other towns for a pawn. And can it be thought he would let Cobham have so great a sum ? "

There could be no answer to this—whatever Raleigh's character, he was not such a fool as to involve himself in so futile and compromising a venture. The clerk went on to read Cobham's second examination, which is merely a short recapitulation of the main charge of the first. And the Lord Chief Justice, fearing lest it be thought that Cobham might have been influenced in his confession, assumed the rôle of witness from his high tribunal and deposed that the confession had been fairly obtained. The proceedings then became extremely muddled.

The foreman of the jury, Sir Thomas Fowler, enquired whether Raleigh had divulged his information regarding Laurency before Cobham's accusation or after (a point of some importance in its bearing on Raleigh's state of mind), to which Cecil, who could have replied in one word, made a speech of several hundred, protesting how much he had once esteemed the prisoner, before he took to his evil courses, and leaving the bewildered juror to extract what meaning he could. Lord Henry Howard next put in his oar with a vindictive but unenlightening comment, and to prevent Raleigh from clearing up the point, Coke resumed his legal argument, which becomes so involved as to be beyond following ; in it he quotes the remark about " the king and his cubs " which in any event did not apply to Raleigh, as it was mere hearsay. And when Raleigh attempted to verify the Attorney's authority for this bit of irrelevant evidence, the latter quickly shifted the subject and undertook to answer the other's speech. One gem of argument in it may be extracted therefrom :

" Whereas you say Spain is so poor discoursing so largely thereof ; it had been better for you to have kept in Guiana, than to have been so well acquainted with the State of Spain."

Coke then took up Raleigh's statement that two witnesses were necessary before a conviction for treason could be had. In support of his contention Raleigh cited both the law of England and that of Scripture to prove that two witnesses had always been necessary to support such a charge, that conviction on mere circumstantial evidence was a method of the Spanish Inquisition. This brought out a storm of angry denials and explanations from his accusers and judges alike, but no refutation— their conflicting assertions have been examined by keen legal minds for three hundred years, but no one has yet brought forward a satisfactory explanation of why an old pillar of the Common Law, which is still valid in trials for treason and explicitly contained in the American constitution, was then suppressed. Coke was so much put out by the prisoner's knowledge of his legal rights that he suspected him of having studied law, an insinuation which the latter indignantly denied.

Having lost this plea he next asked that at least his single accuser be brought face to face with him, a not unreasonable demand. For it appeared that Cobham had declined to sign his own examination, and it would seem that whatever little value it had was entirely negated by this refusal. Raleigh felt certain that Cobham would not maintain his accusations before his face, and went so far as to offer to plead guilty to every count in the indictment if his accuser in open court would repeat his charges. Again a wrangle ensued. Cecil seemed to be in favour of granting the request, or at least of considering it.   But the judges utterly denounced it as capricious, dangerous and unreasonable. The learned Chief Justice expressed fear lest Raleigh before all the hostile watchful eyes in that court should be able to practise upon the witness if he appeared in person. Even he appeared dubious of his position, for later on, *when actually sentencing the prisoner*, he suddenly remembered why Cobham could not be brought forward. His colleague Gawdy explained that the statute was no longer in force, it having been found inco nvenient and repealed, and another colleague, Warburton, endeavoured to enlighten the accused by a somewhat strained analogy, " If one should rush into the King's Privy Chamber, whilst he is alone, and kill the king (which God forbid) and this man be met coming with his sword all bloody, shall he not be condemned to death ? "   He too feared that Raleigh's influence would sway Cobham before all that multitude.

And Coke explained that Cobham's statement was of more force than the oaths of interested persons, for by incriminating Raleigh he was incriminating himself. His experience of the plots now under investigation should have taught the Attorney, if his long career had not already done so, that none are so eager to divulge as the guilty, if by means of confession, true or false, they may hope to mitigate their own punishments.

Raleigh was beaten ; he saw it. All his astuteness, his knowledge, his wit, was unable to break that impenetrable front of prejudice, toadyism and dishonesty. When the Law had thus marvellously been expounded to him he commented simply, " I know not how you conceive the Law."

Popham's answer should be framed in every judicial chamber in the world, " Nay, we do not conceive the Law, we *know* the Law."

Various other examinations, of Brooke, of Copley and of Watson, were read, none of which had anything to do with Raleigh, save for casual remarks, given by the deponents as pure hearsay. Then the question of the book came up. The volume in question, by Robert Snagg, was one of a number which had been circulated at the end of Elizabeth's reign to prove the title of one or another of the possible successors to the throne. All that the evidence advanced was that Raleigh borrowed it from Burghley while searching for some cosmographical tracts in the latter's house, and that Cobham had in turn taken it from his table while he was arranging his papers in preparation for a duel with Sir Amyas Preston, which was never fought. Both borrowers, it seemed, had neglected to ask permission of the preceding owner. Cecil hastened to add that, by virtue of his position, there was no censure attached to his father's possession of the book, and was constrained to admit that the same exemption applied to Raleigh, who was frequently called into consultation by the Privy Council. To which Coke caustically, though somewhat inaptly, remarked,

" You were no Privy Counsellor, and I hope never shall be."

The prosecuting attorneys all immediately raised an uproar about the nefarious nature of the book, which had nothing to do with the case if the accused could not be proved to have published it. (Publication in the legal sentence does not imply printing, merely exhibiting.) During the exchanges a gentleman in the room was heard to remark that this evidence did not appear to him material, and was sternly rebuked by Coke for so unseemly a remark, which he hastily denied having made. At that Raleigh had a chance to say a word and declared categorically, " Here is a book supposed to be treasonable ; I never read it, commended it, delivered it nor urged it."

" Why, this is cunning," ejaculated Coke, as if the denial astounded him.

Raleigh's long patience with his overbearing tormentor was nearing its end, for his answer came tartly, " Everything that doth make for me is cunning, and everything that maketh against me is probable."

Over and over the same ground they went, getting no nearer to proof. So lame was the prosecution's case that it was eventually reduced to calling as a witness one Dyer, a pilot, whose total testimony is as follows :

" I came to a merchant's house in Lisbon to see a boy that I knew there ; there came a gentleman into the house, and enquiring what countryman I was, I said an Englishman, whereupon he asked me if the king was crowned ? And I answered him ' No, but I hoped that he should be shortly.' ' Nay,' said he, ' He shall never be crowned, for Don Raleigh and Don Cobham will cut his throat ere that day comes.' "

Was ever so ludicrous evidence admitted into a court of law—the opinion of an uninformed foreigner on the state of mind of a person he had never even seen, and only heard of by distorted rumours. Raleigh justly asks, " What infer you upon this ? " and Coke triumphantly answers, " That your treason hath wings."

All the frailty and inconsistency of the case Raleigh exposed in a few concluding words. The accusation rested entirely on the word of Cobham, who had retracted. In its very nature it was improbable. " If," he concluded warmly, " you would be contented to be so judged, judge so of me."

The case now neared its conclusion. Raleigh asked as his right, since his life was at stake, that he be allowed the last word, which was denied him. His persistence angered Coke, who sat down in a huff, and would not be persuaded to go on with his address to the jury until the commissioners had coaxed him into a better humour. He began to recapitulate the evidence, and when Raleigh interrupted to correct him the following interesting interchange took place :

COKE. Thou art the most vile and execrable traitor that ever lived.

RALEIGH. You speak indiscreetly, barbarously and uncivilly.

COKE. I want words sufficient to express thy viperous treason.

RALEIGH. I think you want words indeed, for you have spoken one thing half-a-dozen times.

COKE. Thou art an odious fellow, thy name is hateful to all the realm of England for thy pride.

RALEIGH. It will go near to prove a measuring cast between you and me, Mr. Attorney.

This passage itself is a measuring stick between the two ; it goes far to explain why the defeated combatant in this court won so overwhelming a victory in the greater one of mankind's opinion.

Coke was now ready for his last dramatic coup. Reaching into his pocket he produced a letter from Cobham in which the latter reveals the means that

Raleigh had employed to get his recantation out of him (" Oh ! it was Adam's apple, whereby the devil did deceive him," is Coke's pious aside), and now withdraws that recantation.

Coke had finished.   With a grand outburst against the " damnable atheist," he sat down, convinced that at last the prisoner was crushed by his own devices.

But he had reckoned without his man.   In the matter of dramatic strokes he was dealing with a master.   Raleigh also had a letter to pull out of his pocket, and he quietly handed it up to Cecil to read on the ground that the latter could identify the writer's hand.   It was from Cobham, the very last one, and ran :

" Seeing myself so near my end, for the discharge of my own conscience and freeing myself from your blood, which else will cry vengeance against me ; I protest upon my salvation I never practised with Spain by your procurement—God so comfort me in this my affliction as you are a true subject for anything I know. So God have mercy on my soul, as I know no treason by you."

" Now I wonder how many souls this man hath ! " reflected Raleigh aloud.   " He damns one in this letter and another in that."

The reporter of the trial remarks, " Here was much ado."   Coke vociferated that the second letter had been extracted from Cobham by pressure and the Lord Chief Justice uneasily brought forward evidence that the first one had not been so extorted.   One would have thought the matter very puzzling indeed, but apparently the jury did not, for within a quarter of an hour of their retirement they were ready with the verdict of " guilty."

The prisoner was then asked if he had anything to say, why judgment of death should not be passed upon him. His reply was that he threw himself on the king's mercy, confident that His Majesty would appreciate how un-justly he had been used.

It is discordant to the modern ear to hear Raleigh's sycophantic references to the wisdom and graciousness of the perverted creature called James I, and at times his adulation of the sovereign, as now and later when he pleaded with him for his life and estates, is nothing less than disgusting. But it must be remembered that that day had a different conception of royalty than has ours. "There's such divinity doth hedge a king," wrote the greatest of Jacobean poets, and even the civil war did not completely destroy this idea of the Lord's Anointed. Raleigh himself in his later writings completely subscribes to the dictum laid down by Shakespeare. A century and a quarter later we find the cynical courtiers of the eighteenth century still humble before the silly little German monarchs they had recently imported, and a memorable picture is that of the powerful Robert Harley abjectly on his knees to the grotesque George II, informing him of the death of his father and his own succession. There is excuse for Raleigh in that the atmosphere about royalty was rarer in his day than it is in ours and a judgment of his humility based on the latter is not altogether fair. Yet, of course, the very finest spirits of any day would not so have degraded themselves before any monarch whatsoever.

The Lord Chief Justice then addressed the prisoner. He expresses regret that one who had risen to such great heights should have fallen so grievously. His remark that " It is best for man not to seek to climb too high, lest he fall " is curiously reminiscent of Elizabeth's sturdier apothegm quoted in Chapter III. He reproves the convicted man for covetousness in having sought an additional £1500 a year in the form of a treasonable pension when he already enjoyed an income of £3000 (about £30,000 in spending power of to-day). He gives his own testimony as to the truth of Cobham's charges and suddenly remembers why the latter might not face his accuser—because if traitors confront each other the one may wish the other to live that he may be revenged by committing the like treason again.   His concluding words, " I never saw the like trial and I hope I shall never see the like again," are pregnant with the seeds of a future verdict on the whole proceedings.   Then he uttered the words of the infernal sentence of execution :

" That you shall be had from hence to the place whence you came, there to remain until the day of execution ; and from thence you shall be drawn upon a hurdle through the open streets to the place of execution, there to be hanged and cut down alive, and your body shall be opened, your heart and bowels plucked out, and your privy members cut off, and thrown into the fire before your eyes, then your head to be stricken off from your body, and your body divided into four quarters, to be disposed of at the king's pleasure ; and may God have mercy on your soul."

Even in James's day it was rare for the full rigour of this sentence to be carried out.   One strong argument against applying different standards of judgment to that age than to ours is the general outcry which was even then heard against barbarous executions.   It is probable that the priests were treated more or less according to the literal wording of the sentence, but they were only Papists, after all, spies of the Antichrist, and the authorities could in a measure allay the public sensitiveness ; other cases were commuted to simple beheading.

However, only George Brooke suffered even that fate, on the sixth of December.   The executions of Cobham, Markham, and Grey were set for the 10th, Raleigh's for the 13th.   It was during this interval that Raleigh sank to his nadir, a depth too unpleasant to contemplate.   He flung all pride and dignity to the winds and importuned the King and his counsellors, especially Cecil, in the most grovelling fashion for his life.   It is with great reluctance that the admirer of Raleigh is forced to contemplate such words as :

" I do therefore, on the knees of my heart, beseech your Majesty to take counsel from your own sweet and merciful disposition, and remember that I have loved your Majesty now twenty years, for which your Majesty hath yet given me no reward.   And it is fitter that I should be indebted to my sovereign Lord than the King to his poor vassal."

He vowed anything, everything, including one promise he did not keep, that he would never trouble any one about the property lost through his attainder, if only he might live.   To all of which the king turned a deaf ear—his only concession was that Cobham might die first.

But at the end, or what he thought the end, the great artist awoke to the fact that he was defacing the image which posterity was to gaze upon, and in the letter to his wife already quoted says :

" Get those letters, if it is possible, which I writ to the Lords, wherein I sued for my life.   God knoweth that it was for you and yours I desired it, but it is true that I disdain myself for begging for it.   And know, dear wife, that your son is the child of a true man, and who, in his own respect, despises Death and all his misshapen and ugly forms."

This was truly Raleigh, even to the not altogether ingratiating excuse for having written the letters he now despises.   He goes on :

" I cannot write much.   God knows how hardly I stole this time, when asleep ; and it is time to separate my thoughts from the world.   Beg my dead body, which living was denied you ; and either lay it at Sherborne if the land continue, or in Exeter Church, by my father and mother.   I can write no more.   Time and Death do call me away. . . . My true wife, farewell, bless my poor boy ; pray for me ; may the true God hold you both in his arms."

The last chapter was to be deferred for another fifteen years, however.   James did not yet dare before his people and the world to give force to the sentences and he commuted nearly all of them. Yet it was not in his nature to bestow mercy generously and graciously. He allowed Grey, Markham, and Cobham in turn to mount the scaffold, to utter their last words and only then to be informed that their sovereign had been so kind as to lend them (it was far from an outright gift) their lives. Cobham repeated his accusation against Raleigh on the scaffold, but only after he knew that he was not to die ; the king had seen to that. All were presently confined in the Tower, whence not one of them ever issued but to die.

There can be no two opinions as to the conduct of the trial and Raleigh's legal guilt. Famous lawyers who have examined the evidence have been virtually unanimous in saying that not a semblance of justice was shown him. Sir John Hawles, solicitor-general to William III, went over the evidence in detail two generations later, and held that Raleigh's judges were in error on every major point. But the final word was spoken by one of the very judges who assisted in the affair, Justice Gawdy, who said before his death, two years later, that " English justice had never been so degraded as at the trial of Raleigh."

It is possible, of course, for a man to be guilty and substantial justice to be arrived at even though his trial be unfair. But on the very pleadings themselves Raleigh was guilty of no overt act, and subsequent evidence has shown that even the plot itself was so vague as scarcely to have deserved that name. As Raleigh himself pointed out fourteen years later, when the Spanish ambassador Gondomar was attempting to keep him from going to Guiana, the best way to have achieved that purpose was for Spain to have published the proofs of the conspiracy of 1603, which she never did. A modern biographer of Raleigh, Martin A. S. Hume, states that he found original documents in Spanish archives to prove the falsity of the alleged design to create disturbances in Scotland. And the Earl of Northumberland, a friend of Raleigh's who threw him over to toady to James, yet admits that he had never been unfriendly to the latter's title. The worst that can be urged against him is that he listened too patiently to the treasonable maunderings of a fool.

The ultimate proof of Raleigh's innocence, it would seem, is the further charge that Cobham made during his own trial a few days later, when he alleged that Raleigh had planned to prepare for the landing of Spanish troops at Milford Haven. The story is so confused that little can be made of it, save that it dated back to a period before James's succession, when it would not have been treason against him at all. But what its introduction does prove is that the Crown knew its case to be so weak that something stronger was needed. For if, as Raleigh pointed out, they had evidence of a genuine treason, an attack on the country by armed forces, why bother to try him merely for receiving a pension (which he never did actually receive, although many others, including his principal accusers, did) to affect the king's foreign policy? James himself seems to have been aware of this doubt, for Cecil, in writing to his successor Winwood about the abeyance of the Winchester sentences, says :

"The king . . . pretended to forbear Sir Walter Raleigh for the present, until Lord Cobham's death had given some light *how far he would make good his accusations.*"

(The italics are mine.)

James and his courtiers had achieved their conviction and extinguished, as they thought, the last great light of Elizabeth's reign behind the damp walls of the Tower. They had stripped him of his offices, plucked from him the baubles of his splendour, swooped down like harpies and carried off his cherished estates one by one.   But they did their work too well, for in making the wealthy favourite into a pauper and a prisoner, they likewise converted the most hated man in England into its most revered hero.   There swept over the country after his conviction a whirlwind of acclamation.   All who had seen the trial hastened to spread the report of the unfortunate prisoner's wit, aplomb and nobility of bearing under the insults and injustices of his prosecutors.   One writes, " Never man spoke better for himself.   So worthily, so wisely, so temperately he behaved himself that in half a day the mind of all the company was changed from the extremist hate to the extremist pity." The two men whom the king had detailed to report to him the proceedings of the trial said respectively, " Never spake man so well in time past, nor would in time to come," and " whereas he (the witness) when he saw Sir Walter Raleigh first would have gone a hundred miles to see him hanged, he would, ere they parted, have gone a thousand to save his life."   That invaluable letter writer, Dudley Carlton, told his correspondent John Chamberlain, " So well he shifted all advantages that were taken against him that were not *fama malum gravius quam res*, an ill name half-hanged, in the opinion of all men he would have been acquitted.   In one word, never was a man so hated and so popular in so short a time."   It is impossible to exaggerate the effect made on his contemporaries by Raleigh's superb battle against hopeless odds.   The verdict against him became at once a verdict against his royal enemy for ever.

The justice of this reversal of the judgment of Popham and his colleagues has been questioned by various authorities.   It is possible, they say, either that Raleigh was actually guilty but that for reasons of state the principal evidence against him was not brought forward, although privately conveyed to the jury, or that he was morally culpable without being legally so. The former alternative will not bear a minute's examination. Whatever evidence James and his tools chose to suppress would long ere now have been dug up and presented ; it has not been. To the other the answer has already been given, that even the indictment against him in substance charges no more than that he considered accepting a pension to favour a new Spanish policy on *which the king had already decided*—it is another touch of irony that Aremberg had, if the charges were true, violated his ambassadorial obligations and left the country loaded with the royal compliments. Raleigh's own defence, that although he listened to Cobham's project he took it to be only more of his foolish vapourings, and that his whole record was against his indulging in a compact with Spain, seems to be conclusive as to his moral implication in the conspiracy.

And yet, agree though one may with posterity's admiration for the man's courage and the felicity of his tongue before the cruel hostility of the authorities, although one may burn with resentment that so gallant a battle against public hatred and official jealousy should have been so hopeless, yet one cannot avoid the suspicion that here again one is witnessing the performance of a very great actor rather than the doom of a very great man. The shrewd Carlton may have had an inkling of this distinction, for in the letter quoted above he says, " save it went with hazard of his life, it was the happiest day ever he spent." There can be no doubt that he was enjoying the situation, exulting in the sense of every faculty keyed up to meet its demands. He saw himself, as we see him, standing with head erect, alone, having only the aid of his matchless mind and tongue in the encounter with the entrenched forces of corruption, bombast and pedantry before him. As at Cadiz, as at

Fayal, he was alert, strong, the observed of men's eyes, and he knew it. He probably realized that if he lost here his triumph would be all the greater in a larger arena. As in at least two other great trials in history the defendant gained his victory by losing his battle.

Of one of these trials it is perhaps irreverent to speak in this connection, but the analogy and the difference will be clear. The other, the trial of Socrates, also involves a man standing alone before the menace of official brutality, and here also the victim is immortal for his brave and eloquent confutation of his accusers. But in the two latter cases there was so much more than that, an infinite sincerity, a desire for right, on the part of the defendants, which altogether transcended their poor parts in the performance for which they had been unwillingly cast. Whether they lived or died, the truth they presented survived as part of their memories. Raleigh fought for no truth, he held a brief for no great imaginative idea. There was no passion in his heart for something which might live though he perished ; its impulses were too complicated and too near to justifying the charges on which he was tried. He was his own sole cause, and bright as is his image as it emerges from that stone-vaulted chamber at Winchester, his going out leaves nothing behind with which to enrich human imagination.

CHAPTER X

THIRTEEN YEARS IN PRISON

In the murk of a London December Raleigh rode through London to the doors of the Conqueror's Tower, which closed behind him and did not open again for thirteen years. He was then not quite fifty-two, physically strong and at the height of his intellectual vigour. When he came forth he was an old man, tired and ill, but he had learned one lesson thoroughly—that of all human vanities the emptiest is pride of place and power, and had recorded that lesson in deathless language. And surely no man ever lived who could point to his own life for so perfect an illustration of it. At thirty he had been an ambitious adventurer, with his wits, his courage and his looks as his principal assets. He had become the darling of a Queen, a very great Queen, rich and powerful, an explorer and the planter of an Empire, a statesman and the peer of the mightiest of the realm, a poet and the friend of poets, the hero of memorable contests by sea, as naval strategist the direct successor of the greatest commander his country had ever known. Yet here, at the beginning of his life's prime, he found himself stripped of all his ambition's fruits, " none so poor as to do him reverence." All that was left to him was his genius, and that could only serve him in his despair if he had the character to make use of it.

James had not troubled to wait for the verdict of the

judges before degrading and impoverishing his victim. Rapidly the prized honours were taken away—in May Sir Thomas Erskine succeeded him as Captain of the Guard, in September the High Sheriff of Cornwall, Sir Francis Godolphin, was instructed to perform the duties of Lieutenant of that county. Sir John Peyton, his first gaoler in the Tower, was given the governorship of Jersey in August. The lucrative wine licences went to the Earl of Nottingham, whom, as Lord High Admiral, Raleigh had so ably served. By the beginning of 1605 virtually nothing was left of the accumulation of twenty years save the estate of Sherborne, which of all his possessions, of all places on earth, the owner valued most.

It seemed for a time that this, at least, was safe. Raleigh had in 1602 prudently conveyed the estate to his son, with a life interest to himself, reserving £200 a year to Lady Raleigh during her lifetime. The attainder, consequently, could affect nothing but his own life interest. That was temporarily spared him by a deed which appointed certain trustees to administer the income in favour of Lady Raleigh and her son, so that his revenue was merely turned over to them. Raleigh himself was not altogether easy in his mind, despite this arrangement, for he keeps begging Cecil to secure him a new grant from the king, so that he might dispose of the place to the best advantage—preferably to Cecil himself, if the latter will buy it.

Very early, however, the ravenous favourites whom James had brought from Scotland with him began to regard the pleasant property with covetous eyes, and presently, by the instigation of some unidentified person, the conveyance was examined into, with the result that it was found to be void—a careless copying clerk, it seems, had omitted the essential words " shall and will from henceforth stand and be thereof seised " in engrossing the record, and consequently the conveyance in trust had never been completed. Legal advice on the point was taken from Coke and Popham, but both decided against the legality of the transaction.

Even James did not dare baldly to seize the estates on so outrageous an excuse. He meant to have the place—his adored Robert Carr was begging for it—but he thought it wisest to arrange some sort of conveyance, and in the end bought out the Raleigh interest for eight thousand pounds. At least that was the sum agreed upon ; only part of it was ever paid, and even that was eventually lost in the last voyage to Guiana. For the rest Lady Raleigh was to get £400 from the Treasury—when she could collect it.

Raleigh was now almost literally reduced to destitution, if his own statements can be at all relied upon. In an inventory of his property, which accompanies a letter of 1604 to Cecil, he sets forth in detail his sources of income, and arrives at a net total of £295 a year. Against this must be put the cost of his keep at the Tower, which came to almost exactly that figure. This was before Sherborne was finally taken away from him. Thereafter he was dependent upon Lady Raleigh's private property and her precarious allowance from the Crown. Chamberlain, writing to Carlton (was there ever such a useful and well-matched pair of correspondents ?) on January 10th, 1609, sums up the situation of the prisoner, when after describing the flaw by which Sherborne was lost and Lady Raleigh's frantic importunities to the king, he remarks, " Yet it is past recalling, so that he may say with Job, ' naked I came into the world and naked shall I go out.' "

The first year of his confinement was largely spent in agonized appeals to the king, Cecil, and various other influential persons for freedom or at least mitigation of the consequences of his attainder. He was not a very patient prisoner, and James paid small attention to his perpetual requests and complaints. Even Cecil, to whom he constantly refers with gratitude and who undoubtedly rendered him certain services, seems to have grown weary of these incessant assaults on his pity, for the endorsements on many of the letters indicate that they received only formal acknowledgment.

He had other causes of complaint besides the loss of freedom and property. The Tower was damp and its sanitary conditions vile. The dreaded Plague began there sooner and held on longer than in other spots in the capital because of the filth and the rats. Raleigh reported in 1604 that the tenant of the adjacent room had a running plague-sore and that his own son had been compelled to lie in proximity to her and her child, who subsequently died of the disease. He begged hard but unsuccessfully to be removed. Although transferred to the Fleet Prison, of which he had had experience in his youth for a brief period, it was only because James did not want him in the Tower when he entertained the Venetian ambassador there, as pardons were the order of the day during such festivities.

James had in fact all sorts of troubles because of Raleigh's presence in the Tower. People came from far and near to gape at him as he took his daily walks on the wall, foreign legates were always asking curious questions about the illustrious captive and writing home about him, and it must have seemed to the irate ruler that he was more celebrated than the king himself. Even the latter's eldest son, that ill-fated Henry, whose paternity one would like to question as much as one is inclined to doubt his father's, provoked him by remarking, "only my father could keep such a bird in a cage."

Nevertheless the early period of imprisonment had its compensations. The Lieutenant of the Tower, Sir George Harvey, although he had, like Cecil, been hostile before the trial, now showed himself friendly and allowed his famous prisoner the freedom of his garden, where Raleigh eventually built himself a little house in which to conduct his chemical experiments. His confinement was not close. He was allowed visits from his friends, and some of the best spirits in England were his companions. He had also the almost constant society of his devoted wife, whose second son, Carew, was born in a house on Tower Hill.

Even these mild compensations were seriously abated after Sir William Waad, his old enemy, succeeded Harvey. Waad resented his prisoner's attraction to the populace, whose admiration he accused him of trying to win by showing himself daily, and objected to Lady Raleigh's driving into the Tower in a coach for her visits to her husband. Various privileges were curtailed, until presently the residence in the sombre prison subsided into a something resembling a genuine captivity.

The years went on, and what had once been frantically resented as a temporary restraint began to be accepted as a permanent incarceration. Not that Raleigh ever resigned himself altogether—despite repeated rebuffs he persisted in his efforts to obtain a rehearing from James, and at irregular intervals concocted new proposals that he be allowed to go to Virginia or Guiana or to fight for the king on the Continent. Nor did the world, although most of it must have deemed his active life ended, ever have the chance to forget him. The fame of his chemical researches spread over Europe : he was supposed to be a wizard who had solved the cure for all ills, and crowned heads sought his potions. Later, when his growing infirmities circumscribed these researches, and the warm friendship of the Prince of Wales stimulated him to take up his pen for diversion, he recalled to public attention that he was amongst the ablest of living students of political and naval affairs.

His prose writings in the Tower may be divided into four classes : essays on current political problems, essays in political philosophy, discourses on ships and war by sea, and historical writings of varying degrees of importance.   Nearly all were undertaken at the behest of Prince Henry, who looked constantly during his brief life to his father's prisoner for his education. The veneration of this young man was no small tribute to Raleigh—the Prince was a youth of extraordinary brilliance and precocity for whose future nearly every one predicted great things.   The incomparable poets of the epoch vied with one another in dedicating their works to him, not from mere flattery, but because in him they found a sympathetic patron.   His death at the age of nineteen snuffed out the one hopeful light of the Stuart line.

The writings in the first class, as above divided, were undertaken because of a project which affected Henry directly.   James had gone over more and more to the pro-Spanish party, a movement due in part to his own instincts, which were those of a *parvenu*, in part to the cunning with which Philip III's agents distributed gold amongst the unspeakable favourites of the English court.   As a result he approved the design of a double marriage between his heir and his daughter Elizabeth on the one hand and the daughter and the son of the Duke of Savoy, a dependent of Spain, on the other.   Henry solicited Raleigh's opinion and received by way of answer two discourses which repeated the views the writer had held all his life regarding Spanish alliances. He pointed out how one-sided the bargain was, which pledged England to neutrality whilst the inevitably hostile Catholic power completed the subjugation of the Netherlands, a menace which Raleigh saw as clearly as did Napoleon two centuries later.   He argued as he had for years that the power of England's great enemy was on the wane, that there was no need to placate her, that the alternative match of Elizabeth with the Protestant Elector Palatine was more in accord with England's obvious destiny.   Naturally James detested him the more for these frank objections to the royal projects, but it would seem that history has, on the whole, amply justified his foresight.

To take up in detail the various writings would be impossible in a work of this compass—they are too many and too long.   The essays alone fill the bulk of an eight-hundred-page volume in the collected works, while the *History of the World* requires six substantial ones all to itself.   Yet there is no more certain way of discovering his character than by scrutinizing these miscellaneous papers.   A man may to a certain extent direct his actions, but it is not always fair to judge him by what he does.   But no man can deceive others by what he says, if only he says enough, and of this instrument of judgment Raleigh has left full measure.

There is in his case, fortunately, a strong consistency between his acts and his recorded thoughts.   The latter, like the former, convey at every turn an impression of almost incredible versatility.   His scientific treatises have won the respect of scientific men ; he was not far behind Bacon in his prevision of the new world of science. His lectures on war and shipbuilding are amongst the classics in these subjects.   Few men have ever studied more acutely the causes of military success and failure or predicted more accurately the future progress of tactics and strategy.   As to shipbuilding, he had the whole art, its history and problems, at his finger-tips. As the most industrious student of his life, Edward Edwards, said :

" Raleigh not only made great and enduring improvements in ship-building and naval tactics ; he is the first man of any nation who is known to have set his pen at work upon a complete, practical and systematic treatise of naval service and naval architecture, ancient and modern."

As a student of political phenomena his range is limited by his interests and his temperament. The latter impelled him to an essentially aristocratic outlook, a contempt for democracy, whilst the former led him to express his ideas in language calculated to tickle James's vanity, to the detriment of its appeal to the modern reader. Yet, although we may disagree with his conception of the king as *paterfamilias*, we are beginning apparently to share his distrust of the democratic fetish, and the idea that the king is above all law is inherent in the legal doctrine that the Crown may not be sued. At any rate the cast of his mind leads him to conclusions which now seem highly original, such as the view, put forward in *The Prerogative of Parliaments*, his principal effort in political philosophy, that King John had been wronged by being compelled against his will to sign Magna Carta. And who will dispute his reflection that all revolutions are by their very nature incapable of success, carrying in themselves the seeds of their own destruction and that of their authors. His own examples, taken from Roman times, may be amplified by more recent experiences—after Cromwell came Charles II, after Danton came in turn Napoleon and Louis XVIII.

His mind was not only capable of absorbing and digesting multitudes of diverse facts and of giving to them profound and original interpretations, but, what is always the mark of the really first-class intellect, of applying them to other sets of like facts. The vast storehouse of his memory was principally employed for housing chemicals wherewith he might analyse the living world before him in the test-tubes of his intelligence. A battle or a revolution of a thousand years before cast instant light on a battle or revolution of his own time.   From the specific he argued to the general, and so had a sound principle to apply when the specific arose again.

His weaknesses appear in his discourses on conduct, as we should expect.   Expediency guided his own life all too largely, and it is the corner-stone of his moral philosophy.   All his life he pondered on the soul and its immortality, like a good Puritan, yet his mature conclusions on the subject are worthy of the grossest materialist:

" For we worship God because our souls are made to his image, and we know that he is *a rewarder of them that serve him* . . . now to what end were religion, if there were no reward ? and what reward is there if the souls do not live forever ? "

And in his advice to his beloved son, wherein the wise and experienced father sets forth for the young man's benefit all that he has learned from life, he counsels him never to trust any man too much, to marry for convenience rather than for love, to please God lest he be punished.   There is no suggestion of purity of heart or integrity of character, of the beauty of passionately losing one's self in love for a friend or a woman or one's Creator.   He did not see the humour of warning his son to be careful in marriage, he who went to prison for his espousal of the lad's mother, nor of the man at whose jewels and raiment all the world marvelled saying:

" Exceed not in the humour of rags and bravery, for these will soon wear out the fashion ; but money in thy purse will ever be in fashion ; and no man is esteemed for gay garments but by fools and women."

Luckily, though he preached like Polonius, he could act like Laertes, and it was the practice rather than the precept to which the son for whom this was written paid regard.

The dominant note in all these writings is lack of

humour, especially about himself. It is no less than amazing that a man with his perceptions, with his constant view of the world *sub specie aeternitatis*, should himself have taken so seriously as goals to be sought, respectability and good repute amongst his equals. A man who roamed the stars as did he, should, like the great tragic poets, have had a more smiling conception of earthy man's objectives. Of course, had he had a sense of humour, he might not have exerted himself for glory as he did ; on the other hand he would not have debased himself for the sake of either freedom or property, so perhaps it all levelled itself out.

The greatest of all his achievements in the Tower, was the work which sums up the literary side of his career, *The History of the World*. It is almost beyond belief that a man in his condition, prematurely old, sick, his heart full of despair, his brain occupied with a thousand wild schemes for release, should have conceived so large an undertaking and sat down to its performance. He had had the idea of a history of England in mind for a long time, and tried his hand with *A Breviary of the History of England Beginning at the Reign of William the First*, a short tract which survived him in manuscript only. Later he changed his plan to a complete survey of known history up to the conquest of Britain by Caesar, whereafter he intended to concentrate solely on English history, with only occasional discursions into events on the Continent.

" It was for the service of the inestimable Prince Henry that I undertook this work," says Raleigh, and it was to him that it was dedicated. Henry did not live to see the publication of the finished portion of the *History* ; he died in 1612, the same year as Cecil, so that a further despair settled down on the author as he laboured on toward his conclusion, for these two had been his principal reliances in his struggle to free himself from his prison. Perhaps it was the passing of his patron that finally induced the weary historian to lay down his pen before he had finished his task. There are other stories to explain the book's incompletion, including one that Raleigh, finding himself in disagreement with another eye-witness over the details of a trivial fracas in the Tower, decided that since Truth was so elusive in a current matter, it must be unobtainable in long past ones, and hence decided to give over the rest.

Even if the anecdote on which this latter explanation is based were better accredited than it is, it would still not be convincing, for it misrepresents Raleigh's attitude toward the writing of history. He was not the scientific critic of facts, but the artist working in pictures. He accepts his material indiscriminately, whether it be the Bible or Livy, Herodotus or Plutarch. His aim is not primarily to reconstruct, like an archæologist, an authentic picture of the past, but to examine the moral structure of the world from what he believes the past to have shown. In spirit his *History* is much more like Shakespeare or Sophocles than like Gibbon or Mommsen. He observes the acts of conquerors and kings, describes the means whereby they have risen, draws vivid sketches of their characters, and proceeds to show how each in turn falls because he has permitted pride and vanity to overcome his proper humility toward the Overruler of the Universe. The book reads like a series of dramatic tragedies, save that in the latter the action of Fate is frequently perverse and capricious, whereas Raleigh sees it invariably as just and retributive.

It is probable that he did not at first realize the scope of the work he was undertaking, or else even his courage and industry might have been dismayed. As it exists now, it occupies six volumes of his collected works and embraces, I estimate roughly, well over a million words— about twelve times as many as this biography—and fills

1354 closely-printed folio pages.   Yet it concludes with
the Roman conquest of Greece in the second Macedonian
War.   The divisions are made nationally rather than
chronologically.   The first two books begin with the
creation of the world and end with the Babylonian
captivity of the Israelites ; the third book takes up with
the rise of the Persians and goes on, through the Graeco-
Persian wars, to the conflicts of the Greek City States ;
the fourth traces the rise of the Macedonian power to
the fall of Alexander's empire and the rise of Rome.
The concluding book begins with the first Punic War.

It would be idle to say that all this mass of historical chronicle, metaphysical speculation, and personal
reminiscence is of readable interest to-day.   Our values
of history have changed ; Raleigh's perspective seems
to us distorted, much of what he accepted is to us childish,
the points of his abstractions are often lost.   Yet in many
passages he casts a spell as strong as that of any historian
who ever wrote.   His pictures of times gone and men
dead are fresh and vivid, his point of view is always
original and stimulating.   Where an incident or expression in the past catches his imagination and recalls
to him events in his own stirring life he is irresistible.   If
these personal recollections could be gathered into one
small volume, they would beyond doubt live as a separate
classic.   It has often been deplored that he did not
write a history of his own times, but to this complaint
he has himself, as usual, supplied an answer in his
preface :

" . . . I know it will be said by many that I might have been
more pleasing if I had written the story of mine own times, having
been permitted to draw water as near the well-head as another.
To this I answer, that whosoever in writing a modern history
shall follow truth to near the heels, it may happily strike out his
teeth.   There is no mistress or guide that hath led her servants
into greater miseries."

The subsequent treatment of even the history he did write provided ample vindication of his fears.

The haunting demon of space will not permit me further to complete this all too meagre description of the *History of the World*. With all its archaisms it remains a masterpiece of historical composition, to whom poets such as Milton and historians such as Gibbon have alike paid effusive tribute. It is one of the literary monuments of its time, and a worthy companion to that select group of immortal masterpieces born within the walls of a prison. I have barely indicated its scope and have no time wherein to illustrate its style save by two quotations. The first is from the end of the preface and is merely used to show that in contemplation of his *chef d'œuvre* Raleigh could skirt the edge of that saving humour of which otherwise nature had deprived him. He has just reiterated his innocence of the charges against him and his hopes of freedom. In begging the indulgence of the reader he recognizes that they can never be so unkind as other "more ungentle and uncourteous readers of my love toward them," and adds slyly :

"For had it been otherwise, I should hardly have had the leisure to make a jest of myself in print."

Never, I think, has an author written a more disarming and winning reference to the circumstances in which his book was composed.

The other quotation needs no introduction. It is not only the keynote of the book, but amongst the most celebrated passages of prose ever written—one which is incomparable even in that day of golden words :

"O eloquent, just and mighty Death ! whom none could advise, thou hast persuaded ; what none hath dared, thou hast done ; and whom all the world has flattered, thou only hast cast out of the world and despised. Thou hast drawn together all the far-stretched greatness, all the pride, cruelty and ambition of man, and covered it all over with these two narrow words, *Hic jacet* ! "

Raleigh's life was yet to reach its apogee, but the composition of the above passage marks the greatest height to which his mind ever attained. No doubt the epithets of "villainous adventurer" and "gifted charlatan" which indignant historians have hurled at him are justified if one scrutinizes only his pursuit of riches and power and the means whereby he attained them ; but if one reads again this concluding paragraph of the *History of the World* and remembers the circumstances under which it was written, one forgets the prostitution of his talents, one even forgets the talents themselves, recalling only that here " beating his brilliant plumage against the bars of his cage " was an artist capable of converting the profoundest mood of the spirit into beauty.

The *History of the World* was first published in 1614, by Walter Burre, and had an instantaneous success. Three editions appeared in 1617, and in all a dozen in English alone within seventy years, four of them during the Restoration era. The king seems to have been almost alone in his disapproval of the work. Despite Raleigh's precautions in dealing with ancient history only and his gratuitous compliment to James's views on the rights of monarchs, the latter found the strictures on the conduct of kings intolerable—the author was " too saucy in censuring princes," says Chamberlain— and objected especially to the verdict on his near predecessor Henry VIII :

" If all the pictures and patterns of merciless princes were lost in the world, they might all again be painted to the life out of the story of this king."

The result was that he ordered the book suppressed. A letter from the Archbishop of Canterbury to the

Stationers' Company, of December 22nd, 1614, directs
that all copies be brought to himself or the Lord Mayor.
Evidently public opinion forced the removal of the
edict, for the work did circulate, although deprived of
its title-page bearing the author's portrait ; if the king
could not keep his prisoner's opus out of circulation he
was determined that he should not, at any rate, have
public credit for having written it.

There has been more gossip of one sort or another,
outside of simple literary criticism, about the *History*
than about most books which have lived.   It has puzzled
many that a man of so active a life should have been
able to store up the information necessary for so monu-
mental a work, and various efforts have been made to
trace his collaborators.   Isaac D'Israeli, in his *Curiosities
of Literature*, attributes the bulk of the labour to Dr.
Robert Burrell, a former chaplain of Raleigh's and a
large measure of assistance to Hariot and Ben Jonson.
But this argument only rests on inference—Burrell
knew Hebrew, whereas Raleigh did not, and Jonson
later made some reference to his own part in the *History*.
Undoubtedly Raleigh called in help where he found his
own equipment insufficient, as does every author of so
extensive a work, but that does not deprive him of both
credit and responsibility for his creation.   Too much
stress is laid by these critics on Raleigh's many occupations as a bar to his possession of the necessary knowledge.
Somehow he found time to acquire it.   His early
biographers repeatedly dwell on his voracious reading.
" Five hours he slept, two he read, two he discoursed,
allowing the rest to his business and necessities," records
one : " in his sea-voyages he always carried a trunk of
books along with him," says another ; and Sir Robert
Naunton, who knew him, calls him " an indefatigable
reader by land and sea."   There is a letter extant from
him in the Tower to the learned Robert Cotton ask-

ing the loan of various now almost unknown books of early chroniclers, principally by medieval churchmen. D'Israeli forgot, as have others who do not consider primarily the nature of the *History of the World*, that it was not a labour of original research, but the result of the application of an original and philosophic mind to an extensive and well-digested reading.

There have been various theories also as to the reasons why the *History* was never completed, although the author, on his own testimony, had blocked out the rest.   Beside the one mentioned a few pages earlier, there is another to the effect that the bookseller Burre reported to Raleigh in the Tower that the book was selling slowly, whereupon Raleigh threw the unpublished manuscript in the fire with the remark, " The ungrateful world is unworthy of it."   Outside the fact that the story is totally uncharacteristic (little Raleigh cared whether the " world " liked his book or not, much as he may have wanted his equals' good opinion) the explanation is palpably false, because at the time this conversation with Burre is supposed to have taken place the fourth edition was ready for or just off the press.   One need search no further for a reason for the book's incompletion than the fact that shortly after the first part appeared Raleigh's health broke down completely, and he had a stroke ; when he had partially recovered he turned every energy to obtaining his freedom.

The lever for this final effort was again Guiana. During the whole time of his confinement he had employed that magic word as an open sesame for forcing the massive doors of his prison, and now slowly he beholds them swing open.   But to take no chances, as he has in the past, he lubricates their hinges with gold from his meagre remaining supply.   Too often has he entreated the Queen, her brother, King Christian of Denmark, her son, the dead Henry, and the Lords of the Council

to procure his release on the merits of his case alone ;
too often has he suggested the most fantastic conditions
if only he will be permitted to go once more on his
country's behalf to Guiana—he has even offered to leave
his wife and son as hostages to be put to death if he fails
to return.   Nothing moved James.   Raleigh's principal
advocate, the Queen, lost her husband's confidence when
he caught her in clandestine interference with affairs
of State, and he was too much engrossed in seeking
Spanish favour and Spanish alliances to think of letting
loose the one of his subjects the Spaniards feared most
since the terrible Dragon had passed away.

First in 1609 freedom seemed near, for fresh gold was
found in Guiana ; in 1612 it seemed even nearer as the
inscrutable Cecil died and was succeeded by Sir Ralph
Winwood, a man who saw eye to eye with Raleigh in
public policy.   When Henry Howard died, in 1614,
the last of the old enemies were either dead or discredited.
Even yet the pardon tarried.   And so although in 1616
one would have thought that those doors, released from
nearly all pressure of public dislike and official hostility,
would have opened of themselves, Raleigh took no
further chance but seized the opportunity of doing
business in the typically Jacobean way and bribed Sir
Edward Villiers and Sir Edward St. John, the former
a half-brother of the now reigning favourite, George
Villiers, to obtain the latter's intercession.   What
supplications to justice, pity and the glory of England
had failed to do, corruption has effected in that gracious
court—in March 1616, Raleigh's cousin George, now
Lord Carew by virtue of his services in suppressing the
Tyrone rebellion, is able to write :

"Sir Walter Raleigh is enlarged out of the Tower, and is to
go his journey to Guiana, but remaynes unpardoned until his
retourne ; he left his mansion in the Tower the 19th day of
this monethe."

The story of the bribery has been questioned by the historian Gardiner, but Raleigh's own words of thanks to Villiers, " You have by your mediation put me in the world again," when read with a knowledge of Villiers' character, would seem to supply the answer.

And so the old man left the lodgings he had occupied longer than any other to that pleasant couple, the Earl and Countess of Somerset, Overbury's poisoners, and was driven in his wife's coach, no doubt through the same raw east wind that still blows up the Thames in March, to the little house she had taken in the City. The king's order of release had stipulated that he must not go to any public places or entertainments, but this was now as little in his mind as many other of the vanities of youth which he had sloughed off in the Tower—his first day was spent in walking about London, using his eyes again like a blind man restored, observing the changes which thirteen years had made. He was so much else that one forgets that he was also a genuine lover of old scenes and old buildings, in fact one of the founders of the long-lived Society of Antiquaries of London.

But he had not gained his freedom that he might enjoy his remaining years in peace and the pursuit of gentle hobbies. He was under orders to sail for Guiana, and a keeper was appointed to follow him about on territory over which James ruled. There is no reason to believe that Raleigh would have had it otherwise. It is quite possible, as he said, that he might have bought a complete pardon and been free to do as he pleased. But that was too tame a proceeding—he wanted once more to renew his youth, to show this new generation, by one grand exploit, what it meant to have been a Paladin of Elizabeth.

To claim Guiana finally and shower England with its gold was the obvious way of capturing public attention in the Elizabethan manner, but there were others. The French made approaches to induce him to bring his squadron when completed under the flag of the Bourbons, with freebooting as part of his employment, and the Duke of Savoy attempted to enlist his interest in a raid on Genoa, a port virtually under Spanish dominion. Although the accounts are confused, he listened to the emissaries of France and Savoy as he had listened to Cobham and later had to account heavily for so doing. But the fact remains that he proceeded with the fitting of his ships, begged and borrowed every pound he could lay his hands on, spent every farthing he or his wife could lay claim to and never deviated from his promised venture. So closely did he concentrate on it that he failed to take the precautions against failure which ordinary prudence would have dictated.

By May of 1617 his fleet of seven ships of war and three pinnaces were assembled in Plymouth Harbour. His gentlemen adventurers numbered 90, his seamen 318—impressment was no longer open to him and he had obtained his volunteers by the distribution of broadsides, signed by himself and Keymis, which promised shares in his profits to all who would accompany him. Another such collection of rogues and cut-throats it would have been hard to find in all of England.

The town of Plymouth insisted on paying the drummer who called his company aboard on the eve of sailing, and its citizens gathered to see him off with frantic cheers— for whatever others might think of him, he was the son of whom Devon was proud. On June the twelfth he led his little fleet out to sea—the name of his own ship being the " Destiny."

CHAPTER XI

THE RAINBOW FADES

Never did a man set out on a voyage more hopeless. It is doubtful if Raleigh, realist as he was, appreciated fully how strong was the rope around his neck, and how malicious the hands that held the other end of it. To himself he was an Elizabethan sea-rover in action once more, seeking glory or obloquy through success or failure. But those large simple days were over. There were no more sea-rovers; James did not approve of them. The single sea-action which his reign saw was a minor one against some Barbary pirates. There was thus a complete lack of understanding between the King who granted the commission and the admiral who received it. Raleigh knew perfectly well that James had released him unwillingly and given him permission to sail only under impossible and unprecedented restrictions. What he never fully grasped was that the King of England actually *wanted* his great subject to fail. True, he would have appreciated and used whatever gold Raleigh brought back, and might have been compelled to pardon him if it had been of sufficiently sensational quantity. But his plans were all made on the other supposition. Raleigh was given a commission carrying power of life and death over the seamen under him, but he himself sailed unpardoned from the sentence of death of 1603. He was a supreme commander, yet a dead man in the eyes of the law. His commission, contrary to all precedent, was given under the Privy Council seal only, not under the Great Seal, and the words " trusty and well-beloved " in the document, which might have indicated a royal blessing on his dangerous endeavour, were deliberately erased.

It is a little difficult to fathom James's purpose. He was, it is true, very much under the spell of the Spanish Ambassador, Diego Sarmiento de Acuña, Count of Gondomar, and urgently desirous of bringing to fruition the project of a marriage between his heir, Prince Charles, and a daughter of Philip III of Spain, despite the loathing of his people for the proposed alliance. He would have gone far to oblige Gondomar and bring off the match, yet he permitted Raleigh to sail over the furious protests of the Ambassador. The commission did not even contain directly the usual prohibition against trespassing on land already occupied by Christian princes, merely limiting the object of search to heathen territories. Unless James admitted that Guiana already belonged to England, which by implication he had himself done in sending an earlier expedition there, the act of searching for a mine was in itself an act of trespass. Yet, after sanctioning that very act, he took the astounding measure of frustrating it by informing the Spaniard in detail of Raleigh's organization and designs.

Even granting the assumption that he was taking every precaution to avert hostile measures against his new allies, it was at once a stupid as well as a dastardly act to provoke those very hostilities by putting the Spaniards in a position of military defence. Historians have attempted to exculpate James from the charge of duplicity towards Raleigh by asserting that a new era of peace and international amity had succeeded the bellicose days of his predecessor. But no amount of chop-logic will clear him of having, unbeknown to Raleigh, unbeknown even to his advisers, led a foreign power to act on the presumption that a man who held his own commission was contemplating an act of piracy against it. Every accusation that James later made only involves him deeper in the slimy business of having connived to place his own subject in an inescapable tangle. It is of damning significance that James, much as he wanted money, became extremely uneasy at the early reports that Raleigh was returning laden with gold from Guiana.

Raleigh and his friends, while quite unable to perceive the extent of their sovereign's duplicity, were nevertheless worried by the failure to obtain a complete pardon. He thought at one time of purchasing one through the same sources from which he had bought his liberty, and had a talk on the subject with Francis Bacon, then Lord Keeper of the Seal, in the gardens of Gray's Inn. This conversation, as reported by Carew Raleigh, Sir Walter's son, is that Bacon advised against the expenditure of further money which might be needed for the voyage, and gave it as his opinion that the commission under seal removed the former attaint of treason —a view he himself later repudiated when writing James's defence. Another story relating to Bacon, even if not altogether authenticated, indicates the complete divergence of attitude between king and admiral toward the proposed expedition. Bacon asked the latter curiously what he would do if, after all his expenditure, he failed to find the mine. " We will look after the Plate Fleet," answered Raleigh lightly. " But you will then be pirates," objected the cautious lawyer. " Who ever heard of men being pirates for millions ! " was the classic retort. It was a clash between two worlds, Elizabethan and Jacobean, and although Raleigh's subsequent acts proved him not to have been in earnest, he was stating the *credo* of the Drakes and Cumberlands, who could afford to accept the painless rebukes of their royal mistress for enforcing the doctrine of " No peace beyond the line." But that he thought of himself as a commander of a serious exploration and not as the leader of a gang of pirates is obvious from the orders to his fleet which he published before sailing. They are stern but humane and far-sighted edicts, which naval authorities agree are models for the discipline of a fleet for that or any other day. They forbid any act of rapine or violence, direct regular religious worship, and in every other way suggest to the assorted rabble of scoundrels and gaol-birds which his advertisements had collected that this was no mere freebooting expedition.

The nature of the difficulties between Raleigh and James will be more closely enquired into after the former's return. It is necessary here only to remember that, after his long years of pleading and deferred hope, he was finally allowed his freedom ostensibly on the terms he had suggested, but actually that he might be led from prison into dark labyrinths whose twistings had been elaborately laid out to lead him to the block.

Nature itself conspired from the beginning to make his way more difficult. On leaving Plymouth he at once ran into a gale so terrific that his ships were scattered and several forced back into Falmouth. After they were collected and again on their way, the same thing happened just west of the Scilly Islands, and this time one foundered. The third attempt was no happier, and they were blown into Cork Harbour, where they were compelled to wait six weeks for a favourable wind. Meantime the meagre resources of the expedition were being consumed, idleness was breeding difficulties in his naturally mutinous crews, and sickness, which plagued the adventure from beginning to end, broke out.

The best days of the summer were lost in this way

and when again they set sail, it was to find their provisions running short.   Near the French coast they ran
into four vessels and after a long chase captured them.
They looked like pirates, and Raleigh's captains wished
to treat them as such, confiscating their much-needed
supplies.   But he was leaning backward on this voyage,
to the disadvantage of James's later case against him.
He turned them loose after paying for a few pounds'
worth of necessities he had bought from them.

His first stop was at Lancerota, in the Canaries, on
September 6th.   Raleigh wished to water there, and,
after protracted negotiations with the Spanish governor,
sent ashore a party for that purpose.   The Spaniard
had, however, been dallying on purpose, while causing
the removal of the town's goods inland, although the
Englishmen had made no unfriendly demonstration.
When, after three days, the permission was given, the
natives were informed that the landing party were
Barbary pirates and accordingly attacked them, killing
fifteen.

Their comrades were frantic for revenge, but the
admiral resolutely forbade it on the ground that it would
offend the king and prejudice English merchants trading
in the islands.   Nevertheless one Bailey deserted the
expedition and rushed back to London to report that
Raleigh had turned pirate.   Both Spanish and English
official versions exonerate him completely either of
illegal intent or act, but the deserter's story, although he
himself was in the end discredited, was listened to and
added to the reckoning which was being prepared against
Raleigh's return.

The next port of call was Gomera, where occurred the
first and last agreeable incident of the voyage.   The
Governor's wife was an English lady, on her mother's
side of the well-known family of Stafford.   So pleased
was she at the visit of her celebrated compatriot and a

pair of gloves he sent her by way of compliment (how he happened to be prepared with so suitable a present to a lady is not stated) that she sent to his ships quantities of fruit, bread and sugar, of which the voyagers not only stood in need by way of provisions, but which proved very grateful during the ensuing epidemic of sickness aboard. The governor was so impressed with the exemplary and unexpected conduct of the English seamen, who were constrained to let local property and women alone by their commander's promise to hang them in the market-place if they didn't, that he wrote a letter to Gondomar eulogising his visitors—a communication which the Ambassador naturally received without enthusiasm. With a parting gift of a painting the fleet sailed away to Guiana and less pleasant encounters with the Spaniards.

It was the merest luck that they arrived at all. The entire crossing was one long nightmare of tempest and fever. They no sooner were tossed out of one storm than they were swooped upon by another. Man after man died of fever, forty-two in the "Destiny" alone, including some of the very few subordinates whom Raleigh could trust. He himself barely survived a calenture which rendered him unable to take nourishment save artificially for twenty-eight days. When on November 11th, they arrived at the mouth of the Cayenne River (which he calls the Caliana), he had a relapse and his life was despaired of. But he was not destined, like Drake and Hawkins, to be buried in the far-away waters belonging to his enemy—Fate was reserving him for a more magnificent finale.

On account of his enfeebled condition it was obviously impossible for him personally to lead the exploring party. His second-in-command, Warham St. Leger, being similarly incapacitated, the command was given to his nephew, George Raleigh, while Keymis, who was supposed to know the location of the mine on which he had reported in 1596, was detailed to lead a party to it. His instructions were to avoid hostile encounters if possible, but not to shirk them if unavoidable, and to bring back at least a basket of gold from the mine for the satisfaction of the king, if he found it not so rich as to be worth holding until a relief expedition could come to his support.

These, whatever he may have said in council and despite the king's case against him, are the substance of his instructions and hence the extent of his responsibilities in criminal law. No one can urge, of course, that he was unprepared to force his way to that vague mine, if necessary, for his earthly salvation depended on his getting there. His conception of the existing relationship between Englishmen and Spaniards differed so far from James's that there was no common ground between them. The beneficiaries of Pope Alexander Borgia's grant were natural enemies whom it was a pleasure to fight if his designs were blocked. James's view was that Raleigh, to whom he had given a patent to go to Guiana, was nevertheless a trespasser there and had no more right to resist an attack by force of arms than has a burglar caught robbing a house. There was no hope for him unless the Spaniards amiably stood aside and let him help himself, which they were unlikely to do. And more than he feared the king, he feared the disgrace of a defeat by Spain : that at all events he was prepared to resist, and openly said so.

The expedition up the Orinoco consisted of five vessels, with four hundred men provisioned for a month. Raleigh himself was to stay at his old anchorage near Punto Gallo and promised to remain there, dead or alive, to burn his ships if necessary, rather than run before the galleons of Spain, which were daily expected.

The start into the interior was made on December

10th.   It took three weeks to reach the main course of the Orinoco, during which time two of the ships, under Captains Wollaston and Whitney, were temporarily disabled and left behind.   The Spaniards, who had had news of their coming, harassed them with gunfire from the banks, whilst the governor of Trinidad and Guiana, Diego Palomeque de Acuña, one of Gondomar's ubiquitous relatives, hurried up to San Thomé, a tiny settlement on the Orinoco a little below the mouth of the Caroni.

It is the location of this village of " stakes covered with leaves of trees " which has served as the foundation of the lawyer's case against Raleigh.   An earlier settlement of the same name had existed thirty miles further up the river during the first visit, but had subsequently been abandoned.   The new town was of recent origin, and lay directly in the road to the mine, which was supposed to be three miles above it, near Mt. Aio.   James subsequently accused Raleigh of not having informed him of the existence of this hindrance ;   the latter's defence is that he did not know of the change himself. Certainly he cannot be accused of concealing anything, because in 1611 he specifically mentions in one of his pleas to James the existence of San Thomé ;   and the latter seems quite as likely to have had as recent information on the subject as the man he had kept in prison for thirteen years.   Whatever convicts Raleigh of duplicity on this score *a fortiori* proves James a hypocrite and a liar.

The English account says that the mining party landed above the town, that is, between the town and the mine, on the first day of 1618 ;   the Spanish report says below it.   The dispute is academic, since, even if the English did, in violation of their instructions, land for the express purpose of attack, the others got in the first blow.   They laid an ambuscade and attacked as it was

growing dark. The intruders, prison scum most of
them, showed their mettle by running away before the
smaller force from the town, and only the courage of the
leaders, who did the actual fighting, prevented a wild
scramble into the forest for safety. Eventually the
English got themselves together and drove the Spaniards
back into the town. Their blood now up, the former
determined to settle the affair once and for all. Young
Walter Raleigh led the attack, exhorting his men with
words which were later to tell heavily against his father :
" Come on, my hearts, here is the mine you must expect ;
they that look for any other one are fools." At the
moment of victory, as the Spanish defence began to give
way, he was mortally wounded. His last words show
the strain from which he was bred—" Go on ! The
Lord have mercy upon me and prosper your enter-
prises." His followers rushed on and quickly possessed
themselves of San Thomé, the Spaniards scattering into
the woods, whence they kept up an incessant guerilla
warfare. After a wait of eight days at San Thomé,
Keymis set out on the search for the mine, but his heart
was no longer in the work—it had devolved on him to
write the letter informing Raleigh of the death of his son,
and he knew what the news would mean to his master.
His men as well were discouraged ; discontent had long
been spreading and mutinous gossip urged that it was no
use serving a leader who was certain, anyhow, to be put to
death when they returned to England. The Spaniards
kept plucking them off from ambush, and in a few days
the disheartened and diminished party returned with the
excuse that more soldiers were needed. But they never
returned. It certainly seems that Keymis was at fault
in not persisting further. It was on his report, made
in his account of his 1596 voyage, that Raleigh had
based his representations of the mine, and although he
may have exaggerated its wealth, the discovery of miners'

tools in San Thomé would seem to have at least confirmed its existence. A futile ascent of the Orinoco completed the efforts of the inland expedition. Enraged by the repeated attacks of the Spaniards, which had cost them over half their company, the rest fired San Thomé, carried off whatever they could lay their hands on and began the return voyage. On March 2nd they arrived at Punto Gallo.

Meantime Raleigh had passed his time in repelling feeble attacks launched from St. Joseph in Trinidad, renewing his contracts with his old Indian friends, who still remembered and revered him after more than two decades, and in his favourite pastime of studying local plants and flowers. He hoped for the best from his subordinates, but planned to meet the worst if it happened. Then early in February came Keymis's letter and the sun was blotted out for ever.

No human being had ever approached the place in his proud and solitary heart which young Walter had held. So like his father in his gallantry, so unlike him in nearly every other way, in his recklessness and disregard for consequences, the bond between them was of patriarchal strength. His son's education had been one of the busy father's chief concerns. He had sent the youth first to Oxford, then abroad to study with Ben Jonson ; a favourite story recounts how the younger Raleigh trundled his famous tutor about in a wheelbarrow on one of the not infrequent occasions when the latter was drunk. Another anecdote, although long, is worth quoting for its light on the manners of the day :

" Sir Walter Raleigh being invited to dinner to some great person where his son was to goe with him, he sayd to his son ' Thou art expected to-day at dinner to goe along with me, but thou art such a quarrelsome, affronting . . . that I am ashamed to have such a beare in my company.' Mr. Walter humbled himself to his father and promised he would behave himself mighty mannerly.

So away they went. He sate next to his father and was very demure at least halfe dinner time. Then sayd he ' I, this morning, not having the feare of God before my eies but by the instigation of the devill went. . . .' Sir Walter being strangely surprized and putt out of countenance at so great a table, gives his son a damned blow over the face. His son, rude as he was, would not strike his father, but strikes over the face the gentleman that sate next to him and sayd ' Box about ; 'twill come to my father anon.' "

But this must hardly be accepted as typical of the relationship between father and son—very likely Raleigh himself appreciated the *gamin* humour of this response to his discipline. What his feelings for the boy were appears in such phrases as :

" My son . . . was slain, and, with who, to say the truth, all respect of the world hath taken end in me,"

in his letter of March 21st to Winwood, now six months' dead, and in his words to his wife in a terrible and wonderful letter, written on the following day :

" I was loathe to write, because I knew not how to comfort you ; and God knows, I never knew what sorrow meant until now. All that I can say to you is, that you must obey the will and providence of God ; and remember that the Queen's Majestie bore the loss of Prince Henry with a magnanimous heart . . . comfort your heart, dearest Bess, I shall sorrow for us both. . . . My brains are broken and it is a torment for me to write, and especially of misery."

It was in this mood that Keymis had to comfort him. The depositions of the various witnesses, taken later before the commission which judged Raleigh's offence, vary widely in describing Keymis's reception, but all agree that he was upbraided for having so easily given up the search for the mine and thus thrown away his chief's last hope. Keymis tried hard to justify himself, but Raleigh was deaf to all his excuses. There was no condoning the fact that young Walter's body lay three miles from the mine, a vain sacrifice. Keymis then asked permission to justify himself in a letter to the Earl of Arundel, one of the promoters of the expedition, and asked Raleigh's endorsement of it, which was refused. Seeing that this was the last word he said quietly, " I know then, sir, what course to take," and withdrew to his cabin. A little later a shot was heard. When Raleigh sent to enquire the cause, Keymis said his pistol had gone off by accident. But left once more alone, he drove a knife into his heart, the one expiation he felt he could make for the misery he had caused the man he had so long and so devotedly served.

There was nothing now to do but go home. Various calumnies were later circulated that Raleigh had meant to turn pirate, that he had a commission from the King of France and intended to take refuge with him, and other such tales. He himself declares that he planned to go to Virginia, refit and try again. But all or most of those who so eagerly testified against him later now hastened to desert him, and he was at length left without a company ; otherwise, as he wrote in that same letter to Winwood, " I would have left my body by my son's or have brought with me out of that or other mines so much gold as would have satisfied the king that I had promised no vain things." On June 21st, the twenty-second anniversary of the day on which the " Warspite " had sailed by the batteries of Cadiz with a flourish of her trumpets, the " Destiny " returned to Plymouth Harbour alone.

He knew what was awaiting him. Already, ten days before, James had issued a proclamation which set forth in vehement language the royal detestation of the acts of violence which had been committed and announced the intention of punishing the offender—this before any

examination whatever had been made into the circumstances.   An order had gone out for his arrest, and the
man who executed the order was his cousin, Sir Lewis
Stukely, who had purchased the office of Vice-Admiral
of Devon for £600. He was to recompense himself
and more for this expenditure out of his kinsman's
misfortunes, while adding his name to those of that
select band of traitors whom all mankind agrees for ever
to despise.

So grotesque a figure is James Stuart, King of England,
that even when he moves in a tragic setting it is difficult
not to laugh at him.   There was something ridiculous
as well as disgusting in his methods of playing the
benign tyrant to the condemned at Winchester, and there
is equal absurdity in his attempt now to put on the
judicial wig and ermine for Raleigh's benefit.   The
ermine is spotted, the wig askew. James gravely
approved the discrediting of the traitor and deserter
Bailey ; he austerely rebuked Gondomar when that
gentleman, after the news of the burning of San Thomé,
burst in on him demanding instant and condign punishment on the offender (shouting, so the tradition goes,
Piratas, *Piratas*, *Piratas*).   In fact, on this occasion James
lost his temper, flung his hat on the floor, and burst into
condemnation of the Spanish principle of punishment
without trial.   With this gesture he capitulated and
issued his proclamation, at the same time promising,
still before any trial had taken place, that Raleigh should
be punished in Madrid if Philip and Gondomar insisted,
and that any Spanish subject damaged by the raid should
be reimbursed.   This latter promise came home to
roost all too quickly to please him, in the form of a
demand for £40,000 for tobacco.   There is, however, no
record of its payment.   Smaller claims were settled
out of Raleigh's estate, so here at least he could feel
that he had acted righteously.   And somehow the trial,

about the need of which he grew so excited in the name of English justice, never took place. Nor for that matter did that Spanish marriage for which he spotted his high ideals and sacrificed Raleigh. Spain used the bait and then withdrew it, leaving James to melancholy reflections on the frailty of kingly promises.

A number of minor incidents which occurred after Raleigh's return assume significance in the light of later aspersions. He was actually on his way to London with his wife and a friend, Captain King, when he met Stukely, who had come to arrest him. Although his captor was without a warrant Raleigh submitted to being placed in custody and returned to Plymouth. There he momentarily lost courage and engaged two French pilots to take him across the Channel. Yet, when quite clear, ready to board the waiting vessel, he voluntarily returned to Plymouth. The ease with which he might have escaped rather makes it seem that high authority would have been glad to see him do so, as the shortest way out of future embarrassment. Two of the most serious charges against him is that he plotted to seek asylum in France, both before and after returning to England. But the fact remains that he did come back, as he had promised, and that he did not escape to France when he might have done so.

Once more they started on the road to London, the original party reinforced by the addition of one Dr. Manourie, a quack French physician, whose mission it was to assist Stukely in obtaining damaging admissions from the latter's prisoner. It was the last journey the great wanderer was ever to take in this world, and its sadness was intensified by the fact that his way lay through Sherborne. One of the pieces of hurtful testimony which Manourie later offered was that the former owner of Sherborne had said of it in passing, " All this was mine, and it was taken from me unjustly."

Raleigh's principal concern at this stage was to have the opportunity of putting his case before the king. What good this would have done him is not apparent, but he had faith in the art of his pen, a faith often justified in the past even when his cause was less sound than it was now.   He began to be overwhelmed by a sense of the speed with which he was being rushed to his doom, and devised a stratagem which, were it not so funny, might be somewhat discreditable in the circumstances. But it is more satisfactory to regard it as comic relief rather than as a blot on this last, catharsis stage of his tragedy.

It was part of Raleigh's strange inconsistency of character that he, the worldling, trusted nearly everybody.   All his life he had done so, with the result that his servants often cheated him and his colleagues played him false.   He now trusted Manourie to the extent that he confided to him a plan for securing delay.   It was that the physician should give him an emetic and an ointment which should make him appear to be seriously ill, so that he might be compelled to pause at Salisbury whither the king was now travelling.   He hoped that this coincidence would yield him an interview with James, or at least a chance to present him with the *Apology for the Voyage to Guiana* which he was then composing.   The emetic and ointment did their work ; Raleigh became faint, vomited and broke out in purple spots on his body and arms.   His alarmed servants rushed in to Stukely to announce that their master had gone mad—he was hopping about on all fours, clad only in his shirt, and eating grass.   The Bishop of Ely, who happened to be in Salisbury, called a consultation of physicians, who muttered gravely and failed to diagnose the disease—it might, apparently, have been leprosy, but the symptoms were puzzling.   While all this excitement was going on, the patient, who was compelled to refuse food in order to keep up appearances, was having healthy quantities of bread and mutton smuggled in to him, and was composing the *Apology*, a document on which his defence and our knowledge of the second Guiana voyage largely, although not entirely, rest.

Of course Manourie in his subsequent reports gave away the deception, and it was held as a reproach to Raleigh. He himself was not ashamed of it, pointing out that David had pretended insanity and dribbled on his beard in order to escape from his enemies. He might also have added that the hero of the most famous play in the world, written a bare dozen years before, had adopted a similar ruse in order to entrap his.

The king declined to give the desired interview and ordered the prisoner to be moved on to London. He received the *Apology* and apparently read it, for he answered it in an official paper when it was too late for its author to continue the argument.

Manourie quitted the party at Staines and proceeded to write his own contribution to the affair, for a consideration. In it, beside revealing the feigned illness, he makes various other charges against the man he had spied upon, including two to the effect that the former tried to bribe him to aid his escape and had spoken hard words of the king. It may bewilder the reader that I am at pains to record accusations which must seem to him trivial even if true (and whatever comes from Manourie is subject to doubt), but it was on trivialities like these that the case against Raleigh was built up by James and elaborated by a certain school of historians.

There is no doubt that he was now brooding incessantly upon escape, but a curious hesitancy, a kind of fatality, seems to have settled down upon him—the self-certainty and resoluteness of action of his Elizabethan days had completely abandoned him. He had had a chance at Plymouth and passed it by for no apparent

reason. Now he had another. The French resident
Le Clerc sent a message to him through one de Novion
as he passed through Brentford, saying that he wished to
see him. Manifestly this was impossible if he were
going directly to the Tower—an order for his committal
there had already been signed. But the officials, in a
moment of leniency, which is unaccountable unless they
were either trying to trap him into an intrigue with the
French or assist him in getting away, permitted him to
go to his wife's house in Broad Street. There he held
one or more conferences with Le Clerc, who offered to
place a French vessel at his disposal and carry him in
safety to a Channel port.

The Frenchman's motives are not hard to comprehend.
His country admired Raleigh and thought he might be
serviceable against Spain, concerning whom the court
of Louis XIII had cause to be worried—an Anglo-
Spanish alliance would neutralize the advantages anticipated from the double Franco-Spanish matrimonial
arrangement of 1615. Equally Queen Anne, James's
consort, detested the idea of the Spanish match and
preferred a French one for Charles. Just what end
Raleigh could serve in these dynastic complications it
is difficult to see, but in any event it is clear that the anti-
Spanish faction at Whitehall wanted to aid his escape,
and the equivalent faction at the Louvre would gladly
have received him.

Raleigh gratefully accepted the offer of asylum, but
refused to effect his escape with foreign aid. The one
result of his negotiations with Le Clerc was that James,
who had secretly encouraged them, at least passively,
sent the envoy home when they had come to naught and
the peace between the two countries was nearly ruptured.
The result to Raleigh personally was another grave count
in the growing indictment against him.

He had already laid his own plans for escape, however,

Captain King, who had gone ahead to London from Salisbury with Lady Raleigh, had, with the help of a false servant of Raleigh's, Cottrell, found a former seaman of King's named Hart, who was prepared to carry Raleigh across the Channel. The arrangement being completed Cottrell at once communicated it to Stukely, who threw himself with zest into the business of deceiving his prisoner. He protested the deepest loyalty to him, asserted his readiness to accompany him anywhere, and his affection even went so far as to borrowing money from him. Naturally one cannot endorse Raleigh's willingness to accept Stukely's services, spurious as the latter's offer was, since it meant that he was being a traitor to his employers, any more than one can consider the attempt to escape praiseworthy. The one palliation is that he was hopeless and desperate, conscious of his own failing resources and willing to turn anywhere for help to carry him temporarily past this crisis. He never had the intention of deserting his country and serving a foreign power, even a friendly one. He merely wanted to hide himself with the aid of his friends until the storm should blow over.

The escape was attempted that night. By various routes he, King, Stukely and his son, and one or two servants, set off for the appointed rendezvous on the Thames, near the Tower, where Hart was waiting for them with two wherries. The party got aboard and started down the river. Presently Raleigh's suspicions were excited by the sight of another and larger boat following them. He demanded of Stukely who their pursuers were, but the other merely laughed away his fears, asserting that they would never get anywhere if Sir Walter turned faint-hearted. His protestations to his cousin became more and more effusive : he even embraced him openly. Both the pursuers and the doubt persisted, however, and the oarsmen themselves grew alarmed that they were engaged on illegal business, since an assurance had previously been given them that their passenger was merely going to Holland because of a trivial dispute with the Spanish Ambassador. The pace slowed down, the tide began to turn and at length it was evident that Tilbury could not be reached that night. The order was given to turn back. The suspicious boat turned at the same time ; at Greenwich it came up and Raleigh found that one of the two leaders of his pursuers was the same St. John to whom he had paid money two years before for his freedom. At first he hoped to escape arrest at the strange party's hands by declaring himself in Stukely's custody and turning over to the latter the contents of his pockets, most of which the latter retained. The truth then came out ; Stukely arrested him and King in James's name and turned them over to St. John. Raleigh at last saw, and turning to his perfidious kinsman said reproachfully, " Sir Lewis, these actions will not turn out to your credit." His natural consideration for his followers showed itself in his effort to induce King to represent himself as an accomplice of Stukely's and so avoid punishment. But the stout-hearted captain would not demean himself by even feigning an alliance with a wretch whom he despised.

No scoundrel has ever received his retribution more completely, and few more quickly, than Raleigh's betrayer. He attempted to justify himself in print for his conduct, urging in part that Raleigh had cheated his father of certain money due from Grenville's buccaneering expedition of 1586, but no one listened to him, and he soon became generally known as Sir Judas Stukely. Two months after Raleigh's death the Treasury finally reimbursed him in the amount of £566, the balance due to him for his services and expenditure as gaoler and spy ; he had already appropriated nearly £400 worth of goods from the "Destiny" and no one knows what else besides in the way of articles from Raleigh's person. Amongst the latter was the diamond ring which Elizabeth had given Raleigh when at the height of her favour, now his most treasured personal possession. The money did Stukely as much good as it did that most celebrated of all traitors, after whom his contemporaries renamed him. He and his confederate Manourie were very soon afterward caught clipping the edges off gold coins, an offence then equivalent to forgery, and only the king's contemptuous pardon saved him from an abrupt end then and there. Even James, who was not above using such a tool, could not but despise him. When Stukely complained that every one was avoiding and insulting him and asked his Majesty to do something about it, the latter said drily, "Were I disposed to hang every one that speaks ill of thee, there would not be trees enough in all my kingdom to hang them on." When he had secured his pardon, probably by purchase, he slunk away, impoverished and shunned, and finally died alone and mad, two years after the infamous act by which alone he is remembered.

Raleigh was held in Greenwich the night after the failure of his flight. On the following morning he was taken across the river and once more, after two and a half years of freedom, the gates of the Tower opened to admit him. They would never close behind him again until he went forth to die, and perfectly he knew it.

CHAPTER XII

THE KING'S MISTAKE

Yᴇᴛ though the King had made the promise to his brother of Spain that the object of their mutual dislike should be put out of the way, there still remained the troublesome formality of a suitable pretext. The prerogative of the monarch was by no means supreme and unquestioned in England. Certain restrictions had been laid down for him, and even the most debased and corrupt of judges felt bound to execute his wishes by means of certain prescribed formulæ of the law— trial by jury was one of these. An open offer of Raleigh's head as part of Charles's dowry in the Spanish marriage would have bred violent discontent, at the least; perhaps even more, for already Spaniards were being assaulted in the streets of London.

The necessity for a trial, the indignation against Gondomar for overlooking that necessity, were forgotten. James instructed his lawyers to construct a case. But this was somewhat difficult. There were three possible lines to take; all were tried and all crumbled, as they have crumbled in the highly competent hands of subsequent prosecutors of Raleigh, Hume, Gardiner and Spedding, who respectively stress these three lines. He might be condemned as a traitor to his country who had plotted to accept a commission in the service of a foreign power, as a liar who had never intended to seek out the mine but to use it as a pretext for piratical raids, or as a lawless trespasser who had violated his authority and assaulted a friendly people.

It has been admitted above that Raleigh listened to the offer made by des Marêts, the French Ambassador, before he went to Guiana, that he enlist under the French flag. The offer is said to have been instigated by the famous Admiral de Montmorency. There is extant a letter written to Raleigh in French, to a M. de Bisseaux, asking for permission to put into a French port ; but this letter seems to imply nothing more than satisfaction at the good wishes in France for his venture and the fact that certain Frenchmen under his friend, Captain Faige, were planning to take part in the enterprise. Any further conjecture is invalid. If the French Crown had actually offered him a commission, that fact, and the document itself, would be on record, but no eye has ever seen it. It was charged that as a result of these negotiations Raleigh intended, after the disappointment in Guiana, to desert his country and become a soldier of France. The fact remains that he did not do so, and no satisfactory explanation is forthcoming as to why he did not. His enemies say that, abandoned by his fleet and discredited before men, he would have been of no use to Louis. That may be true, but if it is, it is inconsistent with the outcry over the Le Clerc negotiations after his return. If the French wanted him in August, they wanted him in June : the intervening two months had manifestly not improved his market value. The most that the king's examiners could get out of their inquisition on this subject is that, as always, he liked entertaining propositions. It is impossible to hang a man for listening to talk. Nor should it be forgotten that there was then no Foreign Enlistment Act. There were no limitations to any man's offering his sword to any country with which his own was not at

war.   Thousands of James's subjects were already doing
that for Venice.

The charge of intended piracy also quickly fell to
the ground.   The substance of this accusation is that
Raleigh's representations about a mine in Guiana were
not *bona fide*, that he organized his expedition for buccaneering purposes under the mere pretext of seeking such
a mine.   It was alleged that he took no mining tools,
although he expressly states that he spent £2000 for
miners' and assayers' apparatus.   This part of the
arraignment rests on the evidence of a number of dis-
gruntled seamen who at one time or another quitted the
expedition after they found that it was not going to
yield the profits which they had anticipated.   Again
one may easily believe that Raleigh let careless words
drop without finding him guilty of anything more
serious.   If he had wanted to turn pirate, he had the
right sort of crew to go about it with him.   A number
of them went off on their own for that very purpose—
the suggestion that they virtually restrained him from
so doing is merely ludicrous.   His letters and his acts
at Lancerota and Gomera prove that a sense of responsibility if nothing else would have kept him back.   And
even the unfriendliest of modern critics, some of whom
believe him capable of turning pirate after his return,
acquit him of an unbelief in the mine before he went.
They can scarcely do otherwise.   The testimony of the
long list of hostile witnesses whom James's commissioners
examined is more convincing than anything else that the
mine had become and remained a mania with him—
an *ignus fatuus*, perhaps (though gold has been found in
that territory), but a genuine reality in his mind.   The
last paragraph of the spy Wilson's deposition is eloquent,
not only on this point, but on the meaning of the French
negotiations :

" . . . I fell by occasion into a question with him of his (Raleigh's) end in going to France, albeit he had told me before that it was only to save himself till the storm was blown over, hoping by the Queen or some of his friends to procure his peace. Now he, thinking that I had a bad memory, as perhaps he finds, he told me he would make me his ghostly father, and his hopes in France were that at least with his ships and two pinnaces he might recover again Guiana, and so find the mine, which they failed in by reason of his sickness in his ship, being 80 degrees off, the mine being so far up the river Orenoque ; or else his hope was that he being in France, would procure the king of Spain to write to his M. Majesty to call him home and give him his pardon. This is his last dream."

His last dream—to seek the shelter of a friendly country until he could refit the shattered remnants of his expedition and go once more, a sick old man, to realize the hopes of his El Dorado and so win back his peace before he died. And on this they wanted to hang him.

Almost the entire legal case against him rests on the testimony of spies and hostile witnesses, yet even through their biassed words one cannot see the vaguest elements of a capital indictment. It is rather interesting to observe, in passing, that one of these witnesses, Parson Samuel Jones, states that amongst Raleigh's friends in the expedition were Captain Charles Parker, Sir John Holenden and Captain George Raleigh, *not one of whom was called on to give evidence*—apparently James's Commission was having no witnesses for the defence, although the prosecution supplied itself with many.

The line upon which the examiners then and the critics since have principally rested is the one which asserts that, in violation of a commission which authorized him merely to explore and mine, he trespassed on the territory of and did damage to the subjects of a friendly nation.   This line assumes that the principles of international law which have been painfully built up during three hundred years were as operative then as we would like to make them now and have not yet quite succeeded in doing.   I suspect that even those to whom Raleigh is not the greatest of heroes find it easy enough to forgive him even if the accusation be true.   Most people have small patience with the quibbling *minutiae* of jurisprudence, especially when applied to a man of his temperament and his age.   I believe, however, that he can be vindicated even of this charge, and it seems to me worth doing because it will make clearer what his character was during the last days of his life.

It will be recalled that his commission gave him the right to defend himself, if attacked, but not to seek a conflict.   The language of the commission is explicit " to travel thither . . . with sufficient shipping armour, weapons, ordinance, munitions, powder, shot . . . as he shall think most necessary . . . for the use and defence of him and his company."   In the *Declaration of the Demeanour and Carriage of Sir Walter Raleigh*, a paper drawn up by Francis Bacon for the king after Raleigh's death to justify James's action, the latter asserts that he had always disbelieved in the existence of the mine ; had there been one there, he asserts, "it was not probable that the Spaniards, who were so industrious in the search of treasure, would have neglected it so long."   In other words James thought that Raleigh was going into territory which the Spaniards had the right to exploit if they cared to do so, and yet he permitted the sailing of an expedition sufficient in size and equipment to constitute a strong military unit.   If this were indeed Spanish territory, his commission was tantamount to a declaration of war.

He alleges, however, that Raleigh represented to him that although the mine was in land contiguous to that held by Spain it could be approached without any open breach of the peace. Raleigh's conduct in Guiana warrants his defence on his return that he did not seek to precipitate hostilities. His instructions to Keymis were to avoid a conflict if possible, but not to incur the disgrace of a beating by Spaniards if it were forced on him. In this he probably exceeded James's intentions, the king being devoid of all such national pride, but not a reasonable reading of his instructions. The confused and contradictory accounts of what actually happened at San Thomé certainly warrant the conclusion that Keymis attempted to carry out these instructions, but was attacked by the citizens of the town. What happened thereafter, including the burning of San Thomé, was outside Raleigh's intent or control. The element of *mens rea* was completely absent. He had as much right to disavow Keymis's act as had James to disavow the Lancerota incident, or indeed the entire Guiana affair, which would never have occurred at all save for the patent under his hand and seal. True, Raleigh did not in so many words disavow the acts of his subordinates. His reproaches to Keymis were rather for an act of omission. It may be granted that the killing of a few Spaniards, his country's natural enemies, did not perhaps trouble him overmuch, but this by no means implies that he set out with that end in view. From James's case one would think that Raleigh had sunk his last penny and dragged his weary body through discomfort and illness for the ultimate purpose of destroying one unimportant tropical village. The spark of the old buccaneer remained in him, beyond a doubt, but in that voyage his self-restraint, shown so markedly on the voyage out, proved beyond question that he felt a higher responsibility, that a sense of *noblesse oblige* kept him from indulging in the carefree lawlessness of the days of his youth.

On approaching this question I assumed at first that

James's case was sound in so far as it represented Raleigh to be a trespasser, that the latter's defence must rest on the king's collusion in his trespass and on his own efforts to avoid bloodshed in consequence of it.   In the light of a certain international dispute concluded about thirty years ago, one may go further and say that he was not even trespassing, that he had a perfect right to be where he was and that the entire responsibility for the battle on the Orinoco rests with whoever began it—a point on which the evidence is at least as strong against Spain as it is against Keymis.

In a series of Blue-books published by the British Foreign Office between 1896 and 1899 in connection with the Venezuelan Boundary Dispute, the British Government reviews the history of Spanish settlement in Guiana, from which the claims of the Venezuelan Government were derived.   The conclusions are that between 1596 and 1720 the Spaniards had not extended their possessions beyond the immediate confines of San Thomé ; that from 1613 to 1618 the Spaniards " were definitely excluded to the eastward of the Orinoco " (in other words the right bank, where Keymis landed, was unoccupied territory) ; that the constant trading by the English, and especially the Dutch, systematically and not on sufferance, precludes the idea of Spanish political control ; that, in short, the doctrine of Grotius, *Invenire non illud est oculis usurpare, sed apprehendere*, completely bars any Spanish claim to effective occupation of the disputed territory.   Raleigh's own Government has held, in short, that he had actually done only what his commission permitted him to do, penetrated into the " parts of America . . . possessed by heathen and savage people."   The mine lay outside the " confines " of San Thomé ; hence it was his right to seek it out, and repel the efforts of any one to hinder him in his legitimate occupation.   If his statement, which has not been dis-

proved, be true, that he did not know that San Thomé
had been moved down the river, but thought it thirty
miles further off, James's case on this score collapses completely.   For that matter it collapsed, from an English
point of view, ten years after Raleigh's death, when a
combined Dutch and English force under Admiral
Adrian Jancz Pater demolished and rebuilt San Thomé
on the ground that it had no business to be there at all.
In the Venezuelan case the countrymen of James and
Raleigh have finally adjudicated this matter between
them.   In so doing they have also definitely repudiated
James, whose evidence, quoted by the Venezuelans,
they specifically declare to be of no value.

It is clear, then, that Raleigh was going about his
rightful business, and any attempt to punish him for un-
foreseen consequences arising therefrom was a dishonest
method of appeasing the rage of Spain.   His punishment had little or nothing to do with his alleged offences.
If further proof were wanted there is the fact that, even
if he had been guilty, as alleged, of trespass with hostile
intent against Spain, he would not have been legally
punishable by death.   Statute 33 and 34 Victoria C. 90
first defines the offence in the words " Who, within the
limits of Her Majesty's Dominions, prepares or fits
out any naval or military expedition to proceed against
the dominions of any friendly . . . state," etc., and
proceeds to punish it as a misdemeanour by fine and imprisonment.   Even now this creature of the statute is
not a capital crime ; under the common law it was not
a crime at all.   Yet by means of it the king's lawyers
were trying to hang a man who had not even been guilty
of it !   I have taken legal advice on the one other possible
ground of punishment, namely the violation of the
king's commission, and find that that likewise has never
been a capital crime—it was, it appears, a misdemeanour
under the common law, and that is all.   Even if Raleigh

did commit a trespass, and if that trespass fell within or without the powers granted him, he was at the most punishable by a short term of imprisonment. One is tempted to believe that the wording of Raleigh's commission had been left vague on purpose. None of the restrictions which James had promised Gondomar should be included in it are expressly set forth, and it is not unreasonable to assume that they were omitted in order that Raleigh might more easily be led to violate it. No one reading the language of the commission with fresh eyes and then learning what had been done under it would dream that it had served as an instrument for putting its holder to death.

Those astute gentlemen, the king's lawyers, perceived their dilemma, and presently suggested to James that there was no legal way of putting Raleigh on trial for the Guiana affair. The evidence would not bear it, but this they did not say. Instead they advised His Majesty that Raleigh was already a dead man in law by virtue of the conviction of 1603, and that all the king had to do was to withdraw the reprieve of fifteen years before and have the sentence of Winchester carried out. Once Raleigh was out of the way a declaration could be drawn up informing the public of the new reasons for inflicting the old punishment, which was presently done. But as Carew Raleigh pointed out, the new reasons charged him with having plotted against Spain, whereas he was to be executed for having intrigued in her favour. However, it was time to bring an end to these tiresome technicalities. The King of Spain had been promised Raleigh's head, and that head he should have.

I have argued out the legal aspect of Raleigh's condemnation because it was on such arguments that he was sentenced and subsequently misrepresented and vilified by James and his tool Bacon. The *Declaration* drafted by the latter and revised by the former is a lawyer's document ; the *Apology* prepared by Raleigh is a pathetic attempt to justify himself as a human being against charges which had not yet been openly formulated. He weakened his case later by admitting in a letter to his cousin George, Lord Carew, that :

" It is true that though I acquainted His Majesty with my intent to land in Guiana, yet I have never made it known to His Majesty that the Spaniards had any footing there, neither had I any authority by my patent to remove the Spaniards from thence, and therefore His Majesty had no interest in the attempt on St. Thomé, by any foreknowledge thereof in His Majesty."

But this letter was a plea for pardon and the confession amounted to no more than an attempt to placate James by absolving him of collusion in the alleged trespass. Raleigh reasonably reflected that the king might more readily spare his life if by so doing he did not implicate himself in the hurt to Spain.

In his heart he did not care much one way or the other about the legal aspects of his case. His defence to himself rested on altogether a different basis and is set forth in a letter to the king from the Tower, which is worth quoting at length. It begins with the more obvious line of justification :

" If in my outward journey bound I had of my men murdered at the Islands (Canaries) and spared to take revenge ; if I did discharge some Spanish barks taken without spoil ; if I forbare all parts of the Spanish Indies, wherein I might have taken twenty of their towns on the sea coast, and did only follow the enterprise which I took for Guiana—where without any decision from me, a Spanish village was burnt, which was newly set up within three miles of the mine—by your Majesty's favour I find no reason why the Spanish Ambassador should complain of me,"

—reasoning which, with the amplification given above, seems complete enough. But he then rises above himself and his own affairs into a sheer passion of patriotism :

" If it were lawful for the Spanish to murder 26 Englishmen, tying them back to back and then to cut their throats, when they had traded with them a whole month, and came to them on land without so much as a sword amongst them all ; and that it may not be lawful for your Majesty's subjects, being forced by them, to repel force by force, we may justly say ' Oh miserable English.' "

But that is precisely what the king did not mind saying. The fervour of moral indignation and the itch for revenge with which the old Elizabethan regarded the attempts of Spain to extinguish his country's precarious hold in the New World were utterly beyond the comprehension of the cold, pedantic snob who had inherited the English throne, but not a trace of the English character. No doubt he believed that he had achieved a final triumph over Raleigh's memory by the pedestrian reasoning of the *Declaration*, but he was altogether mistaken. Posterity, especially in English-speaking countries, has declined to listen to his arguments ; the imaginative truth was all on the other side. And now it appears that even on his own ground he was wrong, since the successors of that Parliament which so constantly irritated him have cut it from beneath him by rejecting his essential hypotheses.

On October 15th the wishes of Philip were conveyed to James—Raleigh was to be executed in England, not, as had been offered, in the Plaza at Madrid. If he had committed a crime at all it was the murder of Spaniards in Spanish territory, but the Escurial was too cunning to risk universal execration. The law officers thereupon set to work to devise the proper machinery for the execution in England. As has been said they decided in favour of revoking the reprieve of fifteen years before and making the prisoner, who would by such revocation be a dead man in law, a dead man in fact. Proposals were prepared, which were written out by Coke and handed up by Lord Chancellor Bacon to the king. It provided for a public hearing before a commission of Privy Councillors and judges, whereafter an opinion would be handed down justifying His Majesty, in view of Raleigh's recent crimes, in enforcing the old conviction. To this James took exception. A public hearing might reveal embarrassing facts, such as the complicity of certain persons close to the Crown in the French negotiations. James also remembered painfully the reversal of public opinion in his victim's favour after the Winchester trial. He ultimately decided in favour of a hearing behind closed doors.

This took place on October 22nd. The records of it are meagre, consisting only of a fragment of some notes taken by Sir Julius Caesar, one of the councillors. It appears that the old charges were gone over and several witnesses called to substantiate the charge of Raleigh's original bad faith, amounting in Bacon's opinion to perjury ; at the conclusion the accused made a formal speech in which he entered a general denial. The commissioners then issued the expected recommendation.

Early on the morning of the 28th he was led before the bar of the King's Bench to hear his sentence. He had been troubled with ague and was shivering as he was led before his judges. But that it was not with fear was apparent from a short conversation he held with his old valet Peter, who met him as he was leaving his cell. The hour was so early and Raleigh so ill that he had neglected to comb his hair and beard, to which in normal times he devoted an hour a day. Peter was troubled by this unwonted untidiness in his master's appearance and wished to remedy it. But the latter, who had already explained to his keeper that he would not bestow so much care on his head for the hangman, laughingly put him off with the query, "Dost know, Peter, of any plaster that will set a man's head on again, when it is off?"

The proceedings before the King's Bench were brief. Sir Henry Yelverton, with a tribute to Raleigh's splendid career, called for execution. Raleigh attempted to answer, but his voice was weak, and he asked to be allowed to write his reply. Chief Justice Montagu told him that he spoke audibly enough, and he then argued against the granting of the execution on the ground that his commission had implied a pardon. This being promptly denied, he had nothing left but to throw himself on the king's mercy. After a brief speech, in which he complimented Raleigh on his valour, his wisdom and the Christian virtues of his *History of the World*, the Chief Justice declared, " Execution is granted."

There was nothing more to be said. Raleigh had asked the Court to intervene for him. He had previously tried to enlist the good offices of George Villiers, now Marquess of Buckingham, to secure him a reprieve. No doubt he would have liked to live longer. He still had work to do, a young son to take care of. But these are the only grounds on which he bases his claims to mercy. The appeals are dignified and their denials accepted with resignation. There is none of the anguish and hysteria of fifteen years before. Now that the end was definitely near he was prepared to play his part with dignity.

While being removed across Palace Yard from the court-room in Westminster to the cell in the Old Gate House nearby, where he was to spend his last night on earth, he chanced to see an old acquaintance, Sir Hugh Beeson, who anxiously solicited news of the verdict. Raleigh told him, and asked if he would do him the courtesy of being present at the fatal ceremony on the morrow.   Beeson said yes, whereupon Raleigh gravely warned him to come early in order to make certain of reserving a good place.   " For my part," he added gaily, " I am sure of one."

The room in which he was confined for the night was one which was later to be immortalized by Lovelace, who in it wrote :

> " Stone walls do not a prison make,
> Nor iron bars a cage."

It looked down this night on another and greater poet inditing his last verses :

> " Even such is Time, that takes on trust
> Our youth, our joyes, our all we have,
> And pays us but with age and dust,
> Who in the dark and silent grave,
> When we have wandered all our ways,
> Shuts up the story of our days ;
> But from this earth, this grave, this dust,
> My God shall raise me up, I trust ! "

During the evening there came to visit him various friends, who first attempted to cheer him up and then became alarmed because he appeared to require no cheering.   The old rumours of his atheism arose in their memories and the Dean of Westminster, Dr. Robert Tounson, who attended him as spiritual adviser and to administer the last rites, warned him against too great pride.   But Raleigh quietly assured him that his calmness before death arose not from pride, but from confidence in God's goodness.   He no doubt earnestly believed that, but it is permissible to doubt whether his poise came from such confidence alone, whether it was not the artist's instinct for the right attitude.

After the others had departed his wife entered.   That interview is too painful to describe.   The recorder of the seventeenth century, Chamberlain, has left details of it almost too intimate and touching for the reader of the twentieth.   He repeated to her as he had to his friends the posthumous defence he wished to leave in case he was not permitted to speak on the scaffold. She was so distracted that she could scarcely pay attention and he attempted to console her.   At length the clock on the Abbey Tower across the way struck midnight ; it was the moment of parting.   She clung to him and from her last frenzied words he gathered that she had begged and received from the Privy Council the right to bury his body.   " It is well, dear Bess," he commented smiling, " that thou mayest dispose of that dead, which thou hadst not always the disposal of when alive."   His note was humorous now on this subject ; in 1603 it had been tragic.   As it turned out, poor Lady Raleigh was somehow deprived even of this last boon. She wrote that night to her brother, Sir Nicholas Carew, asking permission to inter her husband's body in the Carews' church at Beddington, where she desired herself ultimately to lie.   The permission was granted, but so far as I can judge from a mass of controversial evidence Raleigh was buried in St. Margaret's, Westminster, which by a modern brass plate makes record of the fact. His son, Aubrey says, was also buried there many years later.   The reason for the change is not known—perhaps it was deemed best by the authorities to leave the corpse in the neighbouring church in which it was placed immediately after execution, lest removing it should provoke public demonstrations in favour of the dead hero.

What, one wonders, did the condemned man think about in those quiet hours between the parting with his wife and dawn ?   Of his future fame, for he took pains to reiterate the points of his defence and his loyalty to the king ; of his family, for he made certain testamentary dispositions.   Not of death, surely, for he was not on the whole unwilling to die—" He was the most fearless of death that ever was known," wrote Tounson less than a fortnight later. As his mind went back and surveyed the stirring and glorious memories of his life, he must have seen that it was a good time for him to die. In him the strain of the great Paladins, of Elizabeth's Round Table, had come to its end. His peers were gone ; he was the last, the lonely one. Spanish bullets had cut off in their prime Grenville and Frobisher ; Drake and Hawkins lay in their leaden coffins under the gold and emerald waters of the Spanish Main. Spenser, Marlowe, Shakespeare, all the great ones who had made the reign of Elizabeth resound in the ears of the world and would do so to the end of time, were where he would be a few brief hours hence. Only one man lived in all the kingdom whom he might salute as equal, and that man, after vilifying him by royal order after his death, would in turn descend to his grave un-honoured and disgraced.

As Raleigh paced his cell that long October night he must have been glad that he had not escaped to France, that the king had not seen fit to let him drag out his old age in imprisonment and obscurity. The morrow would give him his youth back again, to be retained eternally like a masterpiece in marble. As at Win-chester, as at Cadiz, as in Ireland, he would once more be the cynosure of men's eyes, gallant, brilliant, and beautiful.

Just after daylight Tounson returned and talked to him earnestly for a short while, endeavouring to put him in a serious composed frame of mind. But it was altogether unnecessary; Raleigh was more serene than the priest himself. On the matter of the justice of his execution he declined to admit his guilt, but was cheerfully willing to concede that he suffered according to law and had no com-plaint to make—the last scene must not be marred by futile whinings.   He dressed himself carefully, in a black velvet gown over a brown satin doublet, black taffeta breeches and grey silk stockings.   Around his neck he hung a gold chain, and, as he was still suffering from the ague, put a lace nightcap under his hat.   One was going to meet Death ; it would be unseemly to overdress one's part, but unworthy to give no thought at all to one's costume for so unique an occasion.

The execution had been set for eight o'clock.   The day was October 29th, 1618.   Because of the early hour and the fact that it was the day of the Lord Mayor's procession, which would attract the public to another quarter of London, James had hoped to keep away the crowd.   But there was not room to stir in Old Palace Yard as the procession from the Gate House pressed forward to the scaffold where the sheriffs were huddling about a fire to keep off the autumn chill.

Raleigh was a bit out of breath from being pushed through the throng, but his wits were as clear as if he had been going to a conference of friends at the Mermaid Tavern.   There was an old man with an extremely bald head amongst the spectators, whom the attendants were forcing back : observing him, Raleigh asked what he was doing out on such an inclement morning.   He had come to pray for him, replied the other.   Thanking him and with a merry glance at the bald head Raleigh took off his nightcap and tossed it to him with the words, "You need this, my friend, more than I do."

Arrived on the scaffold he could look down on the sea of faces about him and recognize those of the many old friends who had come to render him the courtesy of being present at his taking off—a ceremony which was at least as important, surely, as one's marriage or the christening of one's children.   But what rejoiced him was the fact that he was to be allowed a final declaration—whether this was by royal consent or not is not known, but in any event it would have been impossible before that assembly to have deprived the condemned man of the customary dying declaration.

His great fear was lest his fits of trembling and his weak voice should give the impression that he was suffering from any sort of fear, and he explained his condition, apologizing to any who might be unable to catch his words. The Lords present, who had been standing on Sir Randolph Carew's balcony, thereupon came down to the scaffold, shook hands with him and remained by him while he proceeded with his speech.

He first took up the charge that he had been guilty of an intrigue with France. He admitted his desire at one time to escape, but swore a most sacred oath that he had never had any practices with the French king or his agents. He next denied Manourie's statements that he had spoken disloyally of the king—a small matter when we think of the monarch of whom the words were said to have been uttered, but a large one when one realizes how contemporary eyes regarded the office he held. Next he took up Stukely's accusations, particularly the one that he had offered the traitor a bribe of £10,000 to aid his escape, and ridiculed the idea that he would have spent so much money that way had he had it—he could have used it to better purpose. But he now expressly forgave Stukely and all others who had injured him. And as a final refutation of the slander that he had never meant to come back, he called in the Earl of Arundel, one of his backers on the Guiana voyage, who was standing with the other Lords on the scaffold, to testify that he had given his faith, that whether he made a good voyage or bad, he would return. To which Arundel gave an emphatic assent.

Only one other point remained to trouble him—the common belief that he, as Captain of the Guard, had stood by disdainfully puffing tobacco as Essex was led to the block. This report had pained him deeply, and he now swore that he had withdrawn into the Armoury of the Tower as soon as his official position had permitted him to do so, and from afar, where Essex could not have seen him, had witnessed the execution. He now regretted what he had meant to be an act of kindness, for Essex had asked for him in order to be reconciled. His concluding compliment to his old rival was gracious and tender.

He had had his say—he could not believe that any one would doubt the truth of words he had spoken on the threshold of death. And now he asked them all to pray for him :

" I have many many sins for which to beseech God's pardon. Of a long time my course was a course of vanity. I have been a seafaring man, a soldier and a courtier, and in the temptations of the least of these there is enough to overthrow a good mind and a good man."

The scaffold was cleared, Raleigh, the Dean and the executioner alone being left. Having given his personal possessions to some attendants, he prepared for the block, removing his hat and gown. He was as cool, wrote a bystander, as if he had been a witness rather than the sufferer, and in fact he seemed far less moved than any other person in that multitude. The executioner asked for forgiveness for what he was about to do. Raleigh patted him on the shoulder and assured him that he forgave him with all his heart. He then asked to see the axe, and after running his finger along it remarked, " This is a sharp and fair medicine to cure all my diseases."

One more thought did he give to the world about him. Of Arundel he requested that James would publish no defamatory writing about him after his death—a vain hope. Then turning again to his audience, he said,

"Give me heartily your prayers, for I have a long journey to go."

The executioner spread his cloak out and Raleigh knelt upon it. The former asked him to lie facing the east, to which he whimsically replied "what matters it which way the head lie, so the heart be right." He refused to be blindfolded, with the remark, "Think you I fear the shadow of the axe, when I fear not the axe itself." When he was ready he stretched out his hands, the agreed sign to strike, but apparently the headsman was too overcome and the blow did not follow. "What dost thou fear? Strike, man, strike!" came from the figure on the block. In response the axe was raised, and when it fell he was dead. Another blow severed his head from his body. The head was held up and shown to the spectators; later it was given to his wife, who had it embalmed, and kept it by her in a red leather bag all the rest of her life until it was buried with her in her grave.

Raleigh's death was the great triumph of his life; the impression it made was overwhelming. The verdict of the bystanders was expressed by one who was heard to say "where shall we find such another head to cut off?" James might command his lawyers to write a thousand vindications of himself and an equal number of denunciations of his victim, but his subjects were heedless of both. Their eyes and ears were full of that last superb performance of the man who symbolized the glory of the wonderful past and hatred of the odious present. The great actor's curtain, so perfect in its restraint, had won his audience for ever. James tried hard to draw out the plaudits; his agents suppressed wherever they could the ballads which at once deluged the kingdom, but it was as hopeless as his remote predecessor's effort to stem the tides of the ocean.

For how should even a king efface a memory such as

inspired an anonymous spectator of the execution to write these lines :

> " Great Heart, who taught thee so to die ?
> Death yielding thee the victory.
> Where tookst thou leave of life ?   If there,
> How camest thou then so free from fear ?
> Sure, thou didst die and quit the fate
> Of flesh and blood before that state.
> I saw in all the standers by
> Pale Death, life only in thine eye.
> Farewell, Truth shall this story say—
> We died, thou only livedst that day."

BIBLIOGRAPHY

Archæologica. Volumes 34 and 35. Articles by John Payne Collier on Sir Walter Raleigh.

AUBREY, JOHN. *Brief Lives.* Edited by A. Clark. 2 vols. 1898.

Azores, Papers Relating to Expedition to. B.M. Additional MSS. 5752.

BACON, ANTHONY. Correspondence. Catalogue of MSS. at Lambeth Palace Library.

BACON, FRANCIS. *Letters and Life.* By James Spedding. Vol. VI. 1872.

BIRCH, REV. THOMAS. *Life of Raleigh.* In Vol. I of the 1829 edition of Raleigh's Works.

BIRCH, REV. THOMAS. *Memoirs of the Reign of Elizabeth.* 2 vols. 1754.

BROWN, ALEXANDER. *The Genesis of the United States.* 2 vols. 1890.

BRUSHFIELD, DR. THOMAS. *Bibliography of Sir Walter Raleigh.* Second Edition, 1908.

BRUSHFIELD, DR. THOMAS. Other Papers on Raleigh, in *Transactions of the Devonshire Association.*

BURGHLEY, WILLIAM CECIL, LORD. State Papers at Hatfield House, 1571-1596. Edited by the Rev. William Murdin, 1759.

Calendar of State Papers. Domestic. Elizabeth, 1558-1603.
          ,,   ,,   ,,   ,,   James I, 1603-1618.
          ,,   ,,   ,,   *Ireland* (Elizabeth).
          ,,   ,,   ,,   *Venetian* (Elizabeth and James I).
          ,,   ,,   ,,   *Colonial.*

CAMDEN, WILLIAM. *Annales.* Elizabeth.
          ,,   ,,   ,,   James I.

Camden Miscellany, Vol. 5. Documents relating to Raleigh's Last Voyage, by S. R. Gardiner.

Cecil MSS. Historical MSS. Commission. Vols. 4, 6, 7 (Raleigh's Letters, etc.).

Carew Papers. Calendar of Carew MSS. at Lambeth Palace Library 1575-1588. Edited by John S. Brewer and William Bullen, 1868.

CECIL (ALGERNON). *Life of Robert Cecil, 1st Earl of Salisbury.* 1915.

CAYLEY, ARTHUR. *The Life of Sir Walter Raleigh*. 2 vols. 1806. Useful principally for the papers it reprints in full.

CHAMBERLAIN, JOHN. *Letters by J. Chamberlain during the Reign of Elizabeth*. Camden Society, 1861. See also STATHAM (E. P.).

CHAMBERLIN, F. *The Private Character of Queen Elizabeth*. 1922.

CHURCHYARD, THOMAS. *True Discourse Historical of the Succeeding Governors of the Netherlands*. 1602.

COBBETT. *Complete Collection of State Trials*. Vol. II. 1809. (Known as *Howell's State Trials*.)

Cottonian MSS. British Museum.

CROMWELL, OLIVER. *Letters and Speeches*. Edited by Thomas Carlyle, 1870.

CUST, LIONEL. *Portraits of Raleigh*. In 8th volume of the Walpole Society.

"Declaration of the Carriage and Demeanour of Sir Walter Raleigh," in *Harleian Miscellany*, Vol. III. 1809.

DEE, DR. JOHN. Private Diary. Edited by J. O. Halliwell for Camden Society, 1842.

Dee, Life of Dr. John. By Charlotte Fell-Smith, 1909.

Devonshire Association, *Transactions*.

D'EWES, SIR SYMONDS. *Journals of Elizabethan Parliaments*. Edited by Paul Bowes, 1682.

D'ISRAELI, ISAAC. *Curiosities of Literature*, 1849.

Dictionary of National Biography. The article on Raleigh and the references are highly valuable.

EDWARDS, EDWARD. *Life of Sir Walter Raleigh*. 2 vols., the second containing his letters only, 1868. The most complete data yet compiled on the life of Raleigh.

Encyclopædia Britannica. Eleventh Edition.

FIRTH (SIR CHARLES). *Sir W. Raleigh's History of the World* [in British Academy *Proceedings*, 1917-1918].

Fortnightly Review. Vol. VII. 1867. "The Case against Sir Walter Raleigh," by S. R. Gardiner.

FORSTER (JOHN). *Sir John Eliot : A Biography*. 2 vols. 1864.

FOXE, JOHN. *Acts and Monuments, etc*. (Martyrs). 1877.

FROUDE, JAMES A. *History of England*. Vols. 7-12. 1856-1870.

Fugger News-Letters. First and Second Series. Edited by V. von Klarwill, 1924-1926.

FULLER, THOMAS. *History of the Worthies of England.* 1811.

GARDINER S. R. *History of England, from the Accession of James I to the Outbreak of Civil War.* Vol. III. 1885.

GARDINER S. R. See also under *Camden Miscellany* and *Fortnightly Review.*

Geographical Journal, August 1914. With Raleigh's Map of Guiana.

Gondomar, el Conde de. By F. H. Lyon, 1910.

GOSSE, SIR EDMUND. *Raleigh,* 1886.
      „   „   Sir Walter Raleigh's " Cynthia," in the *Athenæum,* January 2nd and 9th, 1886.

HALLAM, HENRY. *The Constitutional History of England.*

HAKLUYT, RICHARD. *The Principal Navigations, Voyages, etc.* The most useful edition is that published by MacLehose of Glasgow, 1905. In 12 vols.

HANNAH, JOHN. *Raleigh's Poems.* 1892.

Harleian MSS. British Museum. Consult Index. A mine of original documents on Raleigh, especially Harleian 39.

Harleian Miscellany. Second Edition, 1813.

HARRIOT, THOMAS. *A Briefe and True Report of the New Found Land of Virginia.* 1588. Also in Hakluyt.

HAWLES, SIR JOHN. *The Government and Magistracy of England vindicated.* 1689.

HENNESSEY, SIR JOHN POPE. *Sir Walter Raleigh in Ireland.* 1883.

HOLINSHED. *Chronicles.* See HOOKER.

HOOKER, JOHN. *Survey of the History of Ireland to* 1587. Dedicated to Raleigh. (In Holinshed's *Chronicles.*)

HOWELL. *State Trials.* See COBBETT.

HOWELL, JAMES. *Epistolae Ho-Elianae.* 2 vols. 1892.

HUMBOLDT, ALEXANDER VON. *Personal Narrative of Travels.* 1804. Translated.

HUME, DAVID. *History of England.* Vol. IV. 1848.

HUME, MARTIN A. S. *Sir Walter Raleigh.* 1897.

Issues of the Exchequer during the Reign of James I. By Frederick Devon, 1836.

JAMES VI OF SCOTLAND. *Correspondence with Sir R. Cecil and Others in England.* Edited by John Bruce for the Camden Society, 1861.

LAUDONNIÈRE, RENÉ DE. *L'Histoire notable de Floride.* Paris, 1586.

LEE, SIR SIDNEY. *Great Englishmen of the Sixteenth Century.* 1904.

LINGARD, REV. JOHN. *History of England.* Vol. VI. 1855.

Lismore Papers. Edited by Dr. A. B. Grosart, 1886-1887.

LLOYD, DAVID. *State Worthies.* 1766.

Miscellanea Genealogica et Heraldica, Vol. II.

MONSON, SIR WILLIAM. *Naval Tracts.* Edited by M. Oppenheim. Navy Records Society. 5 vols. 1902-1914.

NAPIER, MACVEY. *Lord Bacon and Sir Walter Raleigh.* 1853.

Navy Records Society, Vol. 40, 1912 : *Taking of the " Madre de Dios."*

Navy Records Society, Vol. 20, 1902 : Slingsby, *Voyage to Cadiz.*

NAUNTON, SIR ROBERT. *Fragmenta Regalia.* 1641.

Newes of Sir Walter Raleigh from the River of Caliana. 1618.

OLDYS, WILLIAM. *Life of Sir Walter Raleigh.* In Vol. I of the 1829 edition of Raleigh's Works. The first important biography, containing much material now unavailable elsewhere.

Orders to be observed in the Fleet under Raleigh. 1617. Navy Records Society, Vol. 29, 1905.

OSBORNE, FRANCIS. *Traditional Memoirs* (in Secret History of the Court of James I. 1811).

PRINCE, REV. JOHN. *Worthies of Devon.* 1810.

Privy Council, Acts of, from 1580 *on.* The recently completed volumes, especially that of 1601-1604, have much new miscellaneous information on Raleigh's private affairs.

Privy Council Registers. Elizabeth and James I.

PURCHAS, REV. SAMUEL. *Purchas His Pilgrimes.* 1625.

PUTTENHAM, GEORGE. *The Arte of English Poesie.* 1811.

RALEIGH, SIR WALTER. Works. 8 vols. Published by the Oxford University Press in 1829. Includes the *Lives* by Oldys and Birch and the *History of the World.* Useful, but incomplete for the letters and poetry, and badly edited.

RALEIGH, SIR WALTER. *Report of the Truth of the Fight about the Azores.* 1591. Also in Hakluyt.

RALEIGH, SIR WALTER. *Discovery of Guiana.* See SCHOMBURGK.

READ, CONYERS. *Mr. Secretary Walsingham and the Policy of Queen Elizabeth.* 3 vols. 1925.

RODD, SIR RENNELL. *Sir Walter Raleigh.* 1904.

ST. JOHN, J. A. *Life of Sir Walter Raleigh.* 2 vols. 1868.

SANDERSON, SIR WILLIAM. *A Complete History of the Lives and Reigns of Queen Mary and King James VI.* 1636.

SCHOMBURGK, SIR ROBERT H. *Raleigh's Discovery of Guiana,* with unpublished documents. Edited with introduction and notes by Sir R. H. S. for Hakluyt Society, 1848.

SHIRLEY, WILLIAM. *Life of Sir Walter Raleigh.* 1677.

Smithsonian Institution. *Annual Report,* 1925, pp. 509-532.

SOUTHEY, ROBERT. *Lives of the British Admirals.* Vol. 4. 1837.

SPEDDING, JAMES. See under FRANCIS BACON.

SPENSER, EDMUND. The Complete Works. Edited by A. B. Grosart. 10 vols. 1882-1884. Including *A View of the State of Ireland.*

STATHAM, E. P. *A Jacobean letter-writer : Life and Times of John Chamberlain.* 1920. (Gives interesting extracts from the Chamberlain-Carleton Correspondence.)

STEBBING, WILLIAM. *Sir Walter Raleigh.* 1891. The most valuable biography yet written.

STEPHEN, SIR JAMES F. *History of the Criminal Law of England.* 1904.

STEPHEN, SIR HARRY L. " The Trial of Raleigh," in *Royal Historical Society Transactions,* 1919.

STOW, JOHN. *Annales.* Continued to 1631 by E. Howes. 1631.

STUKELY, SIR LEWIS. *Apology.* In Raleigh's Works, Vol. VIII.

Tenison MSS. Catalogue of Lambeth Palace Library.

Times, The (London), October 28th-30th, 1918.

Times Literary Supplement. December 27th, 1921 ; November 22nd, December 20th, 1923; January 10th, 1924; February 14th, July 16th, 1925.

Trial of Raleigh. *Harleian MSS.,* Vol. 39. Also two MSS. in the Public Records Office, one properly calendared under November 17th, 1603, *S. P. Dom. James I,* Vol. 4, No. 83 ; the other joined to the Essex and Southampton trials, February 19th, 1601, *S. P. Dom. Elizabeth,* Vol. 278, No. 102, entered only under latter date. The latter is shorter than the other and I cannot find that it has ever been printed.

TYTLER, PATRICK F. *Life of Sir Walter Raleigh.* 1833.

Venezuelan-British Guiana Boundary Dispute: Blue-books issued by the British Foreign Office. Arguments, exhibits, etc. 17 vols. 1897-1899.

VERE, SIR FRANCIS. Commentaries. Edited by Edward Arber, in *English Garner*, 1883.

WELDON, SIR ANTHONY. *Court and Character of King James I,* 1651.

WHEATLEY, H. B. *London Past and Present.* 3 vols. 1891.

WILLOBY, HENRY: *His Avisa.* Edited by G. B. Harrison. Bodley Head Quartos, 1926, Reprints. Atheism inquiry from *Harleian MSS.* 6849, B.M.

WOOD, ANTHONY À. *Athenae Oxonienses.*

INDEX

ADELANTADO, the, 133, 134, 136, 143
Aguirre, Lope de, 97
Albert, Archduke of Austria, 153, 159
Alençon, Duc d', 25, 57
Alexander II, Pope, and the Bull of Demarcation, 36, 203
Alfinger, Ambrose von, 96, 108
Allen, Sir Francis, 78
Amadas, Captain Philip, 36, 37, 38
Amazon River, 95, 96
Amazons, the, 95, 96, 110-11
Anderson, Judge, 158
Angra, harbour of, 142, 143
Anne of Denmark, Queen, 42, 194, 195, 208, 214
Anthropophagi, the, in *Othello*, 110
Antonio, Dom, Portuguese Pretender, 66-7
Antwerp, 57
Apology, The, for the Voyage to Guiana (R.), 212, 213, 227
Appleby, Captain, 25
Aremberg, Count of, and the Aremberg Plot, 153-4, 158-9, 162, 163, 177
" Ark Raleigh," the, 33, 70
" Ark Royal," the, 119
Armadillo, the, 104
Aroras, poisoned arrows of, 104
Arromaia, 104
Arundel, Earl of, 209, 235, 236
Astrophel (Spenser), 84
Atlantic Ocean, the, 69
Azores, the, 12, 34, 56, 68, 129, 137

BABINGTON, Anthony, plot of, 52, 60; estates of, bestowed on R., 52

Bacon, Sir Anthony, 72-3, 78, 117
Bacon, Sir Francis, 3, 31, 110, 185, 200, 222, 226, 229
Bailey, the deserter, 202, 210
Barbary, gold of, 109
Barbary Pirates, 52, 198, 202
" Bark Bonner," the, 40
Barlowe, Captain Arthur, 36, 37
Barre, David, 23, 24
Barre's Court, granted to R., 23-4
Basquimento, 97
Bay of Biscay, 41
Bay of Guanipa, 101
Beddington, 232
Bedford, Earl of, 50
Beeson, Sir Hugh, 230-1
Belvoir Castle, miniature at, of R., 4
Berreo, Don Antonio de, 94, 97, 100, 101, 103, 104; capture of, by R., 99
Berrie, Leonard, 113
Bingham, Vice-Admiral John, 16-17
Bisseaux, M. de, 219
Blount, Sir Christopher, 138, 148
Bodleian Library, nucleus of, 129
Borough, Sir John, 70, 71
Brazil, 97
Brentford, 214
Brill, 164
British Guiana, Colony or, 113
Broad Street, London, Lady Raleigh's house in, 214
Brooke, George, 152, 167, and the Priest's Plot, 152 *sqq.*, execution of, 172.
Browne, Richard, tax farmer, 49
Burghley, Lord, Lord Treasurer, 15, 17, 21, 22, 24, 27, 30, 49, 56, 57, 63, 72, 82, 85, 93, 131, 167

Burre, Walter, publisher of R.'s *History of the World*, 192, 194

Burrell, Dr. Robert, 193

Butler family, 14

CABOT, John, 10

Cadiz, 209; Drake's raid on, 62; R.'s raid on, 70, 77, 90, 115 *sqq.*, 177-8, 233

Caesar, Sir Julius, 229

Calais, Drake's strategy at, 136, 164

Calfield, Captain, 106

Cambridge University, 48-9

Canada, France in, 10

Canary Islands, 36, 99

Caño Mañamo, the, 101

Canoloch, 22

Cape Finisterre, 136

Cape Verde, sea-fight off, 12

Cape St. Vincent, 119

Capuri River, 106

Carew, Sir George, later Lord Carew (cousin), 78, 149, 195, 237

Carew, Sir Nicholas (formerly Throgmorton), 232

Carlton, Dudley, 176, 177, 181

Caroni River, 101, ascent of, 105, 107

Carr, Robert, *see* Somerset, Earl of

Catherine de' Medici, 45

Catholic West Country Rising (1549), 4

Cavendish, Thomas, 38

Caworako, 105

Cayenne River, 203

Cecil family, 31, 59

Cecil, Robert, 18, 30, 51, 72, 73, 75-6, 84, 93-4, 112, 116, 117, 131, 132, 135, 136, 145, 148, 149 *sqq.*, 153 *sqq.*, 167, 175, 180, 181-2; death of, 188, 195

Cerne Abbas, 91

Chamberlain, John, 176, 181, 192, 231-2

Champernoun, Sir Philip (grandfather), 5

Charles, Prince (Charles I), Spanish marriage, plan for, 199, 211, 214, 218

Charles II, 186, and the revenue from tobacco, 45

Chatham, 64

Chesapeake site, the, 43

Child, T., 6

Chile and Peru, the potato introduced from, 44

Christian, King, of Denmark, 194

Clifford, ——, 125

Cloths export Licences, 48, 60

Cobham, Lord, and the Aremberg Plot, 152, 153, 154, 156-7, trial of, 157 *sqq.*, and reprieve, 174

Coke, Sir Edward, Attorney-General, 159, 160 *sqq.*, 166, 167, 181, 219

Colin Clouts Come Home Again (Spenser), 79-80

"Colleagues of the Discovery of the North West Passage," 35

Colonial Empire, R.'s dream of, 30, and efforts to forward, 11 *sqq.*, 32 *sqq. passim*

Colonization, Spanish, in the Americas, 10

Columbus, Christopher, 111

Come live with me and be my love (Marlowe), and R.'s verses in reply, 88

Commission on Defence of the Realm, 63

Copley, Anthony, 152, 167

Cork, 15, 18, 20

Harbour, 23, 201

Cornwall, 50, 51, 63, 109

Cortez, Hernando, 100

Cotton, Robert, 193

Cottrell, ——, 215

Courtenay family, 5

Cromwell, Oliver, 89, 186

Cumberland, George, Earl of, 68, 70, 82, 201

Curapan, 99, 106

"DAINTY," the, 71

Danton, G. J., 186

Dare, Ananias, 41

Dare, Eleanor, wife of the above, 41

Dare, Virginia, 41

Darell, Miss, 2nd wife of Walter Raleigh, 5
Davis, John, and the North-West Passage, 35, 36
Decades, the (Eden ; Willes's edition), 11
Declaration of the Demeanour . . . of Sir W. Raleigh (Bacon), assertions in, 222-3, 226, 228
Decline and Fall . . . (Gibbon), 2
Dee, Dr. John, astrologer, 27, 28, 32, 35, 55
Demarcation, Bull of, of Pope Alexander II, 36, 203
Denny, Edward, 15
Deptford, 34
des Marêts, French Ambassador, offer of, to R., 197, 219
Desmond family and faction, 14, 15
Desmond, Earl of, 15
Desmond, Sir John, 19
"Destiny," the, R.'s vessel in 1617, 197, 203, 209, 217
Devereux, Lady Penelope, 85
Devonshire, 68, 149
Devonshire, Duke of, 51
Devonshire seamen, fame of, 5, 35, 38
Discourse of a Discovery for a New Passage to Cataia (Gilbert), 10, 11
Discovery of . . . Guiana (R.), 108, 109, 112, 113, 114, real knowledge in, 97, 112, tall tales in, R.'s attitude to, 109 *sqq.*
" Don Adriano de Armado," 91
Dorado, El, *see* El Dorado
Drake, Joan, 1st wife of Walter Raleigh, 5
Drake, Sir Francis, 5, 12, 30, 65, 84, 105, 130, 203, 233 ; and the Armada, 63, 69 ; and the harrying of Spain, 55, 56, 62, 64, 98, 115, 119, 128, 149, 195, 201, at Cadiz, 62, attack on Lisbon with Norris, 66, 67, lessons from his actions, 133-4 ; Mayor of Plymouth, 69, 71 ; and the "Revenge," 69; and the Virginians, 39-40

"Dreadnought;" the, 125
Dublin Gallery, portrait in, of Raleigh, 4
Dudley family, 59
Durham Palace, R.'s town-house, 48, 144, 148, 158, and turret study, 54-5
Dutch naval allies, 119, 134, 139
Duyvenoord, Admiral Jan, 119

EGERTON, Sir Thomas, 49
El Dorado (*see also* Manoa), 95, 96, 108, 113, 221
Elector Palatine, the, 185
Elizabeth, Queen, 1, 5, 17, 24, 45, 104, 164 ; apothegm of, 26, 171; and the Armada, 62, 63 ; attitude of, to would-be explorers and colonists, 11, 32 *sqq.*, 43, and the Colony of Virginia, 37 ; and the Cadiz expedition, 116, 122, 129, 130 ; and her favourites (*see also under their names*), 28 *sqq.*, her gifts to them, 47-8, 50-1, 217, and wrath at their marrying, 29 ; and the Ferrol venture, 135; fury of, at the Dutch offer to Leicester, 57-8 ; penuriousness of, 21, 28-9, 66, 116 ; and her piratical captains, 201 ; plots against, 52, 60-1 ; portrait of, Caribbean attitude to, 100-1 ; and R., 25 *sqq.*, 61, 67, 70, 71, 98, 145, 179, wrath of, at his marriage, 10, 72, 73, 76-7 ; and Spenser, 81 ; vacillation of, 62, 63 ; and her successor, 145 *sqq.*, and death, 150
Elizabeth Stuart, marriage schemes for, 184-5
Elizabethans, the last of the, 233
Ely, Bishop of, 212
England, naval history of, importance in, of the storming of Cadiz, 129 ; naval policy of, outlined by Raleigh, 63, 64 ; throne of, status of, at accession of James I, 144

English Channel, the, 64, 69, 101
English share in the New World (*temp.* Elizabeth), 10
Erskine, Sir Thomas, 180
Escurial, the, 228
Essex, Countess of, 74
Essex, Robert Devereux, Earl of, 10, 18, 29, 43, 67, 131, 134, share of, in the storming of Cadiz, 116 *sqq.*, and in the Islands Voyage, 135 *sqq.*, fall of, rebellion of, and execution, 144 *sqq.*, 160, 236
Every Man Out of His Humour (Jonson), 9
Ewaipanomas, cowls of, 112
Exeter Church, Raleigh burials in, 173
Exmouth, 5

Faerie Queene, The (Spenser), 24, 79, 81, dedications of, 82
Faige, Captain, 219
"Falcon," the, 11
Falmouth, 201
Fardell, Devon, 4
Faro, raid on, 129
Fayal incident, the, 137 *sqq.*, 177-8
Ferrol, 133, expeditions against, 134 *sqq.*
Fitzgerald, Sir James, fate of, 15
Fitzwilliam, Sir William, 79
Flanders, English contingents in, 8
Fleet Prison, R. in, 10, 182
Flores, in the Azores, 137
Florida, Spain in, 10
Flushing, 164
Fort-del-Ore, butchery at, 16-17, 79
Fort Puntal, Cadiz, 123
Fowler, Sir Thomas, 165
France, R. in, 6-7
Free speech, championed by R., 54, 145
French advances to R., 197, 214 *sqq.*, 219, 220-1, 229
French colonization in America, 10
Frobisher, Sir Martin, 11, 35, 64, 65, 71, 75, 128, 233

Gascoigne, George, 7, 8, 10
Gawdy, Justice, 158, 166, 174

Genoa, 197
Gentlemen adventurers, 105, 197
George I, 171
George II, 171
Gibbon, Edward, 2
Gifford, Captain, 101, 106
Gilbert, Adrian, 5, 35
Gilbert, Katherine, *see* Raleigh, Mrs. Walter (mother)
Gilbert, Otto, 5
Gilbert, Sir Humphrey (half-brother), 5, 8; colonizing expeditions of, 10 *sqq.*, 32 *sqq.*, 98; in Ireland, 10, 13, 14, 22; and the search for the North-West Passage, 10 *sqq.*, 32 *sqq.*; writings of, 10; death of, 35
Gilbert, Sir John (half-brother), 5, 98
Godolphin, Sir Francis, 180
Godwin, Hugh, 105
"Golden Hind," Drake's ship, 34
"Golden Hind," Gilbert's vessel, 34, 35
Gomera, R.'s call at, 202-3, 220
Gondomar, Don Diego Sarmiento de Acuña, Count of, Spanish Ambassador, 18, 56, 174, 199, 203, 205, 210, 226
Gorges, Sir Arthur (cousin), 139-40
Gorges, Sir Ferdinando, 148
Gravelines, 64
Gray's Inn, 200
Greenwich, 216, 217
　　Palace, 152
Grenville family, 5
Grenville, Lieut. ("my cousin"), 106
Grenville, Sir Richard, of the "Revenge," 38, 66; pirate and colonizer, 39, 41, 56, 216; death of, 68-9, 126, 233
Grey de Wilton, Lord, 14, 23, 63, in Ireland, relations with R., 15, 17, 18, 21 *sqq.*
Grey de Wilton, Lord, son of the above, plots by, trial and reprieve of, 152, 153, 157, 174
Grotius, Hugo, 224

Gualtero, *see* Caworako
Guard, the, R.'s Captaincy of, 51,
    53-4, 77, 149, 150, 180
Guiana, 42 ; early explorers of,
    96-7 ; legends on, 95 ;
    mountains of, 103 ; R.'s
    interest in and first venture
    to, 94 *sqq.*, 98, results of,
    106 *sqq.*, 112, 115, poems
    on, 113 ; the last voyage
    to, 181, 183, 194, its failure
    and results, 195 *sqq.*

HAKLUYT, Richard, 55 ; friendship
    of, with R., 31, 37
Hampden, John, 89
Hariot, Thomas, 38, 44, 55, 91, 193
Harley, Robert, 171
Hart, the seaman, 215
Harvey, Sir George, Lieutenant of
    the Tower, 156, 182-3
Hatfield House, 85
Hatton, Sir Christopher, 31, 57
Hawkins, Sir John, 64, 65, 75, 115,
    128, 203, 233
Hayes or Hayes Barton, R.'s birth-
    place, 4
Headless men, tales of, 110, 112
Heale, Serjeant, 160
Heneage, Thomas, 54
Henry VIII, 192
Henry, Prince of Wales, 182, 184,
    194 ; death of, 188, 208
History of the World (R.), 2, 6, 7, 31,
    37, 46, 63, 185, 188 *sqq.*,
    193, 194, 230; preface to,
    191 ; passage in, on Death,
    191-2
Hobby horses, 94
Hoe, the, Plymouth, deserters exe-
    cuted on, 117
Holenden, Sir James, 221
Holland, 61, 64, 129, 216 ; R. in,
    25
Horta, reduction of, 138 *sqq.*, 148
Howard family, 59
Howard-Grenville expedition, 67 *sqq.*
Howard, Lord Charles (Howard of
    Effingham), later Earl of
    Nottingham, Lord Admiral,
    66, 93, 99, 115, 146, 180;

Howard, Lord Charles (*continued*)—
    and the Great Armada, 63,
    64, 128; and the Cadiz
    expedition, 116, 119 *sqq.*
Howard, Lord Henry, later Earl of
    Northampton, 145, 149-50,
    158, 165 ; death of, 195
Howard, Lord Thomas, later Earl of
    Suffolk, 68; Vice-Admiral,
    Cadiz expedition, 116, 119,
    122, 124, 126, 134, 135,
    141, 142, 158, 164
Huguenot wars, R.'s share in, 6-7, 8
Hunsdon, Henry Carey, Lord, 82

IMOKILLIE, the Seneschal of, 17,
    18-19, 20
Incas, the, treasure-house of, 97
Indians, Anglo-Saxon-speaking, tale
    of, 42
Indians of South America, Spanish
    treatment of, 100 ; R.'s
    conciliation of, 43, 97, 100,
    207
    of Trinidad, 99
Ireland, 66, 133, 164 ; affairs in
    (1589 *sqq.*), 79 ; coloniza-
    tion of, 54; English methods
    in (*temp.* Elizabeth), 14 *sqq.* ;
    Essex in, 147, 148 ; Gilbert
    in, 10, 13, 14, 22 ; R. in, 8,
    13, 14 *sqq.*, his epithets for,
    23, estates in, and private
    life there, 24, 78 *sqq.*
Islands Voyage, the, 139 *sqq.*, 144
Isle of Wight, 15
Italy, 133

JAMES VI of Scotland and I of
    England, 3, 26, 61, 145, 146,
    149-50 ; plots against,
    152 *sqq.*; persecution by, of
    R., 150 *sqq.*, 181 *sqq.*, 191-2,
    198 *sqq.*, and R.'s second
    trial, 209 *sqq.* ; Spanish
    policy of, 177, 184, 195
Jamestown Colony, 42
Jarnac, Battle of, 6
Jerkins, R.'s servant, 18
Jersey, 149, 159 ; R.'s Governorship
    of, 54, 145, 150

Jesuits, the, 95, 164
John, King, and Magna Carta, 186
Jones, Parson Samuel, 221
Jonson, Ben, 193, 207

KEYMER, John, and his wife, 48-9
Keymis, Captain, 101, 103, 113, 139,
    156 ; expedition of, up the
    Orinoco, 203 sqq., 223 ;
    suicide of, 209
Kilcolman Castle, 29
King, Captain, 211, 215, 216
King, Edward, elegies on, 82
King's Bench, R.'s last trial before,
    230
Knighthood, order of, 37-8, degrada-
    tion of, 128-9
Knollys, Sir Francis, 63
Kyd, Thomas, 91

LANCEROTA, R. attacked at, 202,
    220, 223, 227
Lane, Ralph, 63 ; colony planted by,
    38, 39, 45
Languedoc, caves of, 7
Laurency, the go-between, 154, 163,
    165
Le Clerc, R.'s negotiations with, 214,
    219
Leicester, Robert Dudley, Earl of,
    25, 29, 31, 57, 61 ; offered
    sovereignty of the United
    Provinces, 57-8
Lie, The (R.), lines from, 31-2, 86
"Lion's Whelp," the, Howard's
    ship, 99, 101
Lisbon, 136, 168 ; Drake's attack on,
    66, 67, 115
Lismore Castle, 52
London, 5
London Bridge, 144
Los Gallos, 101
Louis XIII, 214, 219
Louis XVIII, 186
Love's Labour's Lost (Shakespeare), 91
Low Countries, see Netherlands
Lovelace, Richard, 231

MACE, Captain Samuel, 113
"Madre de Dios," cargo of, rifling
    of, 71 sqq.

Madre del Oro, El, 107
Madrid, 210, 228
Magellan, Straits of, 56
Manoa (see also El Dorado), 95, 103,
    105
Manourie, Dr., 211, 217, 235
Markham, Sir Griffin, 152, 174
Marlowe, Christopher, 55, 88, 91
Martinez, —, 103
"Mary Sparke," the, 56
Mary Stuart, Queen, 52, 60, 145
Medina Sidonia, Duke of, 64, 65 ;
    and the storming of Cadiz,
    119-20, 125, 128
Mendoza, Don Bernardino, Spanish
    Ambassador, 17, 37
Merchant Adventurers, the, 60
"Merhonour," the, 119, 124
Mermaid Tavern, the, 46, 234
Mexico, Spain in, 10, 100
Meyricke, Sir Gelly, 138, 140
Milford Haven, 175
Milton, John, 89
Mississippi Valley, France in, 10
Moile, Henry, R.'s rescue of, 17-18
Monardes, —, 104
Montagu, Chief Justice, 230
Montcontour, Battle of, 6
Montmorency, Admiral de, 219
Morris dancers, 34
Mount Aio, 205
Mount Raleigh, 35
Munster, 19, 21
    R.'s lands in, 48
    Rebellions, the first, 15, the second,
        149

NAPO River, 96
Napoleon I, 184, 186
National Defence, R.'s influence in,
    135, 145
Naunton, Sir Robert, 26, 193
Naval difficulties (temp. Elizabeth), 12
Netherlands (see also Flanders), 153,
    184 ; offer from, to Leicester,
    57
New World, the, colonization in, 10 ;
    England's heritage in, R.'s
    views on, 32, 40, 42, 98
Norfolk Plot, the, 60
Norris, Sir John, 8, 63, 66

North America, first English colony in, 36 *sqq.*

North Sea, the, 64, 69

North-West Passage, the, search for, 10 *sqq.*, Association for, 35

Northumberland, Earl of, 175

Nottingham, Earl of, *see* Howard, Lord Charles

Novion, — de, 214

OCEAN'S LOVE TO CYNTHIA, THE (R.), 79 *sqq.*, 84-5

Old Gate-House Prison, Westminster, 230-1

Old Palace Yard, 234

Orellana, —, descent by, of the Amazon, 96

Oriel College, R. at, 6

Orinoco River, Whiddon's expedition to, 94; explorations of, 94, 95, 97, by R., 101 *sqq.*; Spanish activities on, 113; Keymis's expedition up, 203 *sqq.*

Ormond, Earl of, 14, 16, 19, 21-2, 24

Osorius, Bishop, stolen library of, 129

Othello (Shakespeare), 110, 113

Overbury, Sir Thomas, poisoning of, 158, 196

Oxford, Earl of, 27

Oxford University, 207; the Bodleian Library at, 129; R. at, 6-7

PADILLA, Don Martin de, Conde de Gadea, 133

Palomeque de Acuña, Don Diego, 205

Parima, the White Lake of, 95

Parima River, inundations of, 95

Parker, Captain Charles, 221

Parliament, R. in, 51, championing free speech, 54, 145

Parma, Duke of, 64

Parmenius, 12

Pater, Admiral Adrian Jancz, 225

Peckham, Sir George, and Gilbert, 33

Pembroke, Earl of, 78

Perrot, Sir John, 10, 14

Perrot, Sir Thomas, 10

Peru, 96, 97, 100

Peter, the valet, 229, 230

Peyton, Sir John, 180

Philip II of Spain, 97, 119, 164; reign of, with Mary Tudor, 5; his Great Armada, and its successors, 56, 62, 65, 133; death of, 144

Philip III of Spain, 159, 164, 184, 199, 210, 226, 228

Phoenix' Nest, The, 83

Pineapple intoxication, 103-4

Pilgrimage, The (R.), 87

Piracy, 200

Pizarro, Francisco, 96

Pizarro, Gonzalo, explorer of the Napo, 96, 108

Plague, in London, in the Tower, 182; at Sherborne, 99

Plots detected by Walsingham, 60-1; others against James I, 152 *sqq.*

Plymouth, 12, 13, 34, 38, 40, 71, 117, 118, 144, 197; Drake Mayor of, 69, 71; R.'s half-attempt at evasion from, 211, 213

— Harbour, 64, 118, 143, 197

Point Icacos, 99

Ponsonby, —, publisher of *The Faerie Queene*, 81

Popham, Captain George, 100

Popham, Lord Chief Justice Sir John, 158, 162, 176, 181

Potato, the, introduction of, into Europe, 44-5

Prerogative, The, of Parliaments (R.), 186

Preston, Captain Sir Amyas, 99, 101, 102, 167

"Priest's Plot," the, 152 *sqq.*

Puerto Reale, 127

Punto Gallo, 99, 102, 204, 207

QUITO, 96

RABELAIS, 87

Raleana, 103

Raleigh, Captain George (nephew), 203, 221

Raleigh, Carew (brother), 5, 56

Raleigh, Carew (son), 118, 183, 200, 226, 230, 232

Raleigh, City of, Virginia, 40
Raleigh, Katherine (mother), 5, **173**
Raleigh, Lady, born Elizabeth Throg-
    morton, 72-3, 74-5, 94, 99,
    118, 155-6, 173, 180, 181,
    183, 187, 195, 196, 197,
    211, 214, 215 ; R.'s letter
    to, on the death of their son,
    208 ; R.'s last letter to, 173 ;
    last parting of, from R.,
    231-2
Raleigh, Mrs. Walter (grandmother), 4
Raleigh, Sir Walter, birth of, date,
    and place of, 4, parents,
    ancestors and kinsmen of,
    4-5, 38, education, 5 *sqq.*,
    military experiences in
    France, 6-7, and in Ireland,
    8, 15 *sqq.*, criticisms by, of
    his chiefs, 21 *sqq.* ; residence
    in the Temple, 7 ; com-
    mittal of, to the Fleet
    Prison, 10 ; expedition of,
    with Gilbert, 12-13; at
    Court, 1, rise of, 9, 25 *sqq.*,
    wealth, gifts, offices and
    honours of, 48 *sqq.*, 132,
    patent of, for colonizing,
    36 *sqq.*, raids of, on Spanish
    vessels, 55, 58, 67 *sqq.*,
    and the Armada, 62 *sqq.*,
    marriage, loss of favour and
    commital to the Tower, 10,
    72 *sqq.*, 151, 187, release,
    77, and the first Guiana
    expedition, 94 *sqq.*, others
    sent thither by him, 113; the
    Cadiz expedition, 115 *sqq.*;
    reinstatement at Court,
    131; the Islands Voyage,
    134 *sqq.*; his downfall
    prepared for, 149, arrest,
    committal to the Tower,
    trial for treason, reprieve,
    attempted suicide and life in
    the Tower for thirteen years,
    151 *sqq.*, 179 *sqq.*, enlarge-
    ment of, for the second
    Guiana expedition, 195, its
    failure, his arrest, the French
    offers to him (*see that head*) ;

Raleigh, Sir Walter (*continued*)—
    attempt at escape, return to
    the Tower, 209 *sqq.*, **217**,
    second trial, 218 *sqq.*, con-
    demnation, 230, and exe-
    cution, 234 *sqq.*, on the
    scaffold, 46, 234, his last
    speech, 235 *sqq.*, lines on
    the scene, 238 ; last letter
    to his wife, 74, **173**
Biographers of, 2-3
Bravery and military qualities of,
    7, 17
Chemical researches of, 1, 183,
    186-7
Knighthood of, date of, 37-8
Life of, sequence of, summarized,
    199
Name of, variants of, 38
Naval strategy of, 63, 64-5, **71**
in Parliament, 51, 56 *sqq.*, a
    defender of free speech, 54,
    144-5
Patron of explorers and an explorer
    himself, 11 *sqq.*, 27, 32 *sqq.*,
    44, 50, 93 *sqq.*
Portraits, appearance and attire, 4,
    26-7, 48, 93, 187, 214,
    229-30, 234
Quarrels, 9, 18, 48 *sqq.*, *et alibi*,
    passim
Religious ideas, 90 *sqq.*, 187
Reputation, 1 *sqq.*, *et passim*
Tobacco introduced by, 45-6, 210,
    236
Unpopularity of, bases of, 6, 19, 24,
    48 *sqq.*
Writings
    Poetry, 7, 31-2, 55, 77, 79 *sqq.*,
        the last lines, 231
    Prose, 2, 55, 67, 70, 126-7,
        184 *sqq.*, 212, 213
Raleigh, Walter (father), 4, 173 ;
    wives of, 5
Raleigh, Walter (son), 99, 118, 156,
    173, 180, 182, 187, 195;
    death of, 206 *sqq.*
Relation, A, of Cadiz Action (R.),
    126
*Report of the Truth of the Fight
    about the Azores* (R.), 69-70

"Repulse," the, 119, 121, 122, 134, 140

"Revenge," the, Grenville's ship, last fight and fate of, 68-9

Ridolfi Plot, the, 60

Rimenant, Battle of, 8

Roanoke, Island of, Colony on, 36, 39, 43

Roche, Lord, capture of, by R., 19-20

"Roebuck," the, 71

Russel family, 5

"St. Andrew," Spanish vessel, 123, 125, 135

St. Bartholomew, Massacre of, 7

St. Elmo's Fire, 34

St. Francis, Priory of, 128

St. John, Sir Edward, 195

St. John, Sir Lewis, 216

St. Joseph, Trinidad, burning of, 99, 101; attacks from, 207

St. Leger family, 5

St. Leger, Sir Warham, 14, 15, 22, 24, 203

St. Margaret's, Westminster, burial in, of R., 232

"St. Matthew," Spanish vessel, 123, 125, 135

St. Michael's Island, 142

St. Osmond's curse, 53

"St. Philip," Spanish vessel, 68, 120, 123, 125, fate of, 70

Salisbury, Bishop and Chapter of, 52

Salisbury, 212

Salisbury family, 149

San Domingo, 100

San Lucar, 120

San Thomé, on the Orinoco, 113; the second of the name, the burning of, and fight at, 205 sqq., 223, 224-5

"San Thomé," Spanish vessel, 223

Sanderson, William, 35

Santa Catalina, 120

Sarmiento, Don Diego, de Acuña, see Gondomar

Sarmiento, Don Pedro, 56

Savoy, Duke of, emissaries of, 197

Schomburgk, Sir Robert, 101, 110

Scilly Islands, 201

Scotland, intrigues with, 61, 145 sqq.

Seamen, impressment of, by R., 117

"Serpent," the, 56

Serpent's Mouth, storm at, 106

Seymour, Lord Henry, 64

Shakespeare, William, 31, 87; on the divinity of kings, 171

Sherborne, Manor of, bestowed on R., 48, 52-3, 54, 90, 94, 99, 173, and reft from him, 180-1, 211

Shipbuilding, R.'s work on, 185-6

Sidney, Sir Henry, 14

Sidney, Sir Philip, 17, 74; colonization scheme of, 43; elegies on, by R., and by Spenser, 83-4

Sixtus V, Pope, 65

Slave-trading by Sparrow, 105

Smerwicke, Bay of, Kerry, 16, 79

Smith, Captain John, 42

Smith, Godwin, on R., 23

Snagg, Robert, book by, 167

Society of Antiquaries, R. a founder of, 196

Socrates, trial of, 178

Somerset, Robert Carr, Earl of, 53, 181, and his work, 196

Soul, the, R.'s search for a definition of, 91-2

Southampton, Earl of, 160

Spanish Armada, the Great, 30, 56, 62 sqq., 119, 128, and its successors, 65, 133

Spanish Colonization in the New World, 10

Spanish Indies, wealth from, 164

Spanish Inquisition, the, 165

Spanish Main, the, raids in, of Drake, Hawkins, and R., 36 sqq., 55, 98, 106, 107, 115, 164, 177, 233

Spanish Policy of James I, 177, 184, 195

Spanish Treasure fleet, attempts on, 56, 68, 71, 93, 129, 134, 137, 142-3, 200

Spanish Treatment of Indians, 99, 100, 104

Spanish War 1589-92, R.'s share in, 67

Sparrow, Francis, 105
Spenser, Edmund, 15; and Burghley, 81; R.'s friendship with, 24, 31, 77, 79 *sqq.*; on Court life, 31
"Squirrel," the, 34, Gilbert lost with, 35
Stafford family, 262
Stafford, Sir Edward, on R.'s marriage, 72-3
Staines, 213
Standen, Sir Anthony, 118
Stannaries, R.'s Lord Wardenship of, 50-1, 53
Steel Glas (Gascoigne), R.'s verses in, 7, 82
Stuart, Lady Arabella, plots concerning, 146, 153, 158-9
Stukely, Mr., 39
Stukely, Sir Lewis ("Sir Judas") (cousin), 39, 210, 211, 212, 215, 216-17

TEMPEST, *The* (Shakespeare), 113
Temple, the, R.'s residence in, 7
Teneriffe, 99
Tennyson, Lord, ballad by, on the "Revenge," 70
Terceira, 137
Thames-mouth Defence, R.'s scheme for, 133
Throgmorton, Arthur, 118
Throgmorton, Elizabeth, *see* Raleigh, Lady
Throgmorton, Nicholas, *later* Carew, Sir Nicholas, name changed on inheriting property, 232
Thunderstorms in Guiana, 105-6
Tilbury, 63, 216
Tobacco, introduced by R., 45-6, 236; and the State, 45-6, 210
Toparimaca, Prince, 104
Topiawari, King, 104, 105
Tounson, Dr. Robert, Dean of Westminster, 231, 233, 236
Tower Hill, executions on, 145, 149, 236
Tower of London, Essex in, 148; R.'s two committals to, 10, 72, 73, 151, 187
Treason, English law on, 165-6

Trespass with hostile intent, the law on, 225-6
Trinidad, Island of, Whiddon's visit to, 94; R. at, 99, 102, 106, 107, 109
True Discourse Historical of the Succeeding Governors of the Netherlands (Churchyard), 8
Tyrone, Earl of, Essex's truce with, 147
Tyrone rebellion, the, 195

UDALL, —, 32
Ursua, Pedro de, search of, for El Dorado, 97, 108

VENEZUELA, early exploration in, 96; gold in, 107
Venezuela Boundary Commission, the, 97, R. justified by, 224-5
Venice, English mercenaries of, 220
Vera, Domingo de, Guiana exploration by, 99, 100, failure of, 113
Vere, Sir Francis, and the storming of Cadiz, 116, 118, 123, 124, 125
Vespuccius, Amerigo, 96
Villiers, George, later Marquis and Duke of Buckingham, 195, 196, 230
Villiers, Sir Edward, 195
Virginia, derivation of the word, 37; Virginian plantation, the, 36 *sqq.*, 56, 91, 98, 106, 183, 209; R.'s appeals for leave to go to, 183
Virginian venturers, R.'s patent assigned to, 42

WAAD, Sir William, 158, 183
Walsingham, Sir Francis, 7, 18, 21, 22, 23, 27, 37, 52, 56, 57, 58, 59 *sqq.*, 74, 78, 82, 167
Warburton, Judge, 158, 166
"Warspite," R.'s ship, at Cadiz, 119, 124, 125, 134, 144, 209
Watson, William, plot of, 152, 153, 154, 167

West Indies, the, 10, 36, 41, 134

Whiddon, Captain Jacob, 56; Orinoco expedition of, 94, 99 ; death of, 109

White, John, and the Colony of the City of Raleigh, Virginia, 40-1, 42

Whitney, Captain, 205

William, Prince of Orange, 25

William III, 174

Wilson, the spy, 220-1

Winchester, R.'s trial at, 156, 157 *sqq.*, 178, 226, public opinion after, 176, 229

Windsor Castle, 151

Wine Licence granted to R., disputes on, 48 *sqq.*; transfer of, 180

Wingina, Indian Chief, 37

Winter, Admiral Fitzwilliam, 16

Winwood, Sir Ralph, 175, 195, 208, 209

Wollaston, Captain, 205

Wyngandacoia, meaning of, 37; R.'s settlement at, 36, 37

YELVERTON, Sir Henry, 230

Youghal, R. Mayor of, 54

ZOUCH, Colonel John, 19, 20, 22

Zucchero's portrait of R., 4